AIMING HIGH

The Life of Ski and Travel Pioneer Erna Low

Matador
9 Priory Business Park
Kibworth Beauchamp
Leicestershire LE8 0RX, UK
Tel: (+44) 116 279 2299
Fax: (+44) 116 279 2277
Email: books@troubador.co.uk
Web: www.troubador.co.uk/matador

ISBN 978 1780883 540

British Library Cataloguing in Publication Data.
A catalogue record for this book is available from the British Library.

Typeset in Adobe Garamond Pro by Troubador Publishing Ltd
Printed and bound in the UK by TJ International, Padstow, Cornwall

Matador is an imprint of Troubador Publishing Ltd

To my family and to Erna, thankfully an insatiable hoarder and organiser

Acknowledgements

The author would like to thank the following people for their invaluable help in researching this biography: Clare for her support and cups of coffee and Lola, Seth and Reuben for not disturbing Daddy (too much) while he was writing; Joanna Yellowlees-Bound for commissioning the book and for her enthusiasm for all things Erna, "Bobbie" Shafto, Ellen Fleming, Halina Hodi, Roma Black, John Boyle and Colin Trigger for their fascinating accounts of life working with Erna as well as Roger and Christopher Lloyd Pack for their stories of life growing up with Erna and their memories of their mother Uli. Thanks to Steve Keenan for his sage advice on the book.

He would also like to thank Amy Shulman, Anne Sheridan, Arnie Wilson, Bill Colwill OBE, Bridget Major, Carol Wright, Celia Fielder, Charlie Kemmis-Betty, Christopher Black, Claudio Ambroso, Colin Murison-Small, David Medcalf, Dennis Fabri, Eithne Power, Elisabeth Hussey, Emily Wells, Francois Marchand, Gary Edwards, Giles MacDonogh, Guido Ambroso, Hans-Karl Rhomberg, Hubert Schwärzler, Jane Bolton, Jane Stevens, Jean Yellowlees, John Samuel, John Spero, John Ward, Julian Martin, Leopold Holzknecht, Martina Jamnig, Martin Enne, Martin Riml, Mensun Bound, Michael Pettifer, Patricia Farley, Patrick Goyet, Peter Grohs, Peter Hardy, Peter Kemmis-Betty, Phyll Hendy, Polly Dean, Professor Peter Jost, Riccarda Ruberl, Rob Wrate, Roger Bray, Sarah Ruggles, Sara van Loock, Sharon Parish, the staff of the Ski Club of Great Britain, Sue Himmelweit, the late Sylvia Antunovic, Tim Clarke, Tony Skottowe, Dr Ulrich Nachbaur, Victoria Lincoln and Virginia Archer for bringing Erna to life and making this book a reality.

Photo credits

Many of the photos in this book were taken by Erna Low herself. The author has searched exhaustively for copyright holders for other photos used. The photos on the following pages are thanks to: p27, Cadbury Research Library: Special Collections, University of Birmingham; p43, from Cheshire Country Houses by Peter de Figueiredo, Julian Treuherz (1988), Chichester: Phillimore; p65 Pictorial Records; p. 162, ISBN 0 85033 655 4; p104, Vorarlberger Nachrichten; p98, Riccarda Ruberl; p129, Jack Wilson, Jatony; p145, C O'Gorman, The Times; p166, Flaine – Centre Culturel, p171, Goodchild Pictorial Photography; p184, Jalmar; p204, Tess Musgrave. Photo Section: p1, Rob Wrate; p3, Lisel Haas; p4, Monitor Press Features (top), C. Geralds (bottom); p15, Times Educational Supplement.

Foreword

I knew Erna Low for most of my young life. My mother, famously, walked into her office in 1952 looking for a job and came out with what turned out to be a lifelong friendship. They were both from Vienna and had many shared experiences in their background. But apart from that, Erna took to my mother, Uli, in a way that developed almost to a fixation. Over the course of many years they became devoted to each other. Uli was her stalwart support, both in the office and in her personal life.

Erna specialised in bespoke holidays and my mother accompanied her on many of her trips around the country and abroad, acting as her driver and companion and assisting her in her hotel deals. In due course Erna moved to a house round the corner from ours. She became, to all intents and purposes, an additional member of our family. My father christened her "The Mad Woman of Old Brompton Road (MWOBR)" an affectionate term which later palled into one of abuse when Erna's demands on Uli's time became a contentious issue and she felt unable to visit our house for a while.

Erna was a force of nature. She was indomitable and driven, qualities without which she would never have built her travel business into the success it was. She could be demanding, bullying and impatient, and at the same time generous, kind and loyal.

To my brother, Christopher, and myself she was like a benevolent aunt. We walked her adored dogs, lounged around in her garden, went on her holidays, and kept her company. She was also a source of employment for us as students — we worked in the basement of her office on and off for some years, operating the franking machine and the "Doll's eye" switchboard, and then, annually, I would sit round her table at her home, proof reading her winter sports brochure, often working long hours into the night, as was her wont.

Though she could be an exacting employer I found her easy to work with and those times round her dining table are filled with happy memories. Erna had a good sense of humour and I could make her laugh, an ability which I used to deflect some of her more intimidating qualities. Later in life, when I grew older and moved away and started a family, I became less indulgent towards her whims and caprices and she was more critical of my way of life, always casting doubt on my choice of career as an actor. We drifted apart for a while, but she became devoted to my daughter, Emily, to whom she was a godmother, and took her responsibilities very seriously.

We became closer again towards the end of her life, when she became a victim of Alzheimer's and I witnessed at first hand the sad and cruel progress of that illness.

Mark Frary has written a well researched and exhaustive account of her life, from her upbringing in Vienna, through the heady times of the Erna Low Travel Service, to her final debilitating years. Much of this story is known to me, but I was very interested to know of her formative years, about which she spoke very little, and I was particularly struck by the eloquence and passion of two long love letters, both of which are quoted in full. Erna's love life was always a mystery to me, apart from the fact that her dedication to her business didn't really allow for one, but reading these letters made me realise how little one can sometimes really know of a person. Mark has opened a window into the life of a remarkable woman who changed the face of the travel business in her time and set a benchmark for future generations to follow.

Roger Lloyd Pack
London
August 2012

Introduction

I never met Erna Low.

Just as Erna was leaving her office in South Kensington "to go to watch Wimbledon" in 1996, I was just beginning my career as a ski writer. Of course, I quickly learned about Erna Low, the company.

At that time, I knew very little of the woman behind the firm but what I did know was that every time she was mentioned in a newspaper article she was referred to as either "redoubtable" or as a "doyenne", that slightly disparaging but mostly respectful term that is reserved for those who have made a great contribution to some industry or sector at some point in the dim and distant past.

Having seen pictures of her but never having crossed paths with her, I was forced to reach a similar conclusion to her former employee Dennis Fabri.

He told me "If I were to read an Agatha Christie novel and picture in my mind some very kindly battleaxe mentioned in it, I would think of Erna in both her dress and outlook."

It just shows how wrong first impressions can sometimes be.

When I was asked by my friend Joanna Yellowlees-Bound, the chief executive of the ski company Erna Low, to help her fulfil a long-held ambition – to have a biography written – I jumped at the chance. What I did not know then was that Erna was an inveterate hoarder. The company offices in Reece Mews, South Kensington, the same ones that Erna moved to more than sixty years ago are packed with scrapbooks, photo albums, films and correspondence. As I went through that incredible archive, I began to realise what a remarkable woman she was.

Newspaper cutting after newspaper cutting from the peak of Erna's business years in the Sixties fall over themselves to lay praise at her door.

A 1958 article in the *Birmingham Weekly Post* called Erna Low "the only woman London travel agent...working on a considerable scale". A *Financial Times* article in 1960 called her "dynamic", the *Woman's Journal* of January 1963 dubbed her "the go-ahead travel agent" while an article in *Business Week* called her a "wily sheep dog", referring to her ability to get people and things organised.

Praise too from John Carter in *The Times* in 1973[1]: "Any mention of individuals who have brought a strong touch of personality to the travel world would be incomplete without reference to the redoubtable Miss Erna Low; a woman who knows what she likes in terms of holidays and sells what she knows to people who appreciate her choice."

The correspondence told a story too.

How did she make such a success of the business in a male-dominated world? David Owen of Bovingdon, Herts summed up her success in a letter I came across one afternoon. "I was thinking on the train coming home of the ingredients which you have somehow managed to combine in such a way as to offer package tour facilities without making your clients feel they were being herded with a host of unwanted fellow travellers. Mainly I admire your ability to seek out interesting situations and then negotiate advantageous terms at the best upper-middle class of hotel".

A postcard from a Mr A M Johnson reads "I am one of your clients who admires you very much and believes that you brought a lot of happiness into many people's lives".

Finally, meeting the people who were her colleagues, some of them long-suffering, and people she loved completed the picture for me.

She was immensely hard working and expected those who worked for her to work just as hard, even if that meant staying up until 5am to finish a brochure, sometimes to the detriment of their family lives. She was passionate about finding undiscovered destinations and sharing these discoveries yet was disparaging about the rise of mass tourism which came about partly as a result of her pioneering steps. She was innovative too, pioneering the country house party in Britain, the informal ski parties of groups of friends that led to the creation of the chalet industry, the school ski trip and the concept of the specialist tour operator. That is some legacy.

In her introduction to the autobiography that she started to write in the 1980s and 1990s but never completed, Erna writes "So much has changed in the country of my birth, Austria and in the country of my choice – Britain. Thinking back to my early beginnings in this country is difficult to imagine that I came over here in 1931 as a young student with ten borrowed pounds in my pocket and bags full of optimism. It just never occurred to me that anything could go wrong – the world was there to be explored and England was a country full of promise and opportunities."

These words sum up the secret of Erna Low's success perfectly.

Prologue

Saturday 20 December 1952 was a typical winter's day in London. The temperature hovered a few degrees above zero and there was a light drizzle from an overcast sky; the Great Smog caused by London's coal-burning fires that had throttled the capital and some of its weaker residents earlier in the month had mercifully dispersed.

That morning, a ragtag group gathered at platform 2 at London's Victoria railway station. Among the group was a student from University College, Oxford, a civil servant at the Ministry of Supply, three New Zealanders, a pupil from Ashford Girl's School in Kent and her young sister.

There would have been much to talk about. Earlier in the year, King George VI had died at Sandringham at the age of fifty-six and was replaced as monarch by the twenty-five-year-old Princess Elizabeth. The group may have also been discussing how their mode of transport was perhaps reaching the age of retirement. In May that year, the world's first commercial jet airline service was inaugurated between London and Johannesburg – an event that would bring about the precipitous decline of the international rail travel that they were about to experience.

The group had been brought together by one thing – a love of skiing – and they had a common destination, the ski resort of Lech in Austria's Arlberg region, where they planned to spend Christmas and New Year. The trip had been organised by an Austrian *émigré* who had started arranging ski trips back to her homeland twenty years earlier and had made a successful and growing business of it. That émigré was Erna Low.

Leading the party was Lloyd Campion who had also brought along his eleven-year-old son.

The party had brought their own ski equipment – leather lace-up boots and wooden skis that were getting shorter than those used by the ski pioneers of the earlier part of the century. Some of the most fashionable skis on show even had coloured decorations rather than being plain wood.

At 11.30am, with everyone on board, the "Snow Sport Special" left the smoke-filled interior of Victoria and carved its way through the dark suburbs of South East London and on through Kent.

At Folkestone, the train was loaded onto a specially designed ferry, allowing the skiing group to remain in their sleeper cars for the two and a half hour crossing to Calais.

These Snow Sport Specials were popular because they included air-conditioned "Austropa couchettes of modern design" and there was no need to change trains between the Channel and the final destination in Austria.

From Calais, the train thundered through France to Basle, passing through Buchs and Bludenz before arriving just before 9am on Sunday morning at the small station of Langen am Arlberg, at 1215 metres above sea level in the shadow of the Austrian Alps.

By now the group would have been getting excited because there was plenty of snow and Lech was now very close, with the final 10 mile leg of the journey taken by one of Austria's famous postal cars (coaches).

The bus was full, with thirty-eight people crammed on board, a British group made up the majority but were joined by skiers from the Netherlands, Germany, France and Belgium.

By now the snow was falling very heavily and the local police were considering closing the road up to Lech. Today, travellers on the Arlberg Bundesstrasse go through the PassÜrtunnel built in the 1990s but in 1952, the bus regularly took the PassÜrtobel road along Aflenz river. The police made the fateful decision that the post bus was to be the last vehicle allowed to go through[2].

Just after the road passes the Haus Theresia on the left, it crosses the river and clings to the lower slopes of the 2,548 metre Marolköpfe, traversing the Aflenz several times along the way. At one of the bridges, the road narrows to just six feet wide and it drops away 40 feet to the creek below.

At around 5.30pm, just as the heavily laden bus crossed the bridge, something terrible occurred. An enormous gust of wind, seemingly from nowhere and stronger than a hurricane, lifted the bus as if it were a child's toy and tossed it over the edge of the bridge into the ravine below.

Following the bus into the creek were thousands of tons of snow – the strong blast of wind had been the early warning signal for a dry powder avalanche. The bus was quickly buried.

Despite the heavy snow, a skier happened to be passing by and quickly raised the alarm. Less than fifteen minutes later a group of fifty rescuers were on the scene, pulling people from the wreckage.

The party leader, Lloyd Campion, who had survived the plunge into the ravine told *The Times* what happened inside the bus. He had broken an uncovered corner window and managed to scramble out. "Then we worked with our hands and nails trying to dig the snow away to get out the others," he said.

The terrible severity of the accident meant that there were only a handful of survivors; twenty-four of the thirty-eight passengers on the ill-fated Postbus died, their bodies laid out in the church at Langen. It was later learned that many died instantly, not from the crash into the river but because of extremely high pressure on their lungs caused by the air blast.

The Austrian press reported that of those who died, twelve were English – including Anthony Campion, the young son of the party leader – with the remainder coming from the Netherlands, Germany, New Zealand, France and Belgium. Of those that perished, eight were travelling with the Erna Low Travel Service.

***

Avalanches are a deadly force of nature and we are only slowly getting to understand them. The danger they represent can be mitigated through better design of roads, ensuring that mountain trees are only felled in certain ways and by the use of avalanche barriers and pre-emptive blasts to loosen snow. However, avalanches can never be entirely ruled out and they still kill around 150 people around the world each year[3].

The 1952 Arlberg Disaster, as it came to be known, was an unlucky fluke. Not all avalanches are accompanied by air blasts and the timing of its arrival could not have been worse for the travellers on the Postbus. The avalanche was relatively small by local standards and it was only because the bus passed over the bridge at the exact moment that the air blast arrived that it was pushed into the creek[4].

The disaster, which saw the biggest loss of life in an avalanche in Austrian history, lead to the establishment of the Vorarlberger Lawinenwarndienst (the Vorarlberg Avalanche Warning Service), whose efforts have saved countless lives in the years since.

***

Erna's travel business had started in 1932 as a way to get back to Austria to see her family but had grown into something much more. By 1952, Erna was organising the holidays of hundreds of young, professional people, sending them to house parties in Britain and on skiing trips to Austria and Switzerland. These were people who had emerged from the horrors of the Second World War, many of whom had never ventured far from their places of birth other than for their education.

She may not have known it, but Erna was riding a wave of post-war optimism and prosperity that would soon see millions of people travel overseas on their annual holidays, to go skiing, to make new discoveries or just to lie on a beach. Yet the year of 1952 put all that hard-earned success in jeopardy.

As the year drew to a close, Erna Low might have been tempted to call the year an *annus horribilis* as the newly crowned queen would fifty years later. The Arlberg Disaster, and another shocking event earlier that year, could have destroyed other fledgling businesses and less strong-willed business people.

Yet Erna was strong at a time when few women in the corporate world were, perhaps a reflection of a successful sporting youth and the challenges of a Jewish upbringing in Austria just as the National Socialists were coming to power. Despite what she termed as a "serious setback", the company that bore – and still bears – her name went on to become one of the pioneers of selling holidays in both summer and winter to the British public.

Chapter 1

"I was a replacement, planned after my little brother Ernst had died of diphtheria."

These were to be the opening words of the autobiography of the skiing and holiday pioneer Erna Löw, written by Erna, at the age of seventy-five as she looked back over a remarkably successful and varied life. It was a life that included periods as a champion javelin-thrower, a German teacher and chronicler of a minor Victorian poet, as well as organiser of trains, hotels, ski passes and more for tens of thousands of people over much of the twentieth century.

Sadly, the autobiography – set to be called *Ups and Downs* – never materialised. It remained unwritten at the time of her death and the hundreds of scraps of paper, envelopes and whatever came to hand joined an enormous archive of scrapbooks, photo albums, files and boxes that now fills the cupboards and shelves of the South Kensington offices of the company that still bears her name.

Those thousands of words written by Erna's own hand form the backbone of this biography and it is only right that the opening words are hers too. If you can hear the heavy Austrian accent that Erna maintained throughout her life despite seventy years spent in Britain speaking from these pages, it is because many of the words are her own.

***

Erna Marianna Löw was born on 28 July 1909 in an apartment in central Vienna, the only daughter of Eduard Carl Löw and his wife, Emma.

She was ten years younger than her brother Friedrich, known as Fritz to everyone, and arrived on the scene just over a year after the death from diphtheria of her younger brother. She would be constantly reminded of Ernst throughout her life.

"[Ernst] was eight years younger than our elder brother Fritz and was very much the apple of my parents' eyes," she wrote in 1984. "Apparently, Ernst was a charmer and his death was a great blow both to his parents and to his older brother. When I appeared on the scene Fritz did not want to accept that he had a little sister and to placate him I was called Erna – the female version of Ernst."

The family lived at an apartment owned by Eduard's mother Barbara in a well-built block at 35 Josefstädterstrasse in Vienna's eighth district. The eight district was and is popular with the middle classes; it is close to the Josefstädter Theatre and is a short tram ride from the university and Austria's Parliament. Most of the city's mayors have lived here and Austria's current president, Heinz Fischer, lives just a few doors down from Erna's birthplace.

Josefstädterstrasse, Erna's birthplace in central Vienna

Like many of those living in Vienna at the time, Erna's father had not been born in the Austrian capital. Eduard was born on 21 February 1864 in Roštin, near Brno in Southern Moravia in the Czech Republic. At that time, the city was part of the Habsburg-ruled Austro-Hungarian Empire and was known as Brünn. The family name at the time was Loewy, which Eduard changed to the more Germanic Löw just a few months before Erna's birth.

Eduard had left Brünn "a penniless student" at the age of eighteen and came to Vienna, where he earned a living by giving lessons in typing, shorthand and book-keeping. He then had the idea of running correspondence courses for people living outside the Imperial capital, promoting them using the slogan 'Why travel far away when you can acquire knowledge from home'.

The courses, according to Erna, were aimed at "keen young people who wanted to get on in life especially those who lived in little villages in Hungary, Czechoslovakia and Serbia".

Emma Seling was born in Vienna on 26 April 1874 to Ignaz Seling and Eleonore Ruberl, although Emma's family like Eduard's, were also from what is now the Czech Republic, coming from Boskowitz (now Boskovice).

Erna's mother, Emma Seling

Both Eduard and Emma came from Jewish families although from Erna's descriptions of her early life, she did not have a religious upbringing. In fact, like many people of Jewish heritage, Eduard and Emma had given up their Jewish roots; both had been baptised into the Protestant Church as adults and Erna was baptised shortly after birth.

Historian and author Giles MacDonogh says, "Many Austrian Jews converted, and not always for reasons of anti-Semitism. Middle class Jews like the Löws were increasingly assimilated and no longer felt close to the tenets of Judaism. Some wanted to get on in their professions and found an unofficial *numerus clausus* [a limit on the number of Jewish students at the university, for example] stood in their way. Others (chiefly very rich Jews) used baptism to advance their children and make good marriages."

In his book *Vienna and the Jews*[5], Stephen Beller writes: "The attitude to Judaism among the assimilated bourgeoisie was generally one of indifference… A sizeable number of individuals did take the step out, usually on marriage. As a result some of the former Jewish figures of Viennese cultures, such as Hoffmansthal and Wittgenstein, were brought up as Christians."

***

Emma met Eduard, ten years her senior, in the classroom; he had been her teacher and he wooed her fervently for some time before she accepted his proposal, a written proposal that Erna stumbled across inside a book when she was a teenager. "My friends and I had some good laughs reading it secretly," she said. Her parents were married at 21 Müllnergasse by Rabbi Dr I Gelbhaus on 20 February 1898.

That the two families had both come to the Imperial capital was not unusual. As the 19th century came to an end, Vienna was growing rapidly. As it grew, boosted by the arrival of large numbers of people from across the Empire, it engulfed neighbouring towns, particularly those south of the Danube. According to the Viennese census[6], in 1880 the city had 726,000 inhabitants but this had grown to 2,031,000 by 1910, making it similar in population terms to Paris and Berlin.

Vienna was a magnet for Jews from around the Austro-Hungarian Empire. In 1910, Jews represented 8.6% of the Viennese population of which only one fifth were native. "Slightly over a quarter of the Jewish migrants to this Central European Mecca had come from the Czech lands and a little less than one-quarter from the Hungarian lands"[7].

These included Sigmund Freud, born in Moravia. When Erna was just a baby, Freud was running his practice specialising in nervous and brain disorders at 19 Berggasse, just a mile and a half from the Löw family apartment.

Despite its growing size, Vienna would soon lose its role on the world stage. When Erna was born, the First World War was still five years away and the city was still the beating heart of the Austro-Hungarian Empire. The seventy-nine-year-old emperor, Franz Joseph I, still ruled over what is now modern day Austria and Hungary but also parts of Italy, the Czech Republic, Slovakia, Slovenia, Poland, Romania and Croatia.

Yet already the signs of the great upheaval that was to come were evident. Erna was born in the middle of the so-called Bosnian Crisis, when the Empire annexed Bosnia-Herzegovina. This set off a chain of events that culminated in the First World War.

The seeds for the Second World War were also being sown in the city. A year before Erna's birth, a young Adolf Hitler had moved to the city in an attempt to gain entry to the city's Academy of Fine Arts.

Hitler lived there for the next five years, often in homeless shelters, making money by painting watercolours of famous Vienna landmarks copied from postcards. In *Mein Kampf*, he describes the city at the time. "In the centre and in the Inner City one felt the pulse-beat of an Empire which had a population of fifty-two million, with all the perilous charm of a State made up of multiple nationalities. The dazzling splendour of the Court acted like a magnet on the wealth and intelligence of the whole Empire."[8]

***

The Löw family apartment on Josefstädterstrasse was a busy place. Eduard's father, Leopold, had died at an early age and so his mother had to take in boarders, including her younger brother Karl and various cousins from Brünn and Boskowitz.

Meals, taken around a large tiled stove, sat on benches, were a raucous affair "with up to ten people sitting around the dining room table, mostly relatives of my mother's and not always welcomed by my father."

As a result of the dominance of Emma's family at the apartment, she took on the role of matriarch after Eleonore died. Emma, wrote Erna later, was "loved by everyone" and "offered a shoulder to cry on and valuable advice" to both the extended family and their friends.

There were also two maids who had quarters next to the kitchen. Erna recalled later, "In Austria, a maid is very much part of the family – they are part slave and part confidante, you could see them linger outside a door when there were visitors and interesting gossip could be pinched."

"We lived on the mezzanine floor. The ground floor was occupied by a large sweet shop, a stationers and a small haberdashery," Erna wrote in her autobiographical notes.

Erna wondered later whether that confectioners was the origin of her legendary sweet tooth. "[There was] a delicious variety attractively displayed next to the entrance to the house. I was a frequent visitor and spent my entire pocket money on Ildefonso, Pischinger and Heller sweets."

"The house was guarded by a *Hausbesorgerin*, a watchwoman. Nothing escaped her – she knew exactly what went on in the house and made sure everyone else did too," said Erna. "A large tip at Christmas and others throughout the year bought her goodwill and that was important if you wanted parcels delivered and tradesmen admitted. Strangers were immediately detected by her eagle eye."

Erna's father, Eduard, eventually set up a college at the apartment as the success of his correspondence courses grew. The constant to-ing and fro-ing of students may have given the young Erna a boost later in life when she moved to London as a penniless student herself and realised she could make money teaching German.

Erna wrote later about those early years. "My father did most of the teaching at the college and worked very hard – consequently he was very tired and nervous in the evenings. One had to be very careful not to make any noise and often – very unfairly – I was blamed for interrupting him when he read the newspaper.

"I did not take kindly to being shouted at, a dislike which has followed me right through my life. I remember one special incident when I took my revenge by locking myself in the lavatory in our apartment – there was only one – for several hours and all the family had to go over to the students' lavatories which meant queuing for quite a while. However, my father's temper did improve after this salutary lesson."

***

The first school Erna attended was the Freie Schule (free school) at 23 Albertgasse, within walking distance of the family apartment in Josefstädterstrasse. The school

Prof. E. Löw

Eduard's business card for the commercial college

was free in the sense that children were free to express themselves rather than their parents not having to pay anything. The free school association had been established in Vienna by an educationalist called Otto Glöeckl in 1905 as an apolitical initiative and in an attempt to allow children to be educated in an environment free from the influence of the Catholic Church.

The school, which had the motto *Mehr Licht in die Köpfe, in die Schulstuben* (More light in the mind, in the schoolroom), was run by Josef Enslein. Enslein is now immortalised in a Viennese square, Josef-Enslein-Platz, named in his honour after his death.

Erna was taught by Josef's much younger wife, Klementine.

"All the children adored Klementine and she loved every one of them," remembered Erna. "Her classes were not only very instructive but also great fun. I remember how she taught us to make candles and to draw, which I enjoyed although I am far from artistic.

"Frau Direktor had a special gift to make everything interesting for the children. She was much advanced in her teaching methods and we children were free and happy and uninhibited."

Another piece of school work that was long remembered by the family was an essay on the life of the famous Austrian actor Alexander Girardi, written by Erna in Frau Enslein's class. In an early indication of how Erna was not afraid to upturn

Erna's class at the Freie Schule in Albertgasse. Josef and Klementine Enslein are
in the front row while Erna is third from right

the established order the essay started with Girardi's death and ended with his
birth.

The influence of Frau Enslein on Erna cannot be underestimated and she said
that the security of those early close relationships stood her in good stead
throughout her life. Erna kept a photograph of her teacher alongside that of her
mother in her bedroom. "When I have a problem I often wonder how those two
would have solved it," she later said.

Erna went on to become a governor at Avondale Park Infants school in
Notting Hill and said at the time, "I often think of Frau Direktor and how she
foresaw what teaching of young children was to become so much later."

***

Over the summer holidays from the Freie Schule each year, the family rented a
holiday home in Kaltenleutgeben in the Vienna Woods for two months.

One year, Erna had taken a satchel containing all of her school books there to
work on over the holidays.

Erna recalled, "We got off the train at the terminus and suddenly I realised that my satchel had been left on board. The train was turning round for the return journey to Vienna. I saw it coming and without a word to anyone I took a flying leap and landed on all fours on the platform. Needless to say my mother was horrified and so was the conductor. He stopped the train and I returned triumphantly with my satchel. The reception I received was not exactly enthusiastic."

It was on these long summer breaks that Erna developed the love of animals that would last throughout her life. Keeping a pet in a central Viennese apartment was always going to be difficult so Eduard and Emma solved this by promising Erna she could look after pets during these summer holidays and she raised a succession of white mice, canaries and rabbits here.

One of Erna's favourites was a white rabbit with red eyes called Hansi.

"Hansi grew to a considerable size and I was determined to take him back with me to Vienna," she recalled later. "One day towards the end of the holiday there was no Hansi in the cage. I was told that someone had left the cage open and that he had joined his brothers and sisters in the wood.

"At lunchtime, fried chicken – one of my favourites – was served in an effort to console me. However, I was convinced that it was Hansi and for years I could not bear to eat chicken."

Erna's parents eventually relented on the question of pets and at the age of five she was rewarded with the first of what would become a long line of canine companions.

"My joy was indescribable when my father came home one day with a beautiful auburn coloured Irish setter whom I called Prinz," said Erna.

Erna doted on the new dog, allowing him to sleep by her bed, but the relationship was not to end happily.

"My father had bought him from a kennels and he had not been trained properly. Every effort to train him to do 'his business' outside, which involved long hours of parading with him on the road outside our apartment, were in vain," said Erna.

Prinz's habit of relieving his bowels inside the entrance hall immediately after returning eventually caused the two housemaids to hand in their notice. The ruined hall carpet was the last straw and Prinz had to go back to the kennels from whence he came, an incident Erna called "the saddest episode of my childhood".

Another dog who made a great impression on Erna, in more ways than one, was a white Spitz by the name of Immo who was often found roaming the streets near the family holiday home. Erna adopted Immo, who appeared hungry and neglected, regularly sneaking food to him.

"One day I wanted to put something into his bowl and Immo misunderstood; he thought I was taking away some food. He jumped up and bit me in the leg. There was great consternation, the doctor was called and gave me my first tetanus injection. Poor Immo was banned for ever from our garden."

***

After the tragic death of Ernst at a very young age, Emma doted on her son Fritz. He was a sickly child and Emma nursed him through many childhood illnesses, including the genetic skin disorder icthyosis, sometimes known as fish scale disease because of the dry, scaly patches of skin it causes. As a result, Fritz frequently missed school and was taught Latin and Greek by his mother, creating a strong bond between them.

Erna, meanwhile, was Eduard's favourite.

"My father was very jealous of this close relationship between mother and son and welcomed the arrival of a little daughter who turned out to be a tomboy full of fun and up to all sorts of tricks," said Erna later.

Fritz was a keen Boy Scout and boys from his group were regular visitors to the Josefstädterstrasse apartment, making the atmosphere very lively.

Erna confessed that her greatest pleasure was to be allowed to play with the older boys and they played table tennis and climbed trees together.

However, Erna's invitation to play with the boys would come to a sudden end.

"[They] had a summer camp in the Salzkammergut [Upper Austria's lake district] and much to my joy I was allowed to go there with my brother. We travelled third class all night – sleeping on hard benches – and when we arrived in the morning I was unable to move and had to be carried to a tent where to my great disappointment I spent a whole week."

Erna had succumbed to an attack of what the Austrians call *Hexenschuss*, literally witch-shot, or lumbago as we tend to know it. It was the last time she was allowed to take part in her brother's activities.

***

Erna's brother Fritz suffered from icthyosis in his young life

When Erna was just five, events that had been brewing for a number of years came to a head when Archduke Franz Ferdinand, the nephew of Austro-Hungarian Emperor Franz Josef and heir to the imperial throne, was shot dead by the Serbian nationalist Gavrilo Princip in Sarajevo, Bosnia.

The Empire declared war on Serbia on 28 July 1914, believing that its scope would be limited. However, Russia quickly announced the mobilisation of its army in support of its smaller ally. In a classic case of political dominoes, Germany – an ally of the Empire – declared war on Russia on 1 August. Russia's treaty with France then drew that country into the war and Germany's armies quickly invaded Belgium in order to open the route to Paris. The threat to France from Germany drew Britain into the war, which felt it had a moral obligation to protect its closest neighbour as a result of the 1904 Entente Cordiale. Britain declared war on Germany, and by extension the Austro-Hungarian Empire, on 4 August.

The fighting that continued for the next four years would see more than fifteen million people die and twenty million wounded. Vienna, far from the sodden trenches of the Western Front and the more fluid battle lines of the Eastern Front in Poland and Galicia, was left relatively unscathed by the Great War. However Vienna's inhabitants faced food shortages and price rises caused by the disruption to supply lines from other parts of the Empire.

As a result of the close bond with her son, Emma was particularly affected by Fritz's call-up to serve in the Great War at the age of seventeen.

She went with Fritz and a few other young boys training to be officers to install them in their first billet, leaving Erna in the care of the family governess Fräulein Valerian, who was around the same age as Fritz. Valerian too was distraught about Fritz's departure for reasons that Erna would discover later.

"She was madly in love with him and was frequently in tears," said Erna. "On one occasion when she was at her most unhappy, I wormed it out of her that she was very fond of my brother."

Valerian said something to Erna at the time that would haunt her relationship with her mother for years.

Erna said: "When I asked her whether she thought that my mother loved Fritz more than me this juvenile pedagogue said, 'Yes, she does, after all he is a boy.' I was shocked and for many years to come this unfortunate remark was responsible for a lot of misery. I kept on reminding my mother of what Fräulein Valerian had said and refused to accept her denial."

When Emma died twenty years later and Erna was clearing out the family flat, she stumbled across some correspondence that shed a new light on Valerian's sadness at Fritz's departure.

"From it I learnt that, as was customary in good middle class families, my brother had gathered his first sexual experiences thanks to the willing cooperation of Fräulein Valerian. My mother had had to cope with the fruits of their relationship while my brother was away fighting for his country," wrote Erna in her notes.

By the time Fritz returned from the war, Emma had secured Valerian a good job running a kindergarten in Vienna and was long gone from the Löw household.

***

When Erna was eight, the family bought a villa with a garden full of fruit trees in the spa town of Baden bei Wien. Baden lies sixteen miles to the south of Vienna at the start of the Helenental valley and was a former summer retreat for the Habsburgs as well as composers such as Liszt and Beethoven.

Baden, which now has a population of around 25,000, is a pretty Austrian town in the shadow of the Calvarienberg mountain and still has grand buildings that show the Imperial connections of the past. The town's position on the edge of the Pannonian Plain makes it ideal for wine-growing and there are more than a hundred vineyards, producing white wines in the main, particularly Grüner Veltliner, Pinot Blanc and Neuburger.

Yet the main attraction of Baden bei Wien then, as now, is its thermal waters. It was these early experiences of the town's bathing establishments that engendered in Erna a belief in the efficacy of spa treatments, which would play a major role in her later life.

The family's holiday home was on Karlsgasse, in a lovely location close to the beginning of the sinuous road through the Helenental. However, Erna was less impressed with the family's new holiday destination.

"Everyone told me how lucky I was to spend my holidays there," she later wrote, "I did not feel lucky at all. Because it was a spa, Baden was full of old people going for thermal cures and I missed my friends and young company – much more important to a child than beautiful scenery."

One summer, Erna believed her luck had changed, spotting a poster for a children's fete with competitions to be held in the town.

She picks up the story. "I was determined to take part. My mother pointed out to my great chagrin that one had to put one's name down a day earlier and that we were just too late. I simply refused to accept this in spite of my mother's protestations.

"Next morning – a Sunday – I crept out at 8am and made my way to the hotel where the organiser of the fete was staying. I found out the number of his room, went upstairs, knocked at the door, got the poor man out of bed and handed him a slip of paper with my name and age. He was so horrified that he readily agreed to add my name to the list. I returned home triumphantly. My mother tried to explain to me that one does not invade a strange gentleman's bedroom at 8am on a Sunday but to no avail."

These were early signs of Erna's doggedness of getting exactly what she wanted, a skill that would come in very handy in her business life. "I cannot remember whether I won any prize but I certainly felt that persistence pays off," she said later.

***

Baden is home to a fine racecourse, designed in the simple but classy Biedermeier style that had its origins in central Europe in the first half of the 19ᵗʰ century. The racecourse opened in 1892 in order to appeal to summer migrants from Vienna. Rather than flat or National Hunt racing, Baden was and is best known for trotting or harness races, in which the jockey sits in a two-wheeled cart known as a sulky and is pulled by a trotting horse. The summer season still operates at the racecourse with meets every weekend in July and August.

The Löw's next door neighbour in Baden was a Herr Kühlsammer, whom Erna learned through eavesdropping on her parents was something of an expert on trotting.

One day, Erna bumped into Herr Kühlsammer on the street and asked him who was going to win the race the following day.

"He told me the name of the jockey and I promptly managed to get some extra pocket money from an unsuspecting aunt," recalled Erna.

"Off I went the next day to the racecourse where the trotting races were in progress. I watched the way people put on their bets and did the same – and I won. My parents were somewhat surprised to see that I always had plenty of pocket money but nobody knew how I had become so flush – until one day a friend of my father's saw me at the racecourse and promptly told my father. There was a terrific rumpus and children from then onwards were forbidden to enter the racecourse without adults and were forbidden to bet."

With this avenue of excitement closed, Erna had to find new outlets for her energies. She eventually met another Viennese family with three daughters, the Ehrenzweigs, one of whom was the same age as Erna, at the local swimming pool.

"Having some young friends made a tremendous difference to my holidays at Baden and I spent more time with them than at our house," explained Erna. "One of the daughters was nicknamed Muckilla, although her real name was Anni. We used to get up to all sorts of tricks. We went and bought large quantities of ham sausage with garlic and then tried to shock passers-by pretending to be sick – great fun although not very ladylike."

Muckilla's older sister Lily was in her late teens at the time and made a great impression on the young Erna, not least in how to conduct a clandestine love affair. Lily asked Erna and Muckla to act as messengers to ferry little notes and bunches of roses between her and her boyfriend. The younger girls were rewarded with boxes of chocolates for their efforts. The romance was not to last, despite Erna's best efforts as a go-between, something at which she excelled in later life.

"One day when Lily was upset about her romance not flourishing the way she had hoped for, I tried to console her with the words, 'But Lily don't be sad you still have me after all'. I don't think this cheered her up but she used to relate this episode in later years to everyone's amusement."

Erna lost touch with Lily and Muckilla after a few summers in Baden but she met Muckilla by chance again in the 1980s. By this time, Muckilla had a house in Cobham, Surrey with her husband Felix, who happened to be one of Erna's mother Emma's bridge partners. Erna and Muckilla spent many weekends together in later life and occasionally went back to Austria together.

***

Erna's first holiday "abroad" – to see her cousin Camilla in Neuhaus (now Jindřichův Hradec) in southern Bohemia in the Czech Republic – came at the age of nine.

Erna's father Eduard was ill and her mother remained at home to look after him. As a result, Erna was put in the charge of the family cook, who came from Prague.

Camilla lived on a farm which had a large pond, or *Weiher*, where you could swim and had plenty of horses. Animal-loving Erna desperately wanted to learn to ride and was very persistent in her requests to her aunt, who was under strict instructions from Eduard and Emma not to capitulate.

"I had to get round one of the stable lads and enjoyed my first ride on a horse," said Erna later. "It was my last ride too as promptly I fell off and was carted home but luckily only bruised."

The return journey from this first holiday was rather eventful. The cook returned from Prague to collect Erna but was accompanied by her fiancé.

"They were more interested in each other than in me," recalled Erna. "They promptly lost me – or maybe I escaped from them. At the frontier, I was overcome by thirst and got out of the train to find something to drink; the only thing I could get was Pilsner beer. It quenched my thirst but it made me feel somewhat peculiar and I was violently sick."

Erna never found the cook and her fiancé, and arrived in Vienna safely on her own none the worse for her escapade, despite the effects of the Pilsner. The cook was sacked shortly afterwards and beer – Pilsner or otherwise – never passed Erna's lips again.

Erna remained at the Freie Schule until the age of ten; she wanted to stay an extra year but her father considered it unnecessary and she moved on to the *Realgymnasium für Mädchen* (Secondary School for Girls) at 38 Albertgasse.

At the time, the *Gymnasiums* in Austria were the only form of secondary education institution from which you could gain entry to university; the *Realschule* offered a good education but were usually intended for people seeking entry into technical or trade schools. At the Gymnasium, you learned Latin and Greek; at the Realschule modern languages.[9]

The Realgymnasium opened its doors on 18 September 1905 in the grounds of a former riding school. In its first year, the school welcomed ninety-five pupils, a number that has today grown to 625.

It was a rude awakening for Erna after the easy-going atmosphere of the Freie Schule and her shyness and small size made her very unhappy.

Erna's teacher, Frau Professor Ludvig, was very strict and "had no sense of humour"; Erna was made to sit in the front row and had to ask for permission to go to the toilet.

In fact, Erna expressed a dislike for nearly all of the teachers at the Realgymnasium and all of the pupils lived in great fear of the school's director Professor Dagen. "She used to stand on the corridor and was constantly on the lookout for any misdeeds," said Erna.

Science class at the Realgymnasium für Mädchen on Albertgasse.
Erna is the girl with pigtails on the left looking away from the camera.

Two teachers who escaped Erna's disapproval were Frau Dr Bächer and Frau Direktor Adler. The first taught history while the second was in charge of physical education, which remained Erna's favourite subject throughout her school years – excelling at gymnastics, athletics and ball games and playing in many school teams.

Frau Adler also introduced Erna to a sport which would play a central role throughout her life – skiing. The teacher took the class on many ski trips to the many small ski resorts near Vienna. Later Erna would say: "I stayed a ski enthusiast all my life and am convinced I owe Frau Dr. Adler my enthusiasm for skiing and sports generally."

In an article in *The Independent*[10], Erna told of her first experiences of skiing.

"I used to take the bus out [to local mountains] for the day. I went with school friends, or the Girl Guides. And we just went up and down a slope all day. There were very few skiers and nobody to teach us"

At school, Erna learned English and Latin but no French, which would become an important language for her business in later years. It was something she tried to rectify in the 1980s. Speaking in a *Sunday Times* article[11] at the time she said she would regularly listen to the French programme on the BBC World Service, had taken a course at the Lycée and was reading *Moi aussi, j'etais seule*, a book by French agony aunt Marcelle Segal.

***

Another great sporting influence on Erna in her early years was Herr Juranek, who ran gymnastic classes in leafy Schönbornpark on the Lange Gasse, a road just off Josefstädterstrasse. Erna went twice a week and, despite being small and thin in those early years – the result of two bouts of pneumonia and an appendix operation – she was agile, unafraid and soon become Juranek's star pupil.

"If Herr Juranek would have told me to jump from the top of [Vienna's] St Stephen's Cathedral – I think I would have jumped," she later said.

Erna loved to swim too, learning at an early age and inspired through competition with one of her childhood friends – "a certain Litzi Rabl, tall and thin, who I had to spend my holidays with for many years but was no favourite of mine.

"When I learnt to dive, Litzi finally jumped in with the words 'If she does it – I will do it too even if it kills me'."

Erna's grandmother Barbara, her friend Friedl Apotheker, Erna,
her mother Emma and friend Litzi Rabl

Erna admitted to being no angel as a child, in fact was something of a tomboy, and later recalled what was to become a much-repeated incident in the Löw household.

"Litzi and I were left at home under the supervision of my grandmother," she said. "Litzi kept on boasting that she was stronger than I so I had to show her what's what and throw her to the floor where she lay gasping for breath. My grandmother came running and said, 'How can you do such a thing – she was your guest after all' whereupon I made the famous remark 'I had to entertain her somehow'."

The anecdote lived long in the Löw household but Litzi herself did not – she died in her early twenties as a result of a botched appendix operation.

Erna was mischievous by nature, perhaps to relieve the boredom of city-centre living.

One of her favourite pastimes, she reveals in her autobiographical notes, was to fill a rubber balloon with water and empty it onto people passing by below, although the long arm of the law eventually caught up with her.

"I quickly ducked when the policeman on duty looked up and got away with it for quite some time. Once I was not quick enough and he saw me and came up. My grandmother was not exactly pleased and told me that 'I was a nail in her coffin'."

***

The same year that Erna started at the Realgymnasium, she joined the Girl Guides in Baden. She particularly enjoyed the weekly Sunday excursions with the Guides but at one point she was banned from accompanying them on trips.

Erna wrote later, "Our Girl-Guide leader Georgie became interested in the opposite sex at the age of eighteen. Who can blame her? Instead of taking us on our usual Sunday outings she spent the day with her boyfriend. I greatly resented this as I was very bored staying at home on Sundays."

In an early display of Erna's enterprising and organisational nature and after a couple of boring Sundays without getting out of the house, she started to ring around her friends and suggested a handball game to take the place of the excursions.

"It was a harmless effort but my group leader strongly objected to my enterprise. She removed my treasured Girl Guide badge and forbade me to go on excursions with the group for two weeks," she recalled.

She was castigated but Erna's go-getting spirit was clearly in evidence.

***

One Easter, the family was heading to Baden by train from Vienna. Eduard and Emma sat in one compartment while there were six or seven children, including Erna, in another.

The children were playing a game involving throwing a ball made of handkerchiefs from one to the other when all of a sudden there was a violent collision and the scraping of metal on metal.

"Suddenly there was a terrible crash – our train had collided with another one coming from the opposite direction. The side of the train where we children had been sitting was completely demolished and two children were buried in the debris. There was a great deal of commotion, cries for help and searching for relatives."

Several people died in the collision including a teacher from Erna's school.

"Miraculously we children were not badly hurt," wrote Erna. "We all were taken to the nearby hospital but sent home after a while. The accident with its gory details was reported in the paper and all the names of the injured were given. I remember how proud I was to see my name in print and I carried the article with me for many months."

The shock of the accident stayed with Erna for many years and she subsequently refused to travel alone by train.

Ironically, as someone who ended up travelling so much herself in her career, she admitted that any time there was a sudden jerk or jolt when travelling by train or plane, she was taken back to that day many years earlier.

***

Life to the young Erna would have seemed idyllic in the post-war era but already there were rumbles of discontent across the border.

Germany's defeat in the Great War was seen as an enormous humiliation for the country, one that was made all the more galling because of its forced signature of the Treaty of Versailles in May 1919.

Article 231 of the Treaty was to be a thorn in the country's side for the next two decades. It forced Germany to accept responsibility "for causing all the loss and damage to which the Allied and Associated Governments and their nationals have been subjected as a consequence of the war imposed upon them by the aggression of Germany and her allies."

The treaty articles that followed forced Germany to agree to compensate the Allies "for all damage done to the civilian population of the Allied and Associated Powers" and gave the country a period of thirty years from 1921 to do so, starting with a payment of twenty billion gold marks over the three years 1919-21.

As well as the financial constraints placed on Germany, it was also forced to cede large chunks of its territory to foreign powers, notably Poznan, West Prussia and Upper Silesia to the Poles and Alsace-Lorraine to the French. It was also forced to cede its imperial acquisitions overseas to a League of Nations mandate.

The German armed forces were decimated as a result of the Treaty of Versailles; the army was restricted to just 100,000 soldiers, the air force disbanded and restrictions placed on the type of vessels the navy was allowed to operate.

The Germany that emerged after the Treaty to replace Kaiser Wilhelm's empire is known to historians as the Weimar Republic. It was beset by rioting from both left and right-wing factions and, in the early post-war years, suffered from hyperinflation – the cost of a loaf of bread famously rising from one mark in 1919 to 100 billion marks four years later.

In 1921, Adolf Hitler took control of the National Socialist German Workers' Party and two years later led the Beer Hall Putsch in Munich. Hitler, supported by General Erich Ludendorf, took over a meeting held by the Bavarian state commissioner von Kahr at the Bürgerbräukeller. At gunpoint, von Kahr, the head of the Bavarian police Colonel Hans Ritter von Seisser and General Otto von Losso of the *Reichswehr* (Germany army) were asked to support the putsch, which they reluctantly accepted.

However, the Munich putsch, which was intended to be the starting point of a coup to overthrow the government of the Weimar Republic, soon lost momentum and Hitler and his associates were arrested and thrown into jail. It was here that he wrote *Mein Kampf*.

Despite the failure of the putsch, the publicity surrounding it brought Hitler's ideas to the wider German public and would sow the seeds for a second global war.

The country's hyperinflation problems were temporarily curbed by 1924's Dawes Plan, which saw American bank provide loans to help the country meet its repayment obligations and Allied troops move out of the important industrial centre of the Ruhr Valley, allowing the German economy to restart.

The late 1920s in Germany were relatively calm and this period is often known as the Golden Age of Weimar with Berlin at its frenzied centre. The reason? Hyperinflation had returned and Berliners worried about the slumping value of their currency would spend it at the capital's bar each night, listening to jazz and watching the likes of erotic dancer Josephine Baker.

The Young Plan of 1929 was another American-led attempt to curb the problem but both this and the Dawes Plan had a serious flaw – they made Germany heavily reliant on the health of foreign economies, something that would go disastrously wrong when the Wall Street Crash hit.

Meanwhile, Austria's political scene in the 1920s was dominated by tensions between the bourgeoisie, who were vulnerable because of the collapse of the Empire, and the working classes, who were inspired by the events of the Russian revolution in 1917 and whose main political party, the Social Democratic Workers Party, was growing in influence.

Both sides were armed, the ruling classes through various private, well-funded paramilitary groups and the workers by the Republican Defence Corps. Clashes between the two sides were frequent.

The clashes came to a head in early 1927 when fighting broke out in the village of Schattendorf between a group of Social Democrats and a fascist paramilitary group. During the fighting, a barman fired a gun at the crowd outside his pub and killed a man and a child. The barman was sensationally acquitted at the ensuing trial in Vienna, leading to large scale rioting in the Austrian capital. Workers stormed the Palace of Justice in protest and by the end of the day more than 600 were wounded and eighty-nine dead.

Such violent clashes were symptomatic of the pressures bubbling under the surface and which would soon spill out beyond Europe's borders.

Chapter 2

Erna left the Realgymnasium in June 1927, two years after the death of her father Eduard from a long illness. Her school report on leaving recorded her behaviour as "very good" and noted the successful completion of a project on the Roman chieftain Vercingetorix and the Gallic uprising. She was noted as very good in physical education, physics and geography but only satisfactory in maths and English.

The eight years that Erna spent at the Realgymnasium were tough thanks to its harsh discipline, despite the release she got from the outdoor gymnastics classes in the Landegasse and her trips to the countryside. As a result, when those school years were over she declared a "great sense of relief".

By contrast, the next few years would give Erna some much-wanted freedom. In 1927, after consulting with her friends and family, Erna decided to enrol at Vienna University.

The university, founded in 1365, is the oldest university in the German-speaking world but it took more than 500 years, before it allowed women through its doors, making Erna one of the first of the new vanguard.

The university had long welcomed a high proportion of students from Jewish backgrounds, such as Erna. Between 1881 and 1904, the proportion of students who were from Jewish backgrounds was between 24 and 33%.[12]

"Vienna University was the most prestigious centre of learning in the Monarchy, and, as a national centre, attracted students from a large catchment area of which Vienna was only a part," says Stephen Beller in his book, *Vienna and the Jews*.

At the time, the university was seen to be a place to nurture "official" rather than the "liberal intelligentsia" and provided "the State with enough teachers and civil servants to fill the ranks". As a result, the university offered a large number of courses aimed at students who wanted to become teachers and it was onto one of these that Erna enrolled, looking to become a middle school teacher, specialising in physical education and English.

She was in good company. Just a few years earlier, the eminent 20th century philosopher Karl Popper had enrolled for a teaching course at the university and stayed on as a lecturer in the philosophy department which taught Erna's classes.

The choice of English was to change the course of Erna's life, setting her on a course to leave her homeland and spend much of the rest of her life in Britain.

***

It was during this teaching course that Erna made her first ever trip to Britain and it could well have been her last. A violent incident in which the police became involved could very well have put her off the country for good.

In the summer of 1930, the university's travel department organised a four-month trip for a party of fifteen girls, including Erna, to Britain. To modern eyes, the choice of destination seems a little odd; the group opted for a visit to the small village of St Osyth, five miles west of Clacton-on-Sea in Essex.

Dominating the village are the ruins of St Osyth priory. Today, the village has a population of around 4,000 but St Osyth is a popular holiday destination, as it was at the time of Erna's visit, and this number swells to more than 20,000 in the summer, with many staying in chalets and caravans to enjoy the medieval ruins as well as the beautiful Essex coastline.

Erna's group had a different style of accommodation. A local schoolmaster, a Mr Woods, had got in touch with Vienna University and offered to place students who were looking for a reasonably priced place to stay.

Woods was the headmaster of Hill House Catholic boarding school in a mansion on the top of Overdam hill on Point Clear Road. Woods had opened the school in the house after the First World War, taking in boy boarders in the mansion and teaching them in a stable block across the road.[13]

One of the trip's aims was to expose the girls to the English language. However, Erna related, the group spent much of its time in St Osyth's church of St Peter and St Paul during the day and they ended up only hearing a limited amount of the language they were supposed to be studying.

However, the visit soon took a most unpleasant turn.

Erna wrote later: "We really looked forward to going to England but very soon came to the conclusion that Mr Woods was a very cruel man who ill-treated his own children as well as some of the boarders who had been sent to his house on holiday. The accommodation was awful, the food terrible and all the boarders were very unhappy."

"The final straw was when Mr Woods smashed a lamp on the head of one of the boarders, who had to be taken to hospital. The police came and took him away and closed his establishment and we were suddenly homeless."

The local baker – a Mrs Norman – took pity on the group and came to their rescue, invited them to stay until they could find suitable alternative accommodation.

"My Austrian friend who had come to Britain with me decided to return to Vienna but I was determined to give Britain another chance," said Erna. "Little did I know it was to last a lifetime."

Erna's mother Emma, hearing of the group's unhappy experience, asked the university to send through some new contacts. Erna was soon on her way to London to stay with a retired General named O'Callaghan and his Irish wife in Clarendon Road in Holland Park. The couple offered "reasonably priced accommodation with breakfast and supper to students and ex-army officers".

Erna's room was very large but had little furniture, although there was an oversized picture of the Prince of Wales on one wall.

She soon got the size of the O'Callaghans.

"The General was very old and hardly ever visible," she said. "[The wife] would come down to breakfast every morning enquiring 'Is the old boy (her General husband) still alive?'."[14]

Erna added, "It was obvious that he and his wife had seen better days and that they were very hard up; they were mostly interested in the payments their lodgers handed to them every week."

The O'Callaghans' livelihood depended on a match-making business it turned out.

"I was invited to take part and met a number of fairly well-off young people – especially rich young ladies who were introduced to impoverished, young men from good families. It taught me a lot about certain aspects of life in impoverished aristocratic circles."

The stay with the O'Callaghans lasted just a few weeks but the lessons she learned would prove formative for the young Erna, who would soon set up her own business aimed at a similar audience and with which she had similar success in making matches.

She learned another thing from Mrs O'Callaghan too: "She taught me English upper class vowels," she wrote later.

At the end of November 1930, Erna returned to Vienna to resume her studies at the University, but the following July she was back again for another four-month stay, this time staying in Welwyn Garden City.

Erna wrote later, "I had heard of a Quaker family – the Landers – in Welwyn Garden City who offered reasonably priced accommodation to foreign students. Harold Lander, an architect, had been to Vienna and had contacted the department of Vienna University which arranged foreign trips for students."

Erna brought with her an unusual piece of luggage that caused fellow Tube passengers to stare at her after her arrival by train at London's Victoria Station – a javelin. While at university, Erna had taken up the javelin and brought it with her to practise.

"The Landers and their three daughters lived in a pleasant house adjoining Welwyn Golf course. What could be better? I thought this was an ideal place for me to practice throwing. My hosts were not exactly enthusiastic but were too polite to object."

"In due course I practised in a secluded part of the golf course – fortunately nobody objected and I did not hurt anyone – my javelin throwing definitely improved."

In fact, the javelin throwing had improved so much that on 9 July 1932 she represented Austria at the Women's Amateur Athletics Association championships – one of the forerunners of the athletic World Championships – at Stamford Bridge in London.

With a throw of 107 ft 4 inches, Erna came second to the British record holder E. Halstead.

The javelin was not the only sport that Erna was keen on – she also threw discuss, played netball and was a keen handball player, representing WAF, the Wiener Associations-Football club. Despite its name, WAF also had handball and athletics squads as well as the most successful Austrian football team of the time.

Her involvement with WAF lead to a meeting with the most famous Austrian football of all time, the Wunderteam, which won a string of impressive victories in the early 1930s and who were the favourites for the 1934 World Cup.

In late 1932, Erna wrote an article called *The Wonder Team: The Austrians Interviewed by a Fellow Country Woman* about meeting the Wunderteam, who were in London to play a friendly against England at Stamford Bridge.

She decided to pop over to the team hotel in Regent Street in order to present them with "a lucky farthing".

One of Erna's earliest trips to Britain: In the garden with the architect
Harold Lander and his family in Welwyn Garden City

"When I arrived at their hotel and modestly asked for the Austrian team, the receptionist broke into a hymn of joy… he was jubilating over the fact that the Team were out and that he was earnestly hoping they would remain out for a long time, for the continuous stream of calls… to which he had been subjected since their arrival had almost drive him out of his wits."

At that moment, the team returned and Erna joined them for lunch, "I was pleased to see that none of them appeared to suffer in the slightest from 'nerves' or worry on account of the game, as was evident from the enormous lunches they devoured.

One of the players, Miden, confided … that in order to be on the top of his form a man must eat as much as he possibly can; he himself only felt really happy when he had ordered a whole chicken all to himself.

"The Austrians are nearly all small lightly built men and their chief fear is that they will be outclassed by the English players in sheer physical strength to such an extent that their greater speed, agility and tactical science will be insufficient to compensate.

15

Event No. 8. 3.20 p.m. 100 YARDS (Cross Heat).

Winner to compete in Final.

Second in Heats 1, 2, 3, 4, 5.

1st.............. 2nd.............. Time..............secs.

Event No. 9. 3.25 p.m. 440 YARDS CHAMPIONSHIPS.

Heats.

Challenge Cup and Medals presented by Julius Salmon, Esq.

World's and British Record, N. Halstead, B.A.C., 58 4/5 secs.

Standard: 63 secs.

Heat to be drawn up on the ground and duly announced.

1	N. Halstead, B.A.C.	44	H. Beckley, P.A.C.
37	V. Humphreys, Mit. A.C.	29	V. Branch, S. & W.G.
38	E. Squire-Brown, S.H.	45	J. Simmons, P.L.A.C.
39	G. Lunn, B.H.	46	J. Stevenson, P.L.A.C.
40	I. Barber, L.O.A.C.	47	A. Stone, Mit. A.C.
41	R. Christmas, L.O.A.C.	48	D. Bruty, S.C.H.
42	D. Butterfield, M.L.A.C.	49	S. Meurs, L.O.A.C.
43	V. Rudd, P.A.C.	50	E. Jones, Cr.H.

Competitors qualified to run in Final.

1................................. 3.................................

2................................. 4.................................

Event No. 10. 3.30 p.m. JAVELIN CHAMPIONSHIP.

Challenge Cup presented by Sir James Heath, Bart.

Medals presented by Directors of "Daily Sketch."

World's Record (2 hands), Haux, Germany, 57.05m. (190 ft. 9½ ins.)

World's Record (1 hand), E. Braumüller, Germany, 40.27m (132 ft. 2 ins.)

British Record (2 hands), L. Fawcett, L.O.A.C., 171 ft. 4 ins.

British Record (1 hand), E. Halstead, B.A.C., 113 ft. 9½ ins.

Standard: 80 feet.

100	L. Fawcett, L.O.A.C.	105	E. Halstead, B.A.C.
101	R. Davis, Mit. A.C.	106	M. Wilson, M.L.A.C.
39	G. Lunn, B.H.	120	L. Simmins, B.H.
102	M. Curzon, M.L.A.C.	119	E. Otway, L.O.A.C.
43	V. Rudd, P.A.C.	118	N. Purvey, L.O.A.C.
103	C. Jupp, P.L.A.C.	124	E. Low, Vienna, Austria.
104	M. Scorah, P.L.A.C.		

1st.............. ....ft. ....ins. 2nd.............. ....ft. ....ins.

3rd.............. ....ft. ....ins.

The programme from the 1932 Women's AAA meeting,
credit: Cadbury Research Library: Special Collections, University of Birmingham

"Occasionally one of them exclaims, "If we do win, we shall turn London upside down and we'll drink all the 'lager' in the town."

"After promising to come and throw a shoe after them as they leave the hotel for the match, I … wished them *Hals und Beinbruch*, 'that is neck and leg-break', the favourite formula in Austria when one would wish someone particularly good luck."

The farthing proved not quite lucky enough but nearly so. The Austrian team played brilliantly in front of a 42,000-strong crowd at Chelsea's home ground with goals from Matthias Sindelar and Karl Zischek, but eventually lost 4-3.

The article was written for one of the Austrian newspapers and Erna somehow managed to secure a press card and wrote on a number of topics, including why Britons were so in love with the Austrian Tyrol.

Erna returned to Britain for another long stay in July 1932, staying briefly in Balham and Esher in Surrey before ending up in Bloomsbury.

She came armed with the address of an Austrian Boy Scout friend of her brother Fritz who worked in Oxford Street and with a borrowed £10 in her pocket.

Erna, third from left, with the WAF handball team

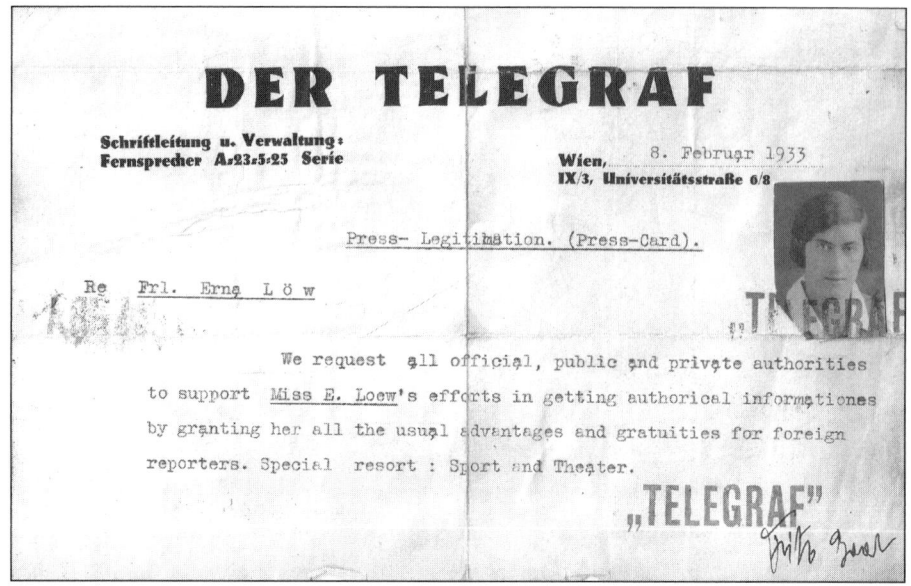

DER TELEGRAF

Schriftleitung u. Verwaltung:
Fernsprecher A.23.5.25 Serie

Wien,   8. Februar 1933
IX/3, Universitätsstraße 6/8

Press- Legitimation. (Press-Card).

Re   Frl. Erna Löw

We request all official, public and private authorities
to support Miss E. Loew's efforts in getting authorical informationes
by granting her all the usual advantages and gratuities for foreign
reporters. Special resort : Sport and Theater.

„TELEGRAF"

Erna's press card

"I promised to call on him and I did – much to his surprise," said Erna.
"Nobody had warned me that it is customary to telephone or write first to make
an appointment before calling – so it was not exactly surprising that my brother's
friend was somewhat astonished when a young lady arrived unannounced. However
in proper Boy Scout manner he dropped everything and listened to my story."

The friend suggested that Erna place an advert in the personal column, then
the front page, of *The Times*, helping her draft it and even paying for it. The ad
read: "Young Viennese lady, graduate (diploma), gives German lessons".

The replies were directed to the friend's respectable office address and filtered
before being forwarded on to Erna, who was much surprised to receive a flood of
letters.

"I finally selected a dozen or so but did not know where to suggest meeting them.
I could not possibly have invited them to come to my humble abode," said Erna.

By chance Erna learned of the Penn Club at 8-10 Tavistock Square in Bloomsbury.
The Penn Club, a club with connections to the Religious Society of Friends (Quakers),
was founded in 1920 with funds from the Friends Ambulance Unit, active during the
First World War. She stayed at the Club for the remainder of her trip.

There Erna met a 23-year-old by the name of Rosamond Jevons, secretary of the Club and a student at the School of Economics in Bloomsbury. Jevons was the grand-daughter of the economist William Stanley Jevons and went on to become a well-known economist herself.

Jevons agreed to allow Erna to use the Club in the mornings to teach her pupils, mostly young, professional people who were keen to learn and paid Erna a small fee.

Between these trips to the UK, Erna would return to Vienna to take further teacher training studies in English and physical education at the university.

The stays in England were clearly helping her grasp of the English language improve dramatically. As part of her coursework she was asked to translate an article from the *Times Literary Supplement* for which she received top marks. Her professor noted, "She speaks English well and with familiarity."

She was also reading English classics extensively as part of her work, such as the *Canterbury Tales, Beowulf* and the works of Coleridge, Marlow, Eliot and Twain.

Erna also garnered high grades for the psychology of the teaching process and in how to teach young girls sports.

***

Yet as Erna progressed through university, the social unrest that had occurred in both Austria and Germany would conspire to put Adolf Hitler into power.

The economic fallout of the 1929 Wall Street Crash and the Great Depression of the early 1930s saw Hitler and his Nazi party make huge in-roads into the political scene. In the 1932 German federal elections, the Nazis won more than 37% of the vote, taking 230 seats and gaining an overall majority.

The following year, the Austrian-born Adolf Hitler was sworn in as Chancellor of the Weimar Republic. He said at the time, "I will employ my strength for the welfare of the German people, protect the Constitution and laws of the German people, conscientiously discharge the duties imposed on me, and conduct my affairs of office impartially and with justice to everyone."

Just what form that justice would take for the Jewish populations of Europe would soon become terribly clear.

Chapter 3

In the final months of 1932 – just as Hitler was about to take control of Germany – Erna made the first step along a road that would lead to her setting up one of Britain's best known travel businesses, a company that would end up taking tens of thousands of people on holiday each year.

She needed to find a way to support her regular trips back to Austria between her stays in England and realised that by putting together a party of people who were interested in the then fledgling sport of skiing – or ski-ing as it was more commonly written then – she could cover the cost of her own trip.

The idea of going for a recreational skiing trip had had an unusual conception just over thirty years earlier.

Dr Henry Lunn was a Methodist minister who organised a series of conferences in the Swiss mountain town of Grindelwald, partly because of the relative ease of access by train and popularity with the British seeking the Alpine air but also because it had been the retreat of the saint Bernard of Clairvaux[15]. Dr Lunn made the travel arrangements and found that he had a flair for it.

In 1898, he took a group to Chamonix, including his son Arnold, on what is generally believed to be the first ever ski package tour. More trips soon followed.

Five years later, skiing was becoming increasingly popular. In early 1903, the barrister and ski jumper EC "Teddy" Richardson founded the Davos English Ski Club and then, at dinner at London's Café Royal in May the same year with fourteen others, founded the Ski Club of Great Britain.

According to the Ski Club, the idea was "to encourage other people to learn to ski, help members improve and take more enjoyment from their skiing while bringing together people interested in the sport."

By 1904-05, Dr Lunn was taking a thousand visitors by train and Channel ferry to the Alps[16], concentrating on Switzerland and developing the resorts of Mürren and Wengen in particular. That year, he established the Public Schools

Alpine Sports Club to provide "all the elective advantages of an English club" and "secure the presence at… Swiss resorts… of a congenial society or people."

"He booked entire Swiss hotels and bought them if necessary to guarantee his customers their homely exclusiveness," writes Huntford in his book *Two Planks and a Passion*. "His customers paid him to take them to the Alps; he included solicitude for their virtue in the price. He censored what came to be known as après-ski… In 1913, on ground of immorality, he banned the bunny-hug, an American dance of the jazz age."

Skiing holidays in the early days were exclusively for the rich; the aristocracy and professionals such as barristers were the only people with the money and the necessary free time it would take to reach the Alps.

***

While the means of getting to the mountains for a reasonable price were being conceived by the Lunns, others were making skiing easier by introducing new techniques.

In 1907, the seventeen-year-old Johann "Hannes" Schneider – born in the town of Stuben am Arlberg in Austria – was offered a job as resident ski instructor at the Post guesthouse in St Anton. Three years later, he had enough clients that he was able to set up his own school.

Until this point, the techniques used by recreational skiers were those that had been developed by early Norwegian skiers, particularly the Christiania turn, named after the Norwegian capital before it was renamed Oslo.

Schneider's revolution was to develop a new type of turn based on the Christiania, the stem Christie, which was easier to teach to beginners. He combined it with a new stance called the Arlberg crouch which replaced the stiff upright stance used heretofore. The learning progression from a basic snowplough through the stem Christie and using the new low position became known as the Arlberg technique, the basis of modern ski instruction.

***

The equipment that skiers were using was changing too.

Skis at this time were made of wood, typically hickory, which was extremely tough but flexible. It was also expensive and by 1893, the Norwegians were experimenting with the idea of making skis from bonded layers of different woods. However, these early attempts were scuppered by problems in finding a sufficiently hardy, waterproof glue to hold them together for long periods. This delamination problem was not effectively solved until 1932.

Skis then were also very long by modern standards – typically measured from the toes to the fingertips of a person standing with their arm raised. Ski poles were long too – they came to shoulder height. The use of a pair of poles – rather than a single one used on both sides – only came about after the publication of Colonel Georg Bilgeri's work *Der Alpine Skilauf* (Alpine Skiing) in 1910.

Keeping your skis on your feet was one of the biggest early challenges. Early bindings consisted of a simple leather strap over the toe of the boot but a second strap was soon added around the heel to allow for the range of movement of the foot.

Later the heel strap would be replaced with a metal cable or spring that gave the heel greater flexibility to move. By 1932, most people were using so-called Kandahar bindings – named after the Kandahar Ski Club and race of the same name founded by Henry Lunn's son Arnold in 1924. The binding was entirely made of metal and included heel clips that allowed the ski to be used for downhill skiing or locked down for cross-country.

***

The final innovation that spurred the development of skiing in the early days was the invention of the ski lift.

In the early days, getting to the top of a mountain meant hiking there on foot with your skis on your back or wearing skis that had been fitted with seal skins to allow movement uphill without backsliding. Sometimes, if you were lucky, a mule or horse would be provided to take your equipment to the top of the hill.

All this was to change in 1908 with the invention of the mechanised lift. Robert Winterhalder owned the Kurhaus Schneckenhof in the Black Forest which also had a water mill which he used to hoist loads up to his loft.

His flash of inspiration was to divert the water to the foot of a snowy slope where it drove a loop of steel wire running up the slope that was hooked over a flywheel. "It was supported by five wooden posts with pulleys, and at intervals were attached a piece of rope to which the skier (or tobogganer) clung by force. It was, in other words, a primitive drag lift… the first ski lift in the world."[17]

The first true ski lift – and which went on to be introduced throughout the

An early ski lift

mountains – was sighted in 1934 in Davos in Switzerland. This included a spring-loaded bar that formed a crook around a person's upper thighs.

It was against this backdrop that in November 1932 Erna decided to put a classified advert into *The Morning Post*, a conservative broadsheet with the motto "The Empire's Senior Daily". The paper was bought and merged into the rival *Daily Telegraph* in 1937. *The Morning Post's* journalists at the time included the legendary W F Deedes, then a cub reporter in his first year of journalism.

A classified ad in the paper cost 7s 6d for the first three lines and then 2s 6d per line thereafter. As was the tradition then, the classifieds took up the entire front page of the newspaper, news stories being relegated to the inside pages.

The ads from the front page of the 17 November 1932 edition[18] are a curious mix. You wonder what disagreement between a girl and her daughter caused her to post the ad "DADDY.—*PLEASE*.—PAM."

Meanwhile, jewellers Mappin & Webb offer to purchase "OLD GOLD FOR CASH", a "widow and linguist" announced she was heading for Alassio in Italy for the winter and sought a travelling companion, while The Pocket Trivet was promoted as "an ideal Christmas present".

WINTER SPORTS.—Austria, fortnight, £15 only, including rail and hotel, arranged by young Viennese Graduette for young people leaving Christmas. Also Swiss Party.—G.R.,1365, " Morning Post," E.C.4.

Erna's *Morning Post* ad

Then, what nearly the last advert in the Personal column reads:

The young graduette's advert is not the only one for skiing trips. One reads, "A party is leaving on January 20th for a fortnight at Grindelwald; special terms; novices and others invited"; another says, "Private party professional class, leaving for Switzerland Dec 29, INVITE OTHERS to join.".

The first Erna Low holidaymakers were four students – Leo 'Baldy' Sassoon, Hutton Williams, Stanley Jordan and somebody with the last name of Fellows whose first name is now probably lost forever.

Erna told a reporter in 1967[19], "I took a handful of students—all boys—and a middle-aged lady (she seemed ancient to us then) as a chaperone [Miss Hudson[20]] and we went to Sölden for Christmas."

Leo Sassoon wrote an account of the trip, saying that "the very term 'Vienesse Undergraduette (sic)' seemed full of romance and aided our decision."

He continued: "The day arrived when we were to meet a Viennese Graduette wearing an orange scarf and to be found by the clock at Victoria Station. We did not openly show ourselves, but from afar surveyed the scene to see what we were in for," he wrote.

After boarding, Leo writes that he and a friend "disliking pleasant remarks" moved to another compartment. However, at the Swiss frontier at Basle, the train split in two and the pair only realised too late they were in the wrong half and ended up becoming separated from Erna and the other intrepid skiers, eventually arriving in Sölden five hours after the others.

Erna recalled this trip later: "We stayed at the Hotel Post, run by Isi Riml, and spent a hilarious Christmas. My party did not like caraway seeds, salami sausage and plumeau beds, I remember, and when I rose in defence of my home country, they used to put a little notice on the table 'Joke in Progress'.

She added, "There were no lifts to Hochsölden, not even a bus to Obergurgl. We just walked uphill on seal skins and enjoyed our *Glühwein* the more for all the exercise we took."

Outside the Hotel Post in Sölden; Erna's first organised ski trip

Erna told ski journalist Stephen Wood in a 1996 article what life was like without lifts[21]: "We were tough in those days: we would climb for two or three hours before skiing down."

"I had no tuition when I started and I remember crashing into a fence because I hadn't learned to stop. When I took groups to the Alps there were individual ski teachers, but it was still all very primitive."

Leo Sassoon says the snow was particularly bad on that first trip. "Snow was only to be found on the Southern slopes, unless one climbed great heights... Joyfully we climbed onto the Southern slopes, here doing every variation of the Christiania, snow plough and Sitzmark [ski turns]."

A Viennese friend of Erna's – Pauli Gstrein, who went on to become a successful hotelier near Kitzbühel – came to teach the group skiing.

"Our evenings were spent dancing, complete with ski-boots [and playing] 'Where are you, Moriarty?' and other games in which one spends a long time on the floor," wrote Sassoon.

For the uninitiated, Where are you, Moriarty? *Is* a parlour game in which participants lie blindfolded on the floor and try to hit each other with rolled up newspapers.

"New Year's Eve was a great success, and the host of the hotel was most proficient on a zither and in yodelling. Our proficiency was in drinking and in very bad imitations of yodelling," he added.

Leo also wrote, "Although not pretty, [Erna] was attractive, could speak French, German and English, [was] a good skier and organiser and showed much patience in enduring the ragging and foolish remarks of her party."

In 1982, Sassoon would write to Erna again after a Life in the Day profile of her appeared in *The Sunday Times*. He said, "As a result of your party in 1939 at Saas Fee, Joan and I are still together after forty-three years".

Erna's match-making skills were pretty well-honed by that stage and would prove to be a regular feature of the trips and parties she would put together over the decades to come.

Her scrapbooks are filled with letters from happily married couples and with birth announcements and baby photos from those that had got together.

Over the next few years, Erna would take more groups to both Austria and Switzerland, with the numbers on her trips growing all the time. She soon got into a routine: a month away in the mountains taking two trips of a fortnight each at Easter and then back to London, the summer months spent on inspection trips, visiting new mountain villages and hotels to arrange good rates for the next winter, and then a month over Christmas and New Year back in the mountains again.

Those early trips visited resorts such as Gerlos, Obladis, Saalbach, Hinterglemm, Galtür, Obergurgl, Lech and Zell am See in Austria as well as Sedrun in Switzerland.

She promoted the trips with a talk at the Anglo-Austrian Club on 13 November 1935 entitled "Austria in winter" with the promise of "lantern illustrations". She was joined by Pauli Gstrein, the "Austrian Ski-ing Champion, exhibiting a recently taken film".

Those early trips led to Erna's introduction to the Kemmis-Bettys, a family of keen skiers from a military background and who would remain friends throughout her life and would invariably be referred to as the K-Bs.

Erna met the first K-B – Mervyn – in a ski hut in Kühtai in 1934. His brother Peter remembers, "For a time, they were the only occupants. The story has it that

Ski group near the Mattmark Hut in Saas Fee

in order to preserve their individual privacy, they hung towels over a rope, dividing the sleeping space into two private halves."

She met Peter K-B in 1935 when the brothers went on trips to Gerlos, Kitzbühel and the Silvretta. Peter, who later became Colonel Peter K-B the secretary of the Army Ski Association, was an early visitor to La Plagne with Erna in the 1980s.

Peter says, "Skiing in those days was hard work but infinitely enjoyable. It normally took the same daily pattern – climbing most of the morning, either on skis or carrying skis on one's shoulder. In Kitzbühel for instance, before the lift was built up the Kitzbühler Horn, one carried skis for the first two hours up through woods, then climbed on 'skins' for the final hour or hour and a half. Then a picnic lunch on top followed by the afternoon run down."

Many of the early trips included stays at mountain huts rather than the upmarket hotels that would appear in Erna Low brochures later.

Speaking to journalist Eithne Power, she recalled, "In later days when I stayed in first class hotels I can never remember laughing so much as in those early days

Skiers relaxing on an early Erna trip to Hinterglemm

when we stayed in basic inns or in mountain huts. Nowadays travellers have become very fussy and the spirit of adventure has gone."[22]

Another early destination for Erna was one that remained a firm favourite throughout her life – Gargellen. Over Christmas 1937, she took a group of at least seventeen people to this village in Austria's Vorarlberg region. The photos of the trip that Erna took are occasionally annotated with the names of those who were there – Hans, Heather, Ditchburn, Pegotty and Nelson Foley (who went on to become chief architect for the Trust House Forte group). As a result of this trip, Erna became one of the first people to take holidaymakers to this corner of the country in winter. Until the 1920s, Gargellen had really been a summer resort.

She wrote in her 1967 brochure, "The great thing about Gargellen is that, in spite of it being a first rate centre, it has escaped over-development and commercialisation. It is, and has been for many years, my favourite centre and, whenever I go to Austria, I always look forward to my visit there."

The Hotel Madrisa, run by the Rhomberg family, was her particular favourite.

"The Hotel Madrisa has been in the hands of the Rhomberg family for many years – since long before the war in fact – and I have known the Rhomberg sons since they were boys. They now assist Frau Rhomberg (senior) with running the hotel and the well-stocked sports shop, and Hans Karl's charming young wife Lilly and their delightful children give a family atmosphere and personal note to the hotel."

Hans-Karl remembers, "Erna was a very good business woman and I can remember that she always tried to get the best conditions for her clients."

***

A couple of years after her first trip to Sölden, Erna gained a long-term rival in the form of fellow Viennese Walter Ingham, born in 1914 and who had come to England in 1932 as a Remington typewriter salesman.

In Ingham's obituary in *The Independent* in 2000[23], ski writer Roger Bray wrote, "Walter's enduring and friendly rivalry was with Erna Low". He quotes Walter in the obituary: "'Very soon I found that selling typewriters gave no job satisfaction and no skiing.' He discovered that if he took a party of fifteen people to the Alps, he could get a free rail ticket and hotel room into the bargain."

He took his first group to the Tyrol in Christmas 1934 and by the end of his first season had taken six groups. From Walter's early tour operation efforts, another of the giant names of the ski industry was born. Inghams (now minus an apostrophe) celebrated its seventy-fifth anniversary in 2009 and today is the second biggest ski tour operator in Britain, taking nearly 100,000 skiers and snowboarders on holiday.

Erna was one of the first to take people to Austrian villages in the winter.
This large group visited Gargellen in 1937

Chapter 4

With the financing of her trips back to Austria solved, Erna could concentrate on her studies. She had by now decided to work towards a PhD in English literature, splitting the time from March 1933 to September 1935 between her mother's apartment in Vienna and various short term let flats in London's Bloomsbury.

The subject of her thesis was the minor Victorian poet Lord de Tabley, suggested to her by her supervisor Professor Kvalik. De Tabley was little known in the 1930s and even lesser known today.

The third Baron de Tabley, John Byrne Leicester Warren, was born at Tabley House, Knutsford in Cheshire on 26 April 1835.

The seat of the Leicester Warren family is Tabley House. This Palladian country house was designed by John Carr of York for Sir Peter Byrne Leicester, the poet's grandfather, and was completed around 1767.

The house has a south-facing, nine-bay central block with an imposing Doric portico reached by curved stairs. This is flanked by pavilions and quadrant passages.

Eton and Oxford-educated de Tabley was a barrister, would-be Liberal MP, numismatist and amateur botanist.

He was also interested in book plates and, in 1880, published a well-received book on the latter called *A Guide To The Study Of Book-Plates*, which the *Sunday Times* called "admirable" and the *Spectator* "solid, trustworthy, and conscientious".

Yet it was for his poetry that de Tabley was best known. He was a friend of Lord Tennyson and Robert Browning and published four slim volumes in 1859 under the pseudonym G F Preston, inspired by the death of his friend George Fortescue. He published further works over the next two decades but did not receive any real acclaim until the release of *Philoctetes* in 1866, again published pseudonymously using the initials M.A. When the critics and public took this to mean poet Matthew Arnold, de Tabley revealed the truth.

In order to research her PhD, Erna managed to secure a ticket for the Reading Room of the British Museum, a more difficult challenge than it is today. She would go to the British Museum most days to write up her thesis and befriended one of the Reading Room assistants, Alf, who helped her selecting books.

"After considerable research I found the address of Lord de Tabley's descendants – the Leicester Warren family," wrote Erna later.

Erna wrote to the family's address in Knutsford, Cheshire with a letter of introduction from the Austrian Embassy.

"They kindly asked me to visit them and allowed me to study Lord de Tabley's letters and manuscripts in their house," said Erna.

Erna's no-nonsense approach to life was typified by her first visit the family seat.

Lord de Tabley and sisters outside Tabley Hall in c1860, from Cheshire Country Houses

"I arrived at the station to find out that Tabley House (the re-built Tabley Hall) was 3½ miles away and that there was no transport to take me. So being the sporting type that I was then, I set off and arrived at the entrance gate. Having had no idea where I was going, I gingerly knocked at the lodge and asked the lodge keeper whether Lord de Tabley was living there. He was somewhat surprised and told me that his Lordship was dead (he had died in 1895) and pointed out that his descendants, the Leicester Warren family, lived in the large stately home at the end of the long drive. So I picked up my rucksack and went on.

"He warned the Leicester Warren family by telephone of the arrival of a strange visitor. The butler opened the door – I had no idea who he was and shook hands with him. Fortunately, the entire Leicester Warren family came to my rescue and invited me to enter the very impressive establishment.

"Col. Leicester Warren asked me 'How did you arrive here?' and I told him that I walked. So the entire family, Col. and Mrs Leicester Warren, their son and daughter exclaimed 'You walked?' Nobody has ever walked here from the station. We always send a car!"

It was the first time that Erna had been in such a palatial residence and she admitted to being overwhelmed. However, she quickly became firm friends with the Leicester Warrens' daughter who was about her own age.

"My first meal with the family was an ordeal but I quickly got used to living in such grand style."

Her *Times* obituary[24] says that when she left Tabley House, "her meagre student's savings did not go far in tips for the many servants, and was embarrassed to be able to do no more than shake hands with the butler."

A year later the thesis was complete and she sent the Leicester Warrens a copy from Vienna. "They were delighted," she recalled later. "It was the only booklet they could send to the many people who asked for details of de Tabley's life."

It would be fifty years before Erna was to return to Tabley House and that in an unexpected manner.

When Erna took on Oxford graduate Joanna Yellowlees as her assistant in 1982, the fact that she was born in Knutsford and her parents lived on Tabley Road clearly struck a chord.

"It was a strange coincidence that Joanna was born in Knutsford and that her parents still lived close to Tabley House," Erna said later. By then, the Leicester Warren seat had become a private school, set up just after the Second World War.

Joanna's parents obtained permission for Erna to revisit. "This brought back many memories of my pre-war visit," said Erna.

Erna remained interested in Tabley House and was particularly concerned when in the late 1980s its future was under threat.

"I received a letter from the land agent, Oliver Beck, who succeeded his father and had been connected with Tabley House all his life, enlisting my assistance in getting support for keeping Tabley House going as a conference centre. Who would have thought that that young student who literally knew no one in Britain – let alone anyone of the standing of the owners of Tabley House – could be of use in the plight to preserve a fine example of one great British heritage?"

She wrote a letter to *The Times* to draw attention to its plight. Although her plan for a conference centre failed, it has been saved from ruin. These days, the house is open to the public several days a week, allowing visitors to see the impressive art collection, while the lower part of the house is a care home for the elderly.

Erna's dissertation – submitted to the university on 7 July 1934 – was dedicated to the Leicester-Warren family "for hospitality and friendly support" and ends as follows:

"It may be said that Lord de Tabley was undoubtedly one of the most interesting poets of the Victorian era. However, it must be regarded as a regrettable loss to English literature that the poet's unhappy disposition, his sense of inferiority and his pathologically intensified sensitiveness, caused him at the height of his creative power to stop all poetic activity, so that relative to his outstanding poetic talent he has only handed on to posterity a small number of works."

***

When Erna was not taking ski groups to the mountains, she was back in London teaching German at the Penn Club and scratching a precarious living.

However, the lessons were proving so popular that Bloomsbury's Penn Club was getting rather overcrowded with the students; club secretary Rosamond Jevons politely asked her to find a new home.

"By chance, I had just become a member of the Ski Club of Great Britain. Skiing was just beginning to become popular and several of my friends and pupils were also Ski Club members," said Erna. The Club's headquarters in Hobart Place in Belgravia was an obvious place to go but she soon outgrew that too.

After many stays in hostels and clubs around Bloomsbury, Erna finally decided that renting a flat was the only suitable alternative.

"I remember walking up and down Bloomsbury, knocking on doors and asking 'Have you by any chance a two room flat to let to a graduate/teacher?' I did not mention that this teacher was having a string of pupils coming to her flat for German lessons. After a considerable time searching for a flat I was eventually given an address at 116 Gower Street – belonging to University College nearby – where a top flat was available for renting. I went to look at the flat, liked it and decided immediately that it was the right place for me – even though it was on the top floor, four staircases up."

"I moved in immediately and befriended the housekeeper – an elderly French lady – who lived on the ground floor. She agreed that I could share the flat with a friend of mine, Dora Tennant, a university graduate. Living on the top floor was very good for our figures as we had to climb four flights of stairs many times a day to answer the postman, let in a cleaner and a regular stream of pupils who came for their German lessons."

Students would arrive at the Gower Street flat, which was "small and simply furnished", and would bring biscuits, flowers and the occasional bottle of wine. Erna called the atmosphere at the 116 Gower Street flat "friendly and easy-going", so much so that "some of the male students started to take advantage of the situation".

We have Erna herself to thank for an account of her life as a German teacher. Among her scrapbooks, there are three pages of yellowing notes in Erna's tight, neat handwriting entitled "The Day of a German teacher [a look behind the scenes]". It reads:

8am. Miss Low to the telefon (sic): "Who is speaking?" "It is you again, what on earth is the matter?"

Caller: "Oh what is the matter with you, I have not rung you up for ages and this is my reception."

EL: "I am so sorry." [It is again Mrs X who always rings up 5 minutes before her lesson to put it off].

10 minutes later. Miss Low to the telefon again. "Who is speaking?"

Mrs X: "I wonder, Miss Low, whether you could come at 12 instead of 9. My dog has been desperately ill all night and we had not a moment's sleep."

EL: "Oh certainly, just as you like."

11am. First pupil arrives.

He: "I am so sorry I could not come last Monday but I was detained at my office and it was too late to communicate with you."

Miss Low: "Oh, that's quite alright. What about your sister?"

He: "Oh, didn't she let you know? She suddenly had to go up to Scotland and I am sure as soon as she will return she will ring you again."

EL: "I hope she will have a good time and see the Loch Ness Monster. Can you show me your homework?"

He: "You **would** ask me for that."

EL: "Yes, I am afraid some homework is necessary."

He: "If one works in the office all day long and has to attend to social duties as well, believe me, Miss Low, es ist sehr schwer, homework zu machen. But the next time I'll do my best for you."

Another playlet written by Erna, A Day in the Life of a German Teacher, gives another account of this time:

An old man (OM) arrives at the top floor and after five minutes' rest on the window sill starts off: "Can I see Miss Low?"

EL: "Yes, that is I."

OM: "I have come to arrange German lessons."

EL: "Will you please sit down."

OM: "You come from Vienna, don't you? That is a place I have always wanted to go to – music, wine, vocab – you do speak German there, don't you? And there is not much difference between Viennese German and other German?"

EL: "Oh no certainly not. Much less than between a person from the Midlands and one from London."

OM: "That's fine. Are you fond of cinemas?"

EL: "Yes, I quite like cinemas."

OM: "You people in Vienna are so gay – take life easy, don't you? I thought to myself, you could come to my place and we could have a lesson and then some food and a little amusement in the evenings. Would you like to do that?"

EL: "I am terribly sorry but at the moment I am so busy that I would only come for the lesson."

OM: "Oh I see. How much do you charge for lessons?"

EL: "That depends on number, time, place."

OM: "Well, Miss Low, I will think matters over. You see I wanted somebody who could keep me company sometimes in the evenings."

In her autobiographical notes, she wrote later, "I soon learned to distinguish between serious pupils and those in search of fun."

As well as those looking for a little company with a cosmopolitan Viennese graduette, there were others with more sinister motives.

She had a bad experience with a pupil who called himself Hamilton Hargreaves but whose real name turned out to be Frank James White and who was a con artist.

A cutting from the papers at the time[25] showed his modus operandi. "Hargreaves" would place an advert in the papers for women to be social hostesses at fashionable East Coast hotels. He would hire an expensive looking car to take them to the hotels and asked them to take their best clothes and jewellery with them. En route the car would "break down" and the women would be asked to push the car. He would then drive off with their belongings.

Erna fell foul of the scam but he was caught, sentenced to five years in jail and most of the belongings returned.

Whether it was her trusting nature but she seemed to attract scoundrels. She was also convinced to help another person she met at the time who needed money.

"I lent money I could barely spare to a chap called Fritz Jellinek. It was £18, a fortune for me in those days and it went down the drain," Erna wrote.

***

One of the German students made a particularly strong impression on the young Erna and, in her notes, she refers to him as her "special pupil".

He was James Watson Maxwell, originally from Manchester and who ran a glove company in the City of London. He started taking regular lessons with Erna in 1933; he was thirty-one years her senior.

Maxwell clearly took an interest in helping the young Austrian, showering her with gifts on a regular basis and taking her out for tea. He also helped Erna with her English and got his manservant to send her *The Times* each day after he had read it.

In a letter to Erna from December 1933, in response to a letter from her, he wrote, "Your letter was perfect barring one error, one does not "hold a speech" but "makes a speech"; one can hold a conference or meeting but they might "make speeches at them"."

He ended the letter in a much friendlier tone: "I am glad to know that my little gestures are appreciated simply because you deserve them". He ended with some best wishes for the coming New Year. "1934 will be pleasing and happy as

A portrait believed to be of James Watson Maxwell

long as I am learning German from you. You claim gratitude in your letter, I am also very grateful to you but that is a secret, Yours as ever, J W Maxwell".

In May 1935, he wrote that he was feeling much better after an illness which had begun in May and that the doctor was now coming every month rather than weekly. It turned out he had a heart problem.

At the end of September, Maxwell wrote to arrange a meeting for tea – "China for preference" – at 4.15 outside Lillywhite's on 4 October 1935 but it was not to be. Maxwell was taken ill that day and died four weeks later at a nursing home in Watford at the age of fifty-seven, leaving an estate worth £19,474 (around £1.1 million in today's money). Erna would not have known about his being stricken and would have turned up, perhaps standing by the statue of Eros in Piccadilly Circus while she waited in vain.

His obituary said he was a person "of a retiring nature [but] nevertheless did a great deal of useful hospital work, and assisted many good causes". His wife's wreath was dedicated to "dearest Nip"; there was also another wreath from "a grateful friend" – presumably Erna.

A few days after his death, Erna wrote a letter – never to be delivered – which reveals much about how she felt about her "special pupil".

She wrote, "How I miss you, I shan't describe in words. I shall never, never find such a kind and unselfish friend as you have been. I wish I could have done more for you and especially come and sit with you when you were ill and when I was thinking of you day and night. I hope you know me well enough not to believe for a moment that I had forgotten you or let you down, but that I did not come although it almost broke my heart, you must take as the confirmation of my wish to act always as you wanted me to act. How much easier it would have been to rush to your bedside and be with you in your difficult hours than make myself stay away and not even be able to send you some flowers or a message.

"I am sure you never doubted me as I never doubted you. I shall live as you would have liked me to live although it will be so hard without your help and advice. You were the one reliable friend I had in England and I feel more alone and friendless than ever before. You were always so modest and considerate and unselfish in your claims to me and I wish now you had not been so, so that we could have had more of each other's company which I shall miss so much now.

"Now you are gone I went to see your office and house and went for a walk where you probably went on Sundays with your dog and now I have been to the RAC just the day you died and when you were in my thoughts all the time. One coincidence after the other. I wish I had seen you just once before you were taken ill and worst of it is that I wanted so much to see you when I arrived and because of a stupid misunderstanding, and my pride our meeting was delayed until it was not granted to us no more. Your presents to me, always chosen with such care and love, will remind me of you daily and hourly since all I possess you gave me. Every morning I think of you when the clock strikes but there is no need for me to be reminded of you because I shall never forget you.

"I wish you would have let me do more for you and not only showered kindnesses on me without asking any in return.

"But why didn't you tell me about your heart. I wish I could do something for your wife or Mr Morley [the manservant], just to repay a few of your kindnesses to me. Nobody ever will take so much interest and sympathy in me and my affairs as you did. I should have needed you so much in the next years of my life – you, just you – my kindest friend and not your gifts. Tomorrow is your funeral and then you will be taken away from me forever. I shall wear the red dress you saw me in for the first time and which you liked on me and I shall always respect your principles and ideas and act according to them. If ever I shall have a son I will call him after you and if ever I shall write a book I will dedicate it to you. You won't be lonely in your grave because I shall be with you in thoughts and come to you to tell you all my pleasures and sorrows as I did when you came to tea on Fridays. Goodbye, my dearest friend, have peace now which you could not find in life. I send you a kiss – the first and last one – and so well deserved. In love, yours Erna."

Erna met James Maxwell at a time when she was very vulnerable. She had arrived in London just a few years earlier and had virtually no friends in the British capital. Erna's father, Eduard, had died six years before and she missed him dearly. From Erna's perspective, James Maxwell slotted into that surrogate paternal role easily.

James Maxwell probably did not see the relationship in the same way. He was clearly besotted by Erna, in spite of being married and his three decade age advantage. He always wrote to her from his business rather than home address and the letters make it clear that he forbade Erna from writing to or visiting him at his home address in Hertfordshire.

There is a small mystery surrounding James Maxwell that may never be cleared up.

He sent a letter on 30 September 1935, just a few days before his death, which reads, "To commemorate July 19th, I presume you may have now forgotten the date, I bought you something very useful, although I am becoming poorer every day… It is a small travelling alarm French clock from Kendale and Dent in Cheapside."

The shattered remains of this travelling alarm clock still sit in the offices of Erna Low, its red leather now battered and the gold leaf lettering reading "E.L. July 19th 1935" looking slightly worn. We can only speculate on its significance. That day was a Friday, the day of the week that Erna says in her letter she would meet him for tea. Erna may have been wearing the red dress which he liked seeing her in, the colour of the clock perhaps reflecting this. Maxwell's description of the incident makes it sound as though it was something trivial that would have meant little to Erna but an enormous amount to him. Perhaps their hands touched while reaching for a teaspoon.

***

Back in Austria, the situation was becoming more and more tense as violent clashes continued between the various privately funded paramilitary groups.

James Watson Maxwell's gift to Erna

In 1933, Chancellor Engelbert Dollfuss suspended parliament and began ruling by decree, suspending many civil liberties for the next year. The following February, the country descended into what is known as the Austrian Civil War but lasted just four days. However, hundreds died and thousands were wounded in the short-lived conflict and it was used as a pretext to ban the Social Democratic Workers Party. In July 1934, Dollfuss was assassinated and his place taken by Kurt von Schussnigg.

Von Schussnigg drew up a constitution that year stating that Austria "guaranteed the equality of all citizens before the law, regardless of birth, caste, class and promised complete equality to all legally recognised religions."

Despite this, there was an increasing anti-Semitism in the country which, while never proclaimed as "official government policy ... the phenomenon clearly permeated the entire system, with at least tacit support from its highest officials."

This anti-Semitism was increasingly evident. Since the Great War, Jews had been systematically excluded from public sector jobs, including the judiciary and education.

It was a situation that Erna and her family back in Austria viewed with an increasing distaste and apprehension.

***

Meanwhile, Erna was becoming increasingly integrated into upper middle class English society.

In what would become an Erna Low trademark, she quickly mixed work and pleasure and became friends with many of her pupils, some of them inviting her into their homes.

"I was amused at their lifestyle and very impressed when I realised how many staff they employed in their elegant houses," she said later.

Two of her pupils lived in a classy block of flats close to South Kensington station and had a butler and entertained regularly, which impressed Erna no end.

Another pupil who became a good friend was Elizabeth Roscoe, the daughter of a well-known solicitor, who lived in Kensington but also had a country house near Rugby. They got on so well that Elizabeth even moved in to the Gower Street flat for a month before returning to her more comfortable Kensington abode.

These regular invitations to London and country houses for cocktail parties, tennis tournaments and even cross-country races would prove to be an invaluable introduction to the English upper classes, the very people who would soon become clients of her fledgling travel company.

Erna was enjoying this lively existence so much that she decided not to return to Vienna, with her growing concern about the rise of Adolf Hitler and National Socialism in Austria certainly weighing on her mind.

Dennis Fabri, who worked at the French Tourist Office and ended up collaborating with Erna on trips, says, "She had the sense when Hitler had barely been elected to move away. She had strong political views and if she hadn't moved away when she did, we would never have heard of Erna Low I suspect."

Erna wrote later on her thoughts on why her trips proved so successful.

"In the pre-war period the upper class English – especially the young – were very keen on making contacts with visitors from abroad. They also became very enthusiastic skiers," said Erna.

"It was fortunate that I was able to arrange ski parties and they joined them and introduced their friends to me. They learned to ski remarkably quickly and also greatly enjoyed the Austrian way of life."

With Erna's closer integration into British life, she took a greater interest in the events that were taking place in the country.

Rumours in the newspapers at the time prompted Erna to write a letter to Sir G Thomas, the secretary to King Edward VIII.

She wrote: "I should be very grateful if you would kindly convey my deepest sympathy and admiration to His Majesty at this present difficult time.

"I, as an Austrian subject, know of the immense popularity the King enjoys abroad and especially in my own country for which he has done such a lot and we have the greatest trust in him to prevent a war at all cost and admire his genuine concern for the people and their problems.

"It would mean not only a terrible loss to England, but also to Europe and the whole world if such a truly good King would be pressed to abdicate. The young generation in my country as well as in his own admire his courage and honesty in this particular matter and nobody with any human feelings can wish for anything else but that the King is free to marry the person he loves."

Whether the King read the letter is unknown but four days later, as reported on the front page of the *Evening Standard* that Erna kept in her scrapbook, the king announced his abdication in order that he might marry Wallis Simpson.

Erna had started down the road of becoming more British than the British.

Chapter 5

By the late 1930s, Erna's mother Emma was in failing health and she made several trips back to Austria to see her, despite the growing crisis in the country. Emma finally died on 7 September 1937.

Despite, or perhaps because of, the disturbing events in Germany and Austria at this time, Erna's German lessons were going very well.

In 1938, Erna was giving German lessons at various schools around London as well as privately. A booklet promoting evening classes at the Friern Barnet Evening Institute in Ferrand Park showed Erna giving classes in both elementary and intermediate German for two hours on Wednesday and Friday evenings for the price of 10s. She was also giving classes in German grammar and conversation at the Princeton Street School of Languages in Bedford Row on Monday evenings.

A head of department at City of London College on Ropemaker Street, where she also lectured, called Erna "a thoroughly efficient teacher and a woman who has known how to inspire liking and enthusiasm in her students." The principal of Bedford Square Secretarial College said she "gained the affection of her students... I always find that she is very willing to accept any suggestions I may make and to fall in with my wishes", sentiments which would not always be felt by her own staff in later life.

Erna was also doing translations from German into English at this time for Sylvia Pankhurst, the woman best known as a prominent campaigner in the suffragist movement. Oddly, Erna received a kitten in payment.

The German lessons allowed her, in her words, "to start moving in different circles".

"They never ask what anything costs, what they earn, what they do. Amazed that people of opposite political parties could be so friendly – politics not even discussed," she wrote later.

Her school, the flat at 116 Gower Street, was next to the building where animals were prepared for testing, "Their cries and whimpering was not exactly pleasant and my pupils who come to the fourth floor often wondered what was going on next door."

116 Gower Street was shared with various friends over that period, including fellow Viennese Hans Motz, who went on to become a professor at Oxford in the Department of Engineering. Erna wrote later, "He used to have a goldfish called Hans Marie – we could not identify its sex – and he took over the bath. He ended up having a sad death in the lavatory when his owner emptied the water bowl."

Erna later shared the Gower Street flat with the Penn Club's Rosamond Jevons who introduced Erna to her friends, many of whom were "extremely left wing". As a result of this connection, she marched with the Oxford University October Club under the banner "Unite, fight and win" against the impending war. She also played tennis for the National Workers Sports Association. A news report of the time about a championship held by the association noted the unusual entry of "Fraülein Erna Low, of the Wiener Arbeiter Sportsklub and Vienna Labour Party".

"Our income was very small and our meals minute especially as we often fed our Austrian friends who were equally penniless." We had a lot of parties at Gower Street and earned a little extra money by writing articles," wrote Erna.

Erna also indulged her passion for writing by putting together a book to teach her pupils which she described in the preface as "neither a travel guide to Austria nor... a German grammar but [a little of] both." The setting for the book is a party of travellers to Austria and contains chapters such as "At the station in Salzburg", "Arrival at the hotel" and "A Sightseeing Walk through Vienna". One chapter, called "the Mountain Party", includes a dialogue between various young British professionals enjoying a walk in the mountains of Austria.

Daphne Gay: "HORRORS – ich habe mich auf einen Ameisenhaufen gelegt [I have sat on an ant hill]. O Bother."

Michael O'Brick: "Bitte sagen Sie uns ein paar gute Flüche auf Deutsch [Please tell us some good curses in German]."

Gretl Wiener [the guide/teacher]: "Donnerwetter! Zum Kuckuck! Hol's der Teufel! Dann gibt es noch eine Menge anderer, aber diese sag' ich Ihnen lieber nicht. [Damn it! Heck! Go to hell! Then there are a lot of others, but I had better not tell them to you].

***

The "Cleaning-Bath"   or   "Unkraut verdirbt nicht"

It was on a foggy Sunday night when two lone female figures returned from the wilds of Hertfordshire to 116,Gowerstreet.

"I m u s t have a bath",the fair one said.

"Get your damned goldfish out of the bath first",the dark one replied,
                                        little
curtly casting a sour glance at/Hans Marie and then attending to some washing.

Five seconds later: A shriek of terror pierced the air and - alas - a gruesome picture presents itself. Panicstricken rigor overcomes the fair one's slender frame and then gives way to eager activity - she fishes in the W.

"What e v e r are you doing???".
"Poor darling Hans Marie - where have you gone to???How does a

lavatory work ? Can he go down,do you think ? I can't see him anymore

Oh,Hans Marie...!"

Tears glittered in the fair one's eyes,sobs blurred her speech.

Different feelings filled the dark one's heart: "Thank God,this foul
                            one
animal is gone and more the bath is mine...My hat,never have I seen anything as funny as my fair flat-mate fishing in the Lav."   However her heartless attempts were nipped in the bud when the fair one's terrorstricken,but fierce,determined g glance struck her. The evil spirit vanished from her black heart and her better Self prompts her to say: "I'd getter get you a cup to fish the animal out!"

"It is too late. He has dissappeared--- Oh,noooo,here he is again -

My darling Hans Marie - What must you have thought where you have

got to!!! Horrors,he has vanished again - Thank God,our plug does

not work! --- "

The dark one appears with the cup,at last Hans Marie is finally and definit ely rescued and is - "of course" - put into the washbasin for a "cleaning bath".
Five minutes later: (In the kitchen)

"Don't you dare to put that smelling goldfish into the bath

                                                            again

Erna's flair for writing was obvious in this story about a pet goldfish

It was around his time that Erna bought her first car, which she dubbed Slippery Sam and which would take her on numerous scouting trips to the mountains to find new places to go skiing.

"I bought a strange little car, secondhand of course, for a little less than £10," said Erna. "The car, a Morris Eight, broke down a great deal but I found a repair shop close by and made friends with one of their staff who helped me to keep the car on the road for three years."

Slippery Sam's successor was a "Baby" Austin Seven which Erna gave the name Sunshine Susie because of its lack of a roof.

On one occasion when Erna was driving Sunshine Susie down a hill near Farnham, she did a 180 degree skid, causing another driver to end up in a ditch. She asked whether he needed driving somewhere. "I do not want a lift from a lunatic," he replied.

"Slippery Sam", Erna's first car being loaded onto a ship ready to go overseas

Again, the car did not last for long and was soon replaced with a Morris Minor which she bought for £50 – roof and all – and stood her in good stead for several years. "Year by year my income improved and so did my cars," she said.

Erna's excitement at the growth of her fledgling business was increasingly disturbing news from home.

Ever since the early 1930s, there had been an increase in anti-Semitic activities in Austria.

Harriet Pass Friedenreich writes in her book *Jewish Politics in Vienna*, "In December 1932, Nazi newspaper and leaflets, as well as placards posted on churches, announced a formal boycott against Jewish businesses during the Christmas season… In November 1937, the Deputy Mayor of Vienna spearheaded a movement for Christians to buy only from Christians, claiming that Jews only patronized other Jews."

Over the four years to 1938, Chancellor Schussnigg was also coming under increasing pressure from Adolf Hitler to agree to a union between Germany and Austria. Schussnigg eventually decided to run a referendum on the idea of unification in early March 1938. Hitler issued an ultimatum to Schussnigg demanding that he hand power to the Austrian National Socialists or face invasion.

The vote never happened. On 12 March, the German Eighth Army marched into Austria and the country was absorbed into the German Reich in what became known as the *Anschluss*.

On 26 April, a decree was made requiring all Jewish citizens to report their total domestic and foreign assets, where such assets exceeded 50,000 Reichsmarks. Three weeks later, a body called the *Vermögensverkehrstelle* was created to transfer these assets into Aryan hands.

Erna's brother Fritz was still living in the family apartment at Josefstädterstrasse at the time and continued to run the family college from it. Despite the family's earlier baptisms in the Protestant faith, the family assets were seized along with those of thousands of others.

Following Anschluss, the persecution of Jews increased dramatically, culminating in *Kristallnacht* on 9 and 10 November 1938 when synagogues were destroyed, Jewish businesses and homes ransacked. Kristallnacht was particularly severe in Vienna, with its large population of people of Jewish origin. Most of the city's synagogues were destroyed and 6,000 Jews deported to the Dachau and Buchenwald concentration camps.

Those Jews remaining in the city were further victimised and encouraged to leave the country. By December 1939, more than 100,000 of 175,000 Viennese Jews had emigrated with another 25,000 in the next two years.[26]

Fritz was among those emigrants, escaping probable death at the hands of the Nazis by moving over to England, staying at Erna's flat in Gower Street with his young wife Mitzi (Maria). Despite escaping with their lives, the family lost the wealth that Eduard and Emma had accumulated from years of hard work at the commercial college. The Josefstädterstrasse flat and college were sequestered by the authorities.

***

Erna's cousins in Milan in Italy were also forced to move because of their Jewish heritage.

Erna's closest ties were with Rodolfo Ruberl, her mother's youngest cousin, who became particularly close to Erna after Emma's death in 1937. Erna frequently went to him for advice, particularly with regards to her finances, and Rodolfo became a de facto head of the family.

Later, Rodolfo's two daughters, Liana and Riccarda, would become regular visitors to England.

Liana's son Guido Ambroso says, "My mother was married twice: the first was in London with an English Officer [Brian Bliss] not too long after the Second World War and Erna was the main reference point for my mother for a few, and I believe difficult, years."

With Germany's invasion of Austria and Mussolini's enactment of the anti-Semitic Manifesto of Race in summer 1938, the Ruberls were forced to flee to Switzerland.

Erna would soon put Riccarda Ruberl to good use, roping her in to becoming one of her party leaders at house parties.

Riccarda, still living in Milan, remembers having to escape to Switzerland. "Of course, one of the first persons we contacted when we finally reached safety was Erna and that was a great joy."

She says, "She came to Milan very often and I accompanied her in her travels when she was looking for new hotels in new places. I remember she always personally checked the rooms. She drove the car, and women were very seldom seen driving at that time. We were all very proud of her. She had these bright ideas which was at that time something very special – she was an innovator."

***

As a result of the *Anschluss*, Erna was granted an unconditional permit to stay and work in England in March 1938 and in November was issued with a certificate of identity by the Home Office that was "issued for the sole purpose of providing the holder with identity papers in lieu of a national passport." By this time, she had dropped the umlaut from her surname.

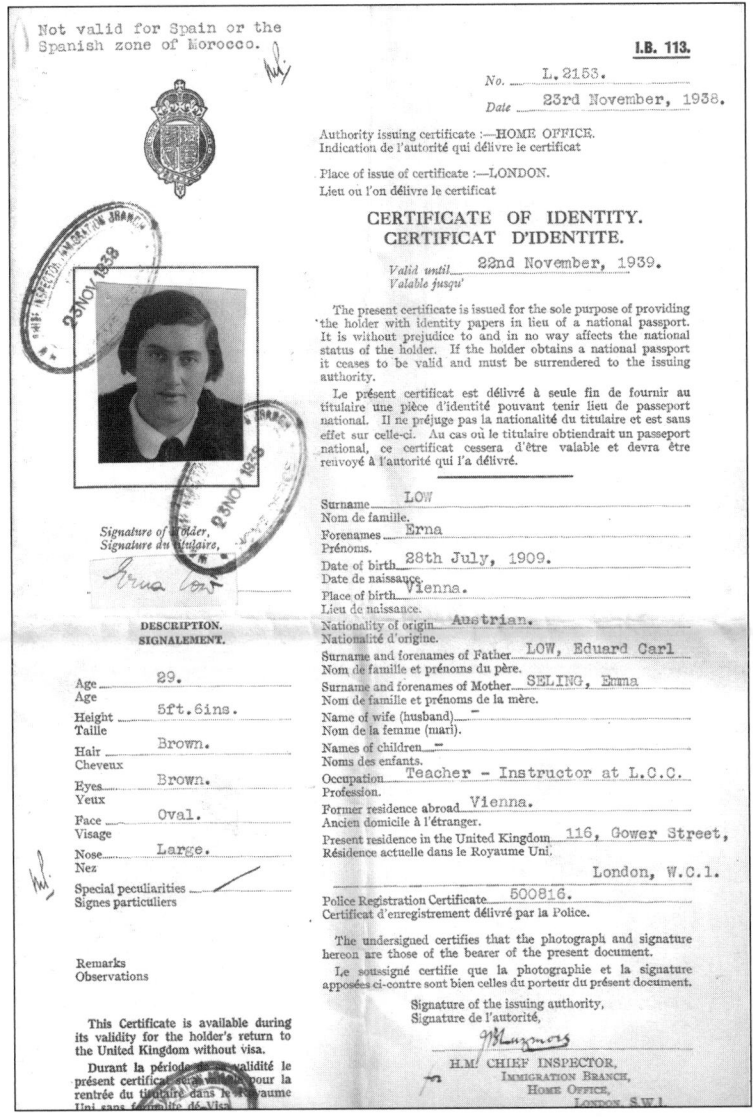

Erna's certificate of identity

It meant that she was able to continue her travels abroad, although Austria was now clearly off limits. With the family assets sequestered, earning a living through her teaching classes and through the fledgling travel business became imperative.

Writing to her clients just two days after *Kristallnacht*, she said, "At last I am able to write to you and to invite you to join my annual Christmas Skiing Party. It was very difficult indeed to get satisfactory accommodation as everybody seems to be going to Switzerland for winter-sports this Christmas" – an understatement to say the least.

The 1938 Christmas party was held in Sedrun in the Grisons, Switzerland. "Sedrun is an absolutely lovely unspoilt village surrounded by a great variety of skiing slopes and about fifteen very good runs for skiers of all grades. I was particularly attracted by the 'local colour' and 'atmosphere' of Sedrun which reminded me of Austria of the old times. Sedrun is 4300 feet high and a so called 'snowhole'."

She also started taking trips to other Swiss stations. "Saas Fee became my favourite centre," she wrote later. Here she befriended the Bumani brothers, well-known ski guides in the resort. The resort featured regularly in her winter sports programmes thereafter.

Family group skiing in Sedrun

In an article in *The Independent*[27], Erna described how they reached the resort. "The only transportation offered for the three-hour ascent to the village of Saas Fee was a mule," she told journalist Stephen Wood.

As well as skiing trips – she had taken 300 people to the mountains by this time – Erna started to turn her hand to trips at other times of the year and to new destinations, taking a party to the stylish Swiss town of Ascona, on the banks of Lake Maggiore, Venice, a windy trip to the Farn Islands as well as one trip to Corsica during which one of her guests, a Mr Danvers-Walker, joined the French Foreign Legion.

At around this time, her friend and pupil Elizabeth Roscoe took Erna on a trip north. "Her sister had a house in Bamburgh in the North of England and often invited us to visit her," wrote Erna. "This was a wonderful opportunity for me to get acquainted with interesting parts of Britain and to experience the comfortable life of the well-to-do upper classes."

With the future of Austria looking uncertain and her work now being based full time apart from the parties abroad, Erna applied for naturalisation in order to become a British Citizen.

A windy boat ride to the Farn Islands

"It was very difficult to achieve as I had so often changed my address in pre-war days," she wrote later.

The British Nationality and Status of Aliens Act 1914 required that the applicant have "resided in His Majesty's dominions for not less than five years" including the year preceding the application in the United Kingdom. The applicant also had to intend to live "in his Majesty's dominions or to serve under the Crown" and be "of good character" and with "an adequate knowledge of the English language".

The fee for application was £10, of which £1 was payable on application with the remainder due on approval. There was an additional fee of "2s 6d payable on taking the Oath of Allegiance". Erna had the father of Mervyn and Peter Kemmis-Betty, who had both been on skiing trips with her in the years before, to sign the papers.

Erna gained her certificate after taking the oath at 42 Bedford Square: "I, Erna Low, swear by Almighty God that I will be faithful and bear true allegiance to His Majesty, King George the Sixth, His Heirs and Successors, according to law."

Erna wrote in her notes, "When my naturalisation was finally approved I was, of course, delighted and celebrated with several of my friends."

***

In the early hours of 1 September 1939, the German *Luftwaffe* began a bombardment of the Polish town of Wielun while the port of Danzig (Gdansk) was shelled by the battleship *Schleswig-Holstein*. A few hours later, German troops from the Tenth Army attached the town of Mokra. By the end of the day, German troops and their Slovak allies were attacking the country from three sides.

Two days later, Erna would have been glued to the radio and would have heard Prime Minister Neville Chamberlain's sombre broadcast:

"I am speaking to you from the Cabinet Room at 10, Downing Street.

"This morning the British Ambassador in Berlin handed the German Government a final note stating that unless we heard from them by 11.00 a.m. that they were prepared at once to withdraw their troops from Poland, a state of war would exist between us.

"I have to tell you that no such undertaking has been received, and that consequently this country is at war with Germany."

Erna takes her oath of allegiance to become a naturalised British citizen,
photo: Pictorial Records

At around this time, Erna received an urgent phone call from one of her friends, Gwyneth Greenacre.

"She was desperate and needed help urgently at her country house, Grey Friars at Dunwich on the east coast," said Erna. "The house was full of evacuee children and there was only one teacher and his wife to look after them. She had asked the Swiss governess in charge of her own children to help in her spare time but this turned out to be unsatisfactory. Could I, please, come to Dunwich immediately?"

What Erna didn't realise and what Mrs Greenacre omitted to tell her was that Dunwich was right on the coast and very exposed to the new threat from Germany.

In blissful ignorance, Erna took the first possible train and went to Dunwich. "It was like the relief of Mafeking," recalled Erna. "I was enthusiastically greeted by the teacher couple and by the Swiss governess whose morale was very low. We

Evacuee children at Grey Friars

were a strange combination but after a couple of days we settled down quite well and looked after the East End children day and night.

"I befriended a pathetic little boy called Billy Gray. He was very pale, thin and unhappy. He missed his mum and was very frightened of bombs. After a week or two Billy settled down, made friends with the other children, gained weight and was more cheerful. He became very attached to me and followed me round the place like a little dog."

After three months at Grey Friars, Erna decided to go back to her flat at 116 Gower Street, feeling that it was safer.

***

When Britain entered the war, German and Austrian nationals on British territory were automatically considered as potential threats and risked being interned in special camps. During the first two years of the Second World War, some 8,000 "enemy aliens", as they were known, were interned in British camps, many of them in the Isle of Man. Many of those interned were deported to places like Canada and Australia, where they would pose no threat. Some never made it, their boats destroyed en route by enemy torpedo[28].

With their backgrounds, Erna, her brother Fritz and his wife Mitzi were all considered potential "enemies" and were required to plead their cases before Enemy Alien Tribunals, Erna in Ipswich – the closest to where she was staying in Dunwich – and Fritz and Mitzi in London.

Erna and Mitzi were both considered not to be dangerous and were allowed to remain at liberty; Fritz, however, was interned for more than a year.

His release, along with thousands of others, came after uproar in the press and in Parliament over the fact that many of those interned were actually Jewish refugees from the Nazis. On 11 January 1941, Fritz was re-categorised as category C – a so-called friendly enemy alien – and released.

Chapter 6

The advent of the Second World War may have slowed the growth of Erna's fledgling travel business but she was soon able to put her background to a different use – listening to radio broadcasts made by the Germans and translating them into English as a monitor with the Special Listening Section of the BBC Monitoring Service.

The BBC Monitoring Service had grown out of policy think-tank the Institute of International Affairs (Chatham House) under the leadership of David Hallett.

In early 1939, the BBC was asked to set up an official monitoring service in the event of a war and, when a national emergency was declared on 26 August 1939, Hallett's staff were invited to move to Wood Norton Hall in Evesham, Worcestershire to form the core of the new service and adverts placed to attract suitably qualified personnel. Erna applied and was soon on her way to Evesham.

"There were Germans and Austrians (including the art historians Ernst Gombrich and Ernst Buschbeck), some Czechs whose mother tongue was German, a few English staff bilingual in German and other nationals who had received a German education… ", according to a contemporary account of the service's activities, *Assigned to Listen*[1].

Finding accommodation in Evesham was no easy task, recalled Erna. "Monitors were not very popular with the Evesham residents".

Assigned to Listen reveals, "War or no war, suddenly to have strangers foisted on you by Government decree, to have to put them up for an indefinite period, to have to provide two meals a day – all for a miserly two guineas a week – would have been bad enough: to have to do so when the strangers were more often than not foreigners to this country… must have been well-nigh traumatic to this sheltered community."

Erna eventually found short-term accommodation in one of the little Evesham houses conveniently situated near a bus stop for the journey to Wood Norton.

Assigned to Listen describes the set-up. "The mansion which was at the centre of the BBC activities stands in the midst of a wooded estate, on a spur of low hills above the Avon as it winds its way from Evesham towards Tewkesbury. The house was bought by the exiled Duc d'Aumale in 1872 and passed on his death to his great nephew Louis-Philippe Robert, Duc d'Orleans, who made extensive alterations… Its plumbing, though not lavish by modern standards, was decorated with fleur-de-lys, which always amused visitors. An enormous pair of iron gates, originally from York House, Twickenham, formed the ceremonial entrance to the estate and were known as the Golden Gates."[29]

Erna's arrival at Wood Norton may have been an odd experience; many new recruits at Wood Norton were greeted "by the blaring sounds of 'If you go down in the woods today, you're sure of a big surprise' – Teddy Bears' Picnic – the test tune used by the engineers for the public address system which reverberated on the trees of the compound every morning at a fixed time"[29].

Erna later described her arrival at Evesham. "A supervisor was waiting for me and conducted me to the German Special Listening Section. There I was attached to a Mrs Hilt who was busily twiddling a knob. I asked her what she was doing but could not get much information from her, especially as she was listening to a strange language – I believe it was Dutch."

"I could not understand why when I was appointed as a German monitor, I suddenly had to listen to languages which I never understood or was able to speak. Gradually I got used to this strange set-up but was always very pleased when German, French or English was spoken."

The monitors, known as "teleprincesses"[29], a term coined by the television personality Gilbert Harding or the historian Gustaaf Renier, worked on six to eight hour shifts throughout the day and night.

Engineers were housed in a hut "up the hill" and looked after the radio equipment houses in big, black boxes. Broadcasts that required translation were recorded on wax cylinder. Recordings were kept for a while and then 'shaved', ready for re-use.

In the early days of the service, the monitors sat in the house itself, listening on earphones to the broadcasts from the hut and working around the clock in a four-shift system. The monitors would have one ear open for the broadcasts and another for the air raid siren as they lived in constant fear that the service would be targeted by German bombers.

The Listener[30] called the listening service "Britannia's Third Ear" and said that in 1941, there were more than a hundred listeners recording and annotating more than a million words a day.

Translated material from Wood Norton was then sent to London by teleprinter in Broadcasting House while important information – known as "flashes" – was phoned through. The service also produced a regular Digest of Foreign Bulletins which, by May 1940, "averaged between 130 and 140 pages and contained some 30,000 words". The digest was supplied to an impressive roster of recipients, including the Admiralty and the War Office but also the Mines Department, the US Embassy, the French Institute, the Polish Ambassador "and a certain officer in Wormwood Scrubs".

Erna recalled, "We had to cover several German stations more or less at the same time; this meant switching from station to station. We battled bravely against falling asleep during our night shifts; fortunately I rarely fell asleep when I would be rudely awakened by one of the supervisors who had a definite 'down' on me who had a nasty habit of unplugging one of my listening devices. God forbid if we missed an important announcement."

"When one of us picked up a 'scoop' there was great excitement. I remember distinctly the night when we heard that a British bomb had fallen on some German key positions and had caused a lot of damage," she said later.

As well as news of British successes, careful monitoring could also avert disasters.

One member of the service, writing in *Assigned to Listen*, recalled: "On one occasion an English speaking announcer in Zeesen was heard to say 'Our bombers are just taking off for Britain. The message was flashed to Fighter Command and a number of German planes were intercepted and shot down."

When Erna's short-term accommodation in Evesham came to an end, she had to look further afield.

"I had met other monitors who were having similar difficulties and we decided to try our luck in a village called Elmley Castle. Elmley Castle is beautifully situated at the foot of Bredon Hill about 10 miles from Evesham. We immediately fell in love with the village and decided to look for accommodation there. We were lucky and our first attempt was successful. We knocked at a cottage door right at the top end of the village.

"The door was opened by a very friendly Meg Kilgour who was always very cheerful although she had little to laugh about. Her husband, Frank, a gamekeeper in peace time, was away training dogs for war service and rarely ever came home. She invited us in and was very pleased at the thought that we would become tenants. She looked after us well, finding local produce and producing good meals in spite of the shortages during the war. When Frank did return, out came the best china and the food definitely improved."

Erna shared the accommodation with three other girls who were working on different shifts. "The four of us who shared the Kilgour cottage had all lived in London before the war and country life was new to us."

"We got on very well with Mrs Kilgour and her family, consisting of two girls – June and Rena, neither of whom owned a pair of shoes – and two boys, all under ten years of age. They were very happy recipients of occasional sweets which we managed to occasionally get. We stayed with them for almost two years," said Erna later.

Rena – "always very pretty" and "the teacher's pet", according to Erna – soon found a husband and they ended up living in a country manor near York. "Who would have thought of such a change in lifestyle?"

One of Erna's fellow listeners at the BBC was Heinz Beran, who had fled the rise of national socialism in his native Vienna. Beran had arrived in Britain just after the start of the war with his wife Trudl, they had been students together at Vienna University.

Erna knew Trudl well – her father had been Erna's doctor back in Vienna and she was a regular visitor to the Grohs family in Poetzleinsdorf, one of the most attractive Vienna districts.

On Erna's regular visits to Vienna before the war, the Grohs family's house was always one of her first ports of call.

"Their house was open to all their friends and we had a lot of fun. Mother Grohs did her best to feed us and we greatly enjoyed her cooking and especially the atmosphere in her house," said Erna later.

"My own mother was a little disappointed but gradually understood that I preferred being with friends in my own age group. The major attraction was the Grohs' son Reinhard, who studied at Vienna University. His tennis was excellent and he won many matches but often failed his exams."

Although the work was challenging, Erna enjoyed at least part of her time at Evesham and that was when she went skiing.

Bredon Hill, south west of Evesham, is just short of a thousand feet high, breaking through that barrier artificially thanks to the 18th Century addition of

Parsons Folly, a stone tower built for the local MP John Parsons. The hill is also the site of an Iron Age hill fort, known as Kemerton Camp.

Bredon Hill's name actually means hill-hill hill; bree in Celtic and don in Old English both mean hill[31] and it is immortalised in an A E Housman poem of the same name, which includes the lines

> *But when the snows at Christmas*
> *On Bredon top were strown,*
> *My love rose up so early*
> *And stole out unbeknown*

In 1967, she told one reporter[32], "I caused quite a stir by walking on skis to Hognorton one night shift when all the buses had stopped because of a heavy snow fall; [I had] a torch fixed to my rear and another in front to comply with the traffic regulations (I was forever in trouble in those days for riding bicycles without lights). On my days off I went up Bredon Hill and enjoyed the odd day's skiing."

When Gloucestershire's snows are sufficiently heavy, locals often take out their ski equipment to the hill. The north slopes down to the village of Great Comberton are the steepest but would have given Erna little trouble.

Erna's skiing jaunts on Bredon Hill eventually came to an end after it was announced that the Monitoring Service was to move from Evesham to Caversham Park in Reading, taking over the buildings of The Oratory School.

The move was as a result of concerns of a German invasion in which case the BBC's main activities might have to move from London to Evesham.

"It was not easy to find good billets [in Reading] and it took quite a few weeks before I found one with an easy going family [on Kidmore Road]. They had a pub in Reading as well as good living accommodation not too far away".

While living in Reading, Erna would spend weekends back at the Gower Street flat; the capital was still suffering under the onslaught of the Luftwaffe. She later admitted that "a top floor flat in Bloomsbury in the centre of London was perhaps not the ideal place to stay during the Blitz but we got used to dashing down to the cellar."

Erna wrote of one of these weekend visits later in life. "One Saturday morning a bomb fell on college premises very close by where an Austrian friend of mine – the artist Lizzi Pisk – lived. I spent several hours looking for her and was greatly relieved when she suddenly appeared. She had a very lucky escape and was not hurt. In spite of my pleading she refused to move from the premises. Bombs continued to fall – especially at night – and we became used to the warning signals 'bombs overhead'."

***

Evelyn Marriott was Erna's "oldest and closest" English friend. "I met her shortly after I arrived in Britain. I owe Evelyn a great deal – not only was she kind and supportive – but she accepted me, a young foreign girl, in her household, discussed her and my problems at great length and gave me a lot of good advice."

Evelyn was married to RAF officer Alfred FP Fane, well known at the time for racing BMW 328s with notable pre-war victories at Donington Park, Nürbrugrung and in the 2.0 litre class of the open-road Mille Miglia endurance race.

When war broke out Flt Lt Fane joined the RAF Photo Reconnaissance Unit and, on one 1942 mission, located and photographed the German battleship Tirpitz.

According to one report[33], on 18 July 1942 Fane "took off from Benson in Oxfordshire on a mission over U-Boat yards at Flensburg however the mission was aborted due to bad weather. He decided to land at Coltishall but eventually decided to head back to RAF Benson even though the cloud level was still extremely low. He crashed following the railway line at low level near Great Shelford, just south of Cambridge. He was thrown out and killed instantly."

After the war, Evelyn remarried, this time to the Arctic explorer Sir George Binney but the marriage only lasted eight years.

Evelyn and Erna stayed close friends, and shared a love of dogs, right until Evelyn's death. She bequeathed Erna a pearl necklace after her death which Erna wore almost daily thereafter.

***

Erna made many lasting friendships during her time at the BBC: fellow German monitor Liesl (Alice) Frank, Dorian Carter and Ellen Fleming, who ended up working for Erna for four decades on and off.

Ellen Fleming was born in Zennor, Cornwall in 1921 and went to school in St Ives and then to Switzerland for eighteen months. Before the Second World War, she spent time in Erna's native Vienna to learn German.

In 1943, Fleming was working in Cambridge where she met her German husband Alec. The couple then both went to work for the Special Listening Service, Alec as a monitor and Ellen as a secretary, when it later moved to Reading.

Ellen, speaking from her beautiful home in Penzance, says: "The BBC taught me to type… terribly badly. The monitors quite liked having me for a typist because my English was so good but hated it because I typed so badly."

The Special Listening Service at Reading was very sociable and it was inevitable that Erna and Ellen's paths would cross which they soon did in the staff canteen.

After the war, Alec died unexpectedly from heart problems. "Erna had heard that he had died and asked me (actually told me) to work for her in the South Kensington office," says Ellen. "I can't remember exactly what I did, probably sticking envelopes, typing and answering the phone, but I absolutely hated it and left after a year."

She didn't know it but she would later return.

Erna left the Service's Y unit on 15 July 1944. A leaving card from fellow monitors reads as follows:

Entranced, four years you've sat, the earphones on,
Revelling in Bach-Chopin-Mozart,
Now doleful tolls the bell; time marches on,
At last arrives the day when we must part.
Leave then, behind, all thoughts of car and pain,
Onward, joyful – to the open plain!
Watcher girl – Viel Glück, Auf Wiedersehen!!
(Note the first letters of this leaving poem.)

The sudden impossibility of taking ski trips to Austria and the necessity of making a living presented Erna with the problem of how to scratch a living.

The war meant that travel was restricted and German classes were suddenly out of favour and she had to find a new way to earn a crust. Erna's growing circle of upper class friends and the country houses they lived in presented her with an opportunity: parties for young professionals in country houses.

Bosigran Count House sits on the cliffs on the road between St Ives and Pendeen on the north Cornwall coast. It is a beautiful granite house overlooking the Celtic Sea and was built in the mid 19th century to service the neighbouring tin mine, whose engine house lies in ruins nearby.

A party at Bosigran Count House, Cornwall

Originally known as the Account House, Bosigran Count House was used to store coal, mining materials and was where miners came at the end of each week to grasp their meagre pay packets. The records of these payments were kept here too – hence the name.

The collapse of the Cornish mining industry meant the tin mine eventually closed but the house was bought as an investment in the mid 1930s by one J L Andrews. At the end of that decade, Andrews leased the house to the Climbers Club as a base to explore the craggy north Cornish coast at the instigation of the owner's nephew, Arthur Westlake Andrews, who eventually became known as the "father of Cornish climbing". The house is still run as a base for climbing the area by the Club today.

Erna came to hear of Bosigran Count House through one of her former German students, Bryan Donkin – of whom more later – and felt that it offered the perfect location for a house party.

"The climbers who normally stayed at the Count House were frequently away on war service and [the custodian] Mr Andrews was glad to have the extra income and we were very happy to rent the accommodation, primitive though it was," recalled Erna later.

She held the first of four summer house parties at Bosigran in 1941, attended by twelve guests whose names and addresses are neatly written in Erna's handwriting in a book along with photos of that first trip. Many of the names listed crop up again and again on the guest list of house parties in the years that followed and by the end of war, the Count House was full to bursting every summer.

In her one page letter inviting people to join her in the fourth year of staying at Bosigran Count House, she described Bosigran Count House as "rather primitive, but… the beds are excellent".

"It is an ideal holiday for people who like a simple out-door life and don't mind 'roughing it'. Everybody shares in the household duties, we make our own beds, keep the place tidy and prepare our own meals… I shall do all the catering for the party, so I shall need your Ration Book with a maximum amount of points. The food is very plentiful, varied and healthy and a farm nearby supplies us with milk, eggs, lettuce etc… You will also have to bring tea and jam for the whole period if these goods have to be collected from the place where you are registered."

She continued, "Bosigran is ideal for scrambling on rocks, walks along the cliffs and in the heather, sunbathing and swimming from the rocks or sandy coves."

In an edition of the Climbers Club journal of the era, Arthur Andrews had this to say about the place. "It is a far cry to Bosigran, but it's a good place when you get there. The house has plenty of room for climbers with its big dormitory, with twelve fitted bunks (with Vi-sprung mattresses) and a Devon fireplace. The upstairs will be converted for lady guests and there would be a separate outside lavatory."

If that all sounds a bit basic for a glamorous 1940s house party, the catering matched too.

"We cooked on a Primus stove which sometimes exploded," Erna recalled. "Once a week we went by bicycle on shopping expeditions to Penzance but mostly we were supplied with milk, butter and cheese by Mr and Mrs Pearce, the farmers who lived close by. Their young daughter, Maureen, often came to Bosigran Count House and enjoyed meeting our parties."

What Erna does not relate in her memoirs is whether the house guests were visited by the Count House 'Knocker'[34], "Bosigran's poltergeist, that emerges from the disused mine to plague the inhabitants of the Count House".

Although not climbers themselves, many of Erna's party guests would clamber over the steep cliffs below the Count House.

"To my horror, enterprising members ventured to climb on the cliffs below. I used to watch them, often warned them, and was greatly relieved when they returned safe and sound."

A poem called Bosigran Cliff, written by an unknown hand, shows that Erna joined in on at least one occasion.

> *The yawning abyss opened*
> *Erna was lowered down*
> *We heard her cry "I mean to try,*
> *But foothold have I none"*
> > *She dangles there upon the rope*
> > *Yet never did she give up hope.*
> *When Erna had succeeded*
> *In getting down the crack*
> *In dread and fear we followed her*
> *Our guide alone hung back.*
> > *Bisecting as he sat at ease*
> > *The dangling form of Marie Louise*
> *It now was nearly lunch time*
> *We stumbled back to eat.*
> *Our knees were bloody but unbowed*
> *We still were on our feet*
> > *And having conquered our first fears*
> > *We deemed ourselves TRUE MOUNTAINEERS.*

Many of the guests who went to these Bosigran house parties would remain firm friends. During her retirement, Erna looked over the names of those who had attended that she had diligently recorded in the many scrapbooks that she filled with memories throughout her life. "I was surprised to see that so many of the people who went to Bosigran are still in touch with me almost fifty years later."

A letter from Erna inviting people to "A Cornish holiday at Bosigran Count House" reveals another element that was to become an Erna Low tradition.

She wrote, "I usually try and meet all prospective members of my parties personally so as to get a party together where everybody fits in reasonably well, as this will not be possible this year – I am in N. Wales with another party – would you please give me some particulars of yourself, interests etc, when writing".

***

The success of the Bosigran parties saw Erna expand the house party business to other locations around Britain, including – in August 1944 – Capel Curig in the Welsh Hills.

Her "brochure" for the trip stated: "I have been very fortunate in finding accommodation for a party of twenty at Capel Curig, an ideal centre for walks, scrambles in the Snowdon district, for gentle walks to Llyn Ogwen, Swallow, Falls, Pen-y-Pass, for lake and river bathing, cycling and fishing."

She pitched the holiday at those people who had taken one of her trips before the war in Austria or Switzerland or had attended the first house parties in Bosigran.

She wrote that it would not be "a super-organised 'Cook's Tour' but a chance to have company when one wants to and privacy when one prefers it… In the evenings we talk, have discussions, play games or go for an occasional pub-crawl or dance."

The eight-day holiday, including accommodation at the Capel Curig Guest House ("more comfortable than a Youth Hostel but not like a luxury Hotel") and third-class rail fare from London, cost £7 7s. She added, "The food will be plentiful and pleasantly cooked, but simple. I shall try to bring fruit and tomatoes as they are very scarce in Wales."

***

Letters from those who went on these early parties show just how much fun they had, perhaps seeking an outlet for their frustrations about the war.

A young lady called Wendy Ball wrote "I think you deserve a lot of praise for collecting such good parties and running them in such a free and friendly way."

Barbara Crowther, who went to a Bosigran house party in 1944, said, "I came on your holiday party feeling very dubious about the whole thing – the thought of being jolly with a crowd of unknown people didn't seem in my line. But it turned out to be the best holiday I ever recollect."

Marie Peel, who worked at Bletchley Park breaking the German Enigma code, was one of those who went to Bosigran and had a fabulous time. After spending a week there, she wrote to Erna, "Should you need the services of a very amateur but willing cook for any of your future parties, do please let me know".

***

Erna's carefully preserved guest book that lists the names of all those who attended the early Bosigran parties also reveals the name of one person who would become a permanent fixture in Erna's life for the next half a century – Ernst Karl Litthauer.

Ernst was born on 17 June 1916 in Germany as part of a "super-bourgeois family"[35] of Jewish heritage. His great grandfather was the Polish embryologist and physiologist Robert Remak and his grandfather the neurologist Ernst Remak. His sister Hilde, who came with the family to England, went on to become the first ever professor of social psychology in Britain, founding that department at the London School of Economics and carrying out one of the earliest in-depth studies into the effects of television on children.

Hilde's mother was sent to England in 1934 because the school she was attending was rife with anti-Semitism.

Hilde's daughter, Sue, says "Uncle [Ernst's] school was much more supportive of the Jews while my mother's school was terrible to her [and others]. My uncle stayed to complete his education and when he finished he went as an apprentice to an industrial firm in Birmingham, which was owned by some relative."

As conditions in Germany worsened, Ernst returned there as he thought there might be some way to take the family's money out of the country.

"He lost his passport and he only just got out of Germany thanks to contacts and connections and trying at numerous border crossings," says Sue. The rest of the family managed to get out in 1939.

Ernst at the time looked something like a matinee film star – slim, with dark, slicked back hair and having a dimpled smile that would have melted anyone's heart in the same way that it would Erna's over the years that followed.

Erna wrote later that "Ernst was a shy young man who had seen one of my advertisements inviting young professional people to join one of my house parties in Cornwall. He arrived by taxi at the rather primitive Climbers Club House. I remember that we were busily dealing with a temperamental Primus stove when a young man in white shorts arrived. He was obviously expecting an upmarket establishment and must have had quite a shock when he entered Bosigran Count House."

***

The actor Roger Lloyd Pack, who knew Ernst well for many years as a result of his mother Uli working for Erna, says Ernst had a "very dry" sense of humour. "He would make rather witty remarks at Erna's expense, but fondly. He was like an uncle but one who didn't play football or talk about anything that I was interested in. He didn't really engage with children."

Roger's brother, the stage manager Christopher Lloyd Pack, recalls Ernst as "kind, generous and soft. He wasn't pushy and was an intellectual and clever man."

Guido Ambroso, one of Erna's Italian family, remembers Ernst well too. "He was of German Jewish origin but, like Erna, was secular and assimilated. Although he had a degree in engineering, he had a wide, humanistic culture. He looked like an old-fashioned (in the good sense) intellectual more than an engineer."

"Like Erna, he spoke perfect English but with a subtle central-European, Germanic accent that he could not hide. He was a very gentle and sweet person (I don't know why, but he reminded me of Primo Levi, whom I had met separately at a conference in London)."

He adds, "Erna rarely said that she had a PhD and it was only very late that I discovered that she did her doctorate on this obscure Victorian poet. If anything, it looked as if Ernst was the PhD in literature and Erna the engineer (appearances can be misleading)."

***

At the outbreak of the war, Ernst faced an Enemy Alien tribunal just as Erna had. Unlike Erna, it was decided that Ernst should be interned on the Isle of Man.

Sue Himmelweit says, "Ernst said it was one of the best times of his life. There were such interesting people there and they even set up a university there. They eventually let some people out to join the army effort. He was stationed in Chiswick and took a part-time engineering degree."

After the war, Ernst went back to Birmingham and started working with another company owned by distant relatives, BKL Alloys. The company had been formed in 1936 by Ernst's German relatives after their German steel company had been forcibly sold to Mannesmann before the war.

Ernst went on to become the company's export sales director, spending a lot of time overseas and eventually gaining an OBE in the New Year's Honours of 1967 for services to export[36].

Ernst would become a regular fixture at Erna's house parties during the war and in the immediate post-war years, watching Erna's fledgling business as an organiser of travel take form. Given their similar backgrounds and his good looks, it was inevitable that they would become a couple and, in 1948, they started seeing each other.

Sue Himmelweit says, "Erna was a constant in his life although they had a stormy relationship. He would come down to London most weekends and he spent most of his time with Erna. I always felt that he was slightly on her coat-tails and she was very demanding."

Chapter 7

After leaving the Monitoring Service in 1944, Erna landed a job at the London Regional Committee for Education among the Forces, initially on a part-time basis but after the war was offered a full-time role with the Committee attached to Southampton University.

The purpose of the organisation was to lecture returning troops on a variety of subjects, including "re-education of the Germans, local government and electoral reform".

One of her lectures spoke about the need for the Allies to put forward "a precise statement of war aims".

She said in one of these lectures, "The time has come to put an alternative to the German people. Casualty lists, retreats, lack of victories, coupled with obvious privations at home made worse by the winter, will soon begin to tell on German morale. A German mother will bear the horrors of war silently only as long as we are not able to convince her that there will be a prospect of a secure life for her children as for the children of the victor countries."

"I also spent my time writing to the German press in the hope of convincing post-war Germans that there would be 'a place in the sun' for a sane Germany. Little did I realise then that Germany would soon be better off than Britain although Britain had won the war," said Erna later.

To deliver her lectures, she toured the country in Sunshine Susie, the Austin Seven that had no roof, visiting many classic British seaside resorts as she went, something that would give her ideas on expanding her business.

***

With the number of house parties and ski trips growing, Erna decided after the war ended that it would be better to have one or two permanent employees than continue to use temporary help and so put an advertisement in *The Times*.

One of the applications – from a young girl called Valerie Jean Shafto – stood out.

During the war, Valerie Jean – whom everyone called Bobbie after the song – had been a FANY, one of the First Aid Nursing Yeomanry which these days is known as the Princess Royal's Volunteer Corps.

The FANY originated in the Boer War. Bobbie says, "They were nurses who used to ride out on horseback in the most glamorous uniform, red jacket with brass buttons and long blue skirt. In the Second World War, I was recruited to be part of what was called Churchill's secret army, a wireless operator attached to Bletchley Park."

Bobbie says, "After the war all of us ex-service lot felt a bit lost without the companionship. One thing we didn't want to do was to be secretaries but we all ended up doing that because our parents wanted us to have a career and we had missed university."

Despite not being able to stand the sight of blood, Bobbie was attracted to medicine and the role of medical secretary in particular. It was this idea that attracted her to the advert to work for a 'Dr Erna Low PhD'.

"I rang up and made an appointment but she was very abrupt on the phone," says Bobbie.

On the day of the interview, Bobbie came to London with her sister and almost did not bother going "because the sales were on and I didn't like the sound of Erna very much".

Her sister convinced her to go against her better judgement.

Erna wrote in her autobiographical notes, "The beginning of the interview was not easy – Bobbie was somewhat shy – but the meeting became much easier when I realised that by a coincidence I had stayed in her parents' hotel when I lectured to the troops on the Isle of Wight. The food had been exceptionally good in the hotel, the staff friendly and her parents helpful. I had no doubt about appointing her. She worked with me for more than forty years and became my right hand."

Bobbie was handed the job of organising Erna's house parties.

Bobbie remembers, "They were very popular for post-war holidays – especially for people who wanted to meet other young people. In those days, people came along and were just happy for the company. They would come along with their own sheets, pillow cases and towels and would help with the chores – and had a very good time."

Bobbie and Erna drove around the country seeking out new schools and country houses to use for the increasingly popular parties.

These stately properties were all suffering after the war – the owners were broke and many of the premises had been badly damaged. "They were all struggling to keep afloat so the rent was very welcome to them," says Bobbie.

"Erna used to say to me, 'You do all the talking because they won't like me and my accent'," says Bobbie. "I would interview the headmasters and bursars but they were so mean about anything precious like a piano. How could you possibly keep a grand piano out of sight? That way I learnt how to organise."

Much of the time Bobbie spent organising the house parties was finding staff. Many of the schools and country houses Bobbie found would not allow the company to use their staff and so she would advertise jobs as kitchen maids, waitresses, servers and cleaners to hard-up students.

Bobbie Shafto (second from left) and group at a house party

Perhaps inevitably, there was the occasional crisis.

"I don't know how I actually coped with that responsibility [of running the company] when I think of it. I always think of one disaster in Dorset where the company organised a sailing holiday for young people. They went out with completely inexperienced sailors and there were children who were washed overboard and it hit the headlines. I thought, 'my God, did I realise what was in my hands when I appointed the leaders?'"

These temporary staff also caused Bobbie headaches with their activities.

"I never really enjoyed the summer because we had a lot of teenage parties and, oh dear, oh dear, what those teenagers used to get up to," says Bobbie with a wry smile and a shake of the head.

"You never knew what crisis would come next," she says. "Once I hired a couple who took off in the night, packing up their car with all the food. The leaders rang me up and said, 'They have done a bunk'.

"I told Erna we had to go down there and all we could find was sausages and onions."

On another occasion Bobbie went down to a school to do an inventory before the house party. "The day before each party I would go down and count all the beds and make sure I had plans with the number of beds in each rooms, which were male and which were female and that all the beds were in their right places," she says.

On this occasion, she turned up at the school and noticed a young man lurking around. She asked the party leader who he was and was told that he was the boyfriend of one of the girls due to arrive the following day.

"Next thing I knew was the leader called me up to say that the young girl in question had come to the house to have an abortion and that the parents had arrived and were blaming me for this. The young man hanging around the house was the father of the child."

There were also regular liaisons between the party leaders. "I used to have terrible complications with the leaders getting entangled in love affairs and husbands coming to complain to me. But what could I do? I suppose they were thrown together and they were bored."

In typical Erna style, her family members were also roped in to lead parties, notably Riccarda Ruberl, the daughter of her favourite uncle Rodolfo. Riccarda's sister Liana was a regular guest as was another cousin from the extended Ruberl family, Franco, who was a student at Birmingham University at the time.

Bobbie started arranging Christmas, Easter and summer parties and weekends at country houses, rented school premises and other interesting locations around the country.

The parties attracted people from the Forces, others in professional jobs where they didn't socialise much as well as many coming from universities and those who had worked with Erna at the BBC Monitoring Service.

One of the very first house parties organised by Bobbie was held at Westwing School in Penzance between June and September 1946.

Among the guests at that first party – neatly recorded in Erna's handwriting – were Roma Black "with her little boy Christopher", now better known as the historian Professor Christopher Black.

"Our very first house party was in a very nice school, except that we discovered that the kitchen was full of rats. The food was very good though," says Roma with a laugh, speaking from the sitting room of her beautifully decorated home in Salisbury.

The sorts of activities on offer at those parties were varied. There was swimming, boating, walking and visits to local sites such as St Michael's Mount when they went to Cornwall.

House parties were simple affairs: rationing meant food was basic and guests often had to cook things themselves. Erna's long term companion Ernst Litthauer is in the back row second from right

The programme from a typical house party in August 1950 shows that tours and visits to local sites of interest were also popular.

August 13th, 2:10pm Party leaves by boat to Windsor Castle and Eton College

August 14th, 10:00am Outing to Lambeth Borough Council (7/6 including lunch)

August 15th, 11:00am South Bank Exhibition

August 16th, 11:00am Official Reception by His Worship the Mayor of Windsor. Visit to Hampton Court

August 17th, 2:15pm Visit to the 'Star' Newspaper and Festival Pleasure Gardens

August 18th, Dance in the evening

August 19th, All day free

August 20th, 10:30am Visit to Huntley & Palmers' Factory (Biscuits)

A note on the entertainment available at these house parties in Erna's unmistakeable tone is included in her scrapbook. It reads: "It is realized that most people don't want to be heavily 'organized', but would rather enjoy themselves their own way. For those who are interested, however, there are plenty of communal activities, fun and games."

This lack of organisation was something of a constant, it seems.

Peter Kemmis-Betty and his wife Gemma attended one of the parties at the time. "It was a hilarious affair," he remembers. "Nothing seemed to be prepared or organised but it somehow worked, largely down to her personality."

Erna said that these were not luxury holidays by any means since they were taking place against a backdrop of rationing. Erna was often referred to by her guests as "the quarter mistress" as a result.

"The accommodation was mostly rather primitive, the food simple but the company good," she said, "and judging by the enthusiastic entries in my log book most of my clients had a good time."

In the latter half of the 1940s, Erna and Bobbie took parties to a breathtaking array of places: Capel Curig in Wales, the Old Vicarage in Aldeburgh, Gaveston and Loxwood Halls in Sussex, schools in Cranleigh, Dockenfield and Runfold in Surrey, St Johns in Budleigh Salterton and Dartington Hall in Devon, Dedham near Colchester and, for Whitsun 1949, at Ringstead Mill near Hunstanton in Norfolk.

There were a number of regular guests – Hella Pick, a fellow Viennese who was put on a Kindertrtansport before the war and went on to become a well-known journalist on *The Guardian*, the Chelsea MP Sir Allan Noble, Alice Frank, Arthur Oram, John Scott, Valerie Bowman, Peter and Margaret Jost and, of course, Ernst Litthauer. The MP Ashley Bramall was among those who went to Rope Hill School for Easter 1950 and several other parties in the following years.

As well as the house parties, Erna would hold regular reunion parties in London, charging 5s for entrance. One party in February 1947 at the Artworker's Guild Hall in Queens Square attracted 150 people.

A handwritten note in one of her scrapbooks reads: "Thinking back to those days, I am surprised that they put up with the frugal meals and the inadequate accommodation. There were large and small dormitories in the schools we rented in Cornwall and all over England. The guests helped with the preparing and serving of the meals and there were hardly any complaints.

"It became obvious that the parties filled a great need in post-war years and made many young people very happy, especially those who had lost friends in the war or stayed in Britain far from home."

An article in *The Lady*[37] explains, "In those days it was quite difficult to meet new people. In war time, social events were few and far between. Friends had been parted and indeed lost forever. The house parties were a way of introducing people to each other."

Many couples met at these 1940s house parties. Her work diary from the era shows details of four "rabbits" who shared the so-called "Rabbit-Hatch" at Redhurst in Cranleigh one Christmas who ended up getting married to fellow guests: Barbara Crowther married Geoff Walton the following June, Geoffrey Hull married Dorion Carter, Mavis Unwin married Peter Unwin while Janette Maxwell married the Norwegian Anders Buraas, who had fled his native Norway as a result of the German occupation and went on to become London correspondent of the daily newspaper *Arbeiderbladet*.

The industrialist Peter Jost CBE was another to wed courtesy of Erna. "After having been introduced to my wife by her uncle, our first outing together, and my first introduction to Erna Low, was an Erna Low trip to the mill near Hunstanton. We were married the year after and naturally had our honeymoon arranged by Erna Low. In 2011, it was purely by chance when on a visit to Sandringham and, losing our way, we found ourselves looking at the very same windmill which had started our relationship. It had not changed much. This year we will have been married for sixty-four years."

Erna later told *Housewife* magazine[38], "Right from the start I made a point of 'matching up' the parties: the sexes have to be more or less evenly distributed: and ages, background and/or interests have to be compatible."

***

The parties became so successful that Erna realised that she needed to set herself up more formally as a business and so, in 1946, Erna Low Travel Service Ltd was formed.

She told writer Stephen Wood in *The Independent*[39], "I didn't want it to become a business; it did it by itself. I used to say to friends: 'I went skiing and it was wonderful.' So they wanted to go, too. I started putting adverts in newspapers; the more people you had, the more fun it was. And it just built up."

Erna recalled later, "After the war several of my early clients, who in the past had stayed at Bosigran Count House, contacted me to inform me of their marriages and divorces, their new jobs, etc. They continued to look to me for holiday suggestions and tried to persuade me to arrange parties in new centres. Finally I gave up my teaching job at the end of the war and made the arranging of holidays my career."

Establishing the new business also meant finding more suitable premises.

The lease on Gower Street came to an end in the summer of 1947; a friend pointed out an advertisement in *The Times* for an "Attractive Mews house to rent in South Kensington", which had become too small for the previous residents.

Seventy years on, that attractive mews house – 9 Reece Mews – remains at the heart of the Erna Low business.

Halina Hodi, Erna's first au pair – even though she had no children – remembers what Reece Mews was like when Erna first moved in.

"Downstairs there was only a garage: one side was for storing things, and the other for her car. Then you had to climb upstairs into a kitchen/dining area; you turned left and there was a bathroom. If you went straight on there was a cubby hole in which was my bed. If I wanted to get dressed I had to open the door – I couldn't move. Then there was her bedroom and from there you got into her living room where she worked, and was nicely furnished in Austrian style."

Over time, the garage was converted into an office while Erna continued to live upstairs.

***

9 Reece Mews

As well as house parties in Britain, Erna expanded her reach overseas, taking a party to Switzerland in August 1946 because it was "not expensive" and that she "had heard that the food there was particularly good".

"We greatly enjoyed salmon, consommé, chicken and mousse – great treats in post-war days," said Erna later.

The party also enjoyed seeing Winston Churchill pass through the country.

"We happened to be there on the day when thousands of Swiss people lined up in Berne to greet Sir Winston Churchill who was travelling in an open Landauer – a cigar in his mouth as usual – from Schloss Almendingen to Berne."

She also took a party of thirty-two to the Hotel Elfverson in Mölle, Sweden on the Royal Danish Mail Service (via Harwich and Esbjerg) and many of those attending became regular clients including Dr Manny Tuckmann and his wife, the sculptor Ghisha Koenig.

Copenhagen in Denmark, Voss, Finse and Stalheim in Norway were soon added to the rapidly growing holiday programme.

One summer trip to Austria caused one guest to come over all poetic, who sent Erna the following poem.

"To Austria, to Austria!"
Cried Erna far and wide,
And we who were quiet home birds
With answering shout replied.
We came, we saw, were conquered,
But found our stay too short,
Then straightway were resolved
Again to sally forth.
In Eichenheim we found it,
The holiday we sought,
By scenes of mountain splendour
Our hearts quite up were caught.
By day we climbed the Berge
Or swam in the Schwarz See,
So full our hours were numbered,
There never was 'nough of day.
Of course by night we wandered
To dives of 'Low' repute,
Where Tyrolean singers
Played zither, harp or lute.
We danced, we drank, we gabbled,
Till dawn's fair rosy light,
And some were quite enamoured
By eyes both dark and bright.
But thirteen days soon ended,
Our duty's bugle heard,
And we to home and office
Return like migrant bird.
Farwell to all our parties
In Rössl, Gams or Reisch,
To Eichenheim, Kitzbühel
Adieu dear Österreich.

However, these overseas excursions would suddenly be cut short.

The idea that British people should be able to take time off from their working lives for a holiday became enshrined in law with the Holidays with Pay Act 1938, which forced employers in industry to give their staff at least a week off each year on full salary.

The Act was to set off explosive growth in the holiday sector and Billy Butlin and his famous camps came along at just the right time to take advantage of the average Briton's new found leisure time.

Although Erna's early trips were not specifically aimed at the working classes as such, the idea that everyone needed a holiday certainly helped with the early growth of the company.

In the immediate aftermath of the Second World War, Britain was almost broke. The incoming Labour government also had grand plans for the immediate post-war years, including the establishment of a national health service, and it needed money to fund that.

The economist John Maynard Keynes was sent cap in hand to the US and Canada for support. The countries offered Britain some US$5.5bn (US$71 billion in 2012 dollars) through the Anglo-American loan, which was only finally paid off in 2006.

The loan came with some stringent conditions which unintentionally worsened the state of Britain's post-war economy and a crisis engulfed sterling in July 1947 which led the government to introduce severe austerity measures.

In August 1947, the government announced a ban on foreign travel except for "travel for necessary business purposes" and also a reduction in the amount of foreign currency that could be exchanged from £75 to £35.[40] A spokesman for Messrs. Thos. Cook told *The Times* that the stoppage of currency "would put an end to winter sports".

It is a tribute to Erna that she survived this challenging time, others did not emerge unscathed. Thomas Cook, one of the earliest names in travel, was nationalised in 1948 because of problems surrounding its operations through the Second World War, remaining in public hands until 1972.

Thankfully for Erna's new business, the ban on foreign travel was lifted in 1948 and she was soon advertising again on the front page of *The Times*. "I can still include you in one of my Swiss Parties, also others in Scandinavia, Italy, France and house parties for professional people in Devon and Eire, including 'Family Party'", she wrote.

By this time, she was scouting out locations in a new car – a Sunbeam Talbot with a personalised EL number plate.

Erna was never a great driver, as anyone who was her passenger will readily admit. One of Erna's assistants, Roma Black, recalls one occasion when Erna was driving in London.

"We were driving in the middle of Soho and the traffic was very bad and there were cars parked on either side of this narrow road and we got stuck. We didn't know what to do about it. There were two hefty young men walking along the pavement and saw that we didn't know what to do. So they got two other men who were walking along the pavement and the four of them just picked the car up and hauled it over the obstruction."

She would eventually hand over most of the driving to her assistants.

***

The quirky language of Erna's advertisements was also reflected in her brochures, the first of which appeared in 1948, showing how quickly the business was growing.

The brochure is entitled "To Sun and Snow with Erna Low".

The first brochure, from 1948

The brochure's introduction immediately turns to the question of foreign currency and sets a precedent that would last for the remainder of her days in charge – Erna wrote everything and in a personal style that worked remarkably well.

Erna wrote, "Winter Sports are back on the map again! The available funds for Switzerland are limited and it really is essential to book for a Swiss Winter Sports Holiday right away… I have tried to make my Winter Sports programme as varied as possible and to include unspoilt places as well as the better known centres with ski-lifts and funiculars… Being a keen skier myself, I have considered each place from four points of view – good ski-ing possibilities, long hours of sunshine, pleasant hotels at reasonable cost and plenty of social or village life."

The brochure included two week trips to Scanfs in Switzerland's Engadin, Mürren, Wengen and Gargellen.

The Gargellen trip ran from 27 December to 12 January and she describes some of the elements of the package: "Under the Austrian Tourist Scheme hotels catering for visitors from abroad get special food allocations and you can be sure of excellent food as well as a pleasant informal atmosphere".

The cost of the trip was £39.0.0, allowing holidaymakers a further £19.0.0 in spending money according to the foreign currency restrictions in place when the brochure was published.

This price covered "fourteen days at the hotel or pension, three meals a day, service charges, taxes, luggage transfer from station to hotel, a reserved seat on the outward journey, II class return fare (I class on the boat, III class in Switzerland)" and the services of a leader if there were more than twelve in the group.

What seems amusing to modern eyes are some of the things you need to pay extra for: tea (1/6 to 3/- per day "depending on the number of cakes you eat"), baths (2/- to 3/-). Tuition was between £2.0.0 and £4.0.0 for two weeks while ski and boot hire was between 1/6 and 2/6 per day.

One of the people who went on these early ski trips was Bernard Weatherill, known as Jack to his friends. Weatherill had enlisted in the army at the outset of the Second World War and rose to the rank of Captain in the 19th King George V's Own Lancers in India. On his return to the UK, he became active in the local Conservative Association and was elected as MP for Croydon North East in 1964, representing it until 1992. In 1983, he became Speaker of the House of Commons.

As was Erna's wont, she wrote at the time to congratulate him on his elevation to one of the highest profile roles in politics. He wrote back saying "So good of you to have written – we must resurrect that long delayed meeting. I hope all goes well with you. Yours aye, Jack".

"Jack" would regularly invite Erna to meetings and parties at the Speaker's House during his career in office.

***

The Ski Club of *Great Britain's Ski Notes and Queries* magazine from the time showed that Erna was competing with the likes of Dean & Dawson, Frames Tours, Fourways Travels and [Walter] Ingham's Winter Sports Bureau for business.

Yet travel abroad was still the preserve of the few at this time and was largely by train and cross-channel ferry. Department for Transport statistics show that in 1950, there were 4.5 million people taking international journeys by boat and 2.1 million passengers at UK airports (including domestic flights). In 2010, there were 23.5 million by boat and 210.6 million at UK airports. The effect of the introduction of regular air services in the 1950s and 1960s cannot be underestimated and as the fledgling Erna Low Travel Service business moved into the 1950s, it faced a challenging future.

***

In the 1950s, skiing, in Austria in particular, was to gain a boost from an unexpected source – the post-war Marshall Plan.

George C Marshall rose through the ranks of the US military and was appointed Army Chief of Staff on the day war broke out in Europe.

After the Allied victory, his grasp of strategy singled him out as the perfect choice to help with the reconstruction of the economies and spirits of Western Europe. In January 1947, US President Harry Truman appointed him as Secretary of State. Truman's brief idea was to come up with a US-financed plan – the country was by then the richest in the world – to engender political stability in Europe but also to act as a buffer against the advance of Communism.

Marshall drew up a plan in just five months that would see the US offer US$13 billion in aid to sixteen nations[41]. The money was initially used for urgently needed supplies – food, fuel and other staples – but eventually the money was used to rebuild Europe's shattered industrial infrastructure. As a result of this cash injection, the European economies grew rapidly in the four years to 1952.

One of the beneficiaries of the European Recovery Program (ERP), as it was officially known, was the Austrian tourist industry.

According to writer Günther Bischof[42], "The Marshall Plan generously financed both investments in the rebuilding and modernisation of hotels, spas, cable cars and ski lifts, and streets and transportation facilities between 1950 and 1955" with "the lion's share… [going] to the three Western Austrian States of Vorarlberg, Tyrol and Salzburg" largely because these areas were occupied by French and American troops rather than Russians.

Over that five-year period, some öS 93.3 million from the ERP funds went towards ski lifts and transportation: cable cars were built in Lech, the Montafon, the Dachstein and the Zillertal and ski lifts in the Arlberg, Montafon, Ischgl, Obergurgl, Lienz, Kitzbühel, Tauploitz, Radstadt and Villacher Alpe. Bischoff concludes "There is nary a prominent hotel or ski resort not funded through ERP."

This investment in skiing also had a knock-on effect in bringing skiing to France.

Austria was occupied by allied forces from 1945 to 1955. The French zone was in the Tyrol and so "tens of thousands of men from all over the country, of all classes of society, were introduced to skiing". This was the kickstart for the French ski industry a few years later.[43]

***

Roy Dawson, who worked for Erna in the 1950s, spoke to Roger Bray for his definitive history of British package tourism *Flight to the Sun*[44].

"I took a group to the Austrian resort of Hochsölden… It was the first time I had ever been to the Ötztal. When we got there it was a filthy night. Erna was buying bulk seats on Ingham's Snow Train and I had to trust they had made all the right arrangements. We got to Sölden in heavy snow and there was just a single seat chairlift to take us on to the resort, which is higher up the mountain. The coach couldn't make it up the hill to the foot of the lift so we had to manhandle the baggage up.

"A single lamp was swinging, as if in a ghost film. These cases were loaded on the lift and disappeared in to the darkness. I didn't know whether to go up first or last but I was assured there was someone waiting at the top, so I let the customers go ahead. They were pretty terrified by this time. When they got on the lift there were big black hooded capes to protect them against the storm. The chairs whacked them on the calves and they went off, swinging wildly in the night. At the top we had to haul the cases another 150 yards across the snow to the Hotel Sonnblick.

"But not a single one complained. They had survived – and it was an experience to remember and talk about. And next morning there was a wonderful winter mountain view and sun and snow such as they had never seen before."

Bobbie Shafto tells an amusing story of one of their scouting trips to see a hotel in the Alps, the Berghotel Körbersee in Schröcken in Austria's Vorarlberg region. Erna's second cousin from Italy, Riccarda Ruberl, drove them to the foot of the mountain.

"We had to go to a place right up the mountain and Erna was mad keen to discover the spot," remembers Bobbie. "We had an appointment up at the top of the lift and a little boy turned up. He had a spanner which turned a handle that was operating a flat soap box with no sides. We had to get in and lie down flat.

"Erna was at one end and I was at another and her build and mine were rather different; it was a bit uneven and bumpy and we swung around in all directions."

The *Materialbahn* or goods lift – for that is what it was – eventually got stuck, leaving the unbalanced pair stranded. After some time, the lift was restarted and the couple reached the hotel where they were greeted warmly.

The incident is fondly remembered in a cartoon drawn by Riccarda, who remained safe and sound at the bottom of the lift.

As well as driving Erna on some of those early scouting trips, Bobbie had another important role to play at those meetings with hotel owners.

"Erna didn't drink at all and I used to wait for this little phrase to come out with a gesture towards me: 'Nein, nein, meine Sekretär' . The drinks would come to me so I used to get cheered up," she remembers with a laugh.

***

Erna Low Travel Service was advertising extensively in the early 1950s using slogans such as "Interesting holidays for professional people", "Original holidays with a personal note" and "A Foreign Holiday in England". The range of publications was immense, from the *Daily Telegraph* and *New Statesman* to *London Teacher* and Germany's *Die Welt* (*"Englisch lernen ein Vergnügen"* – English learning a pleasure).

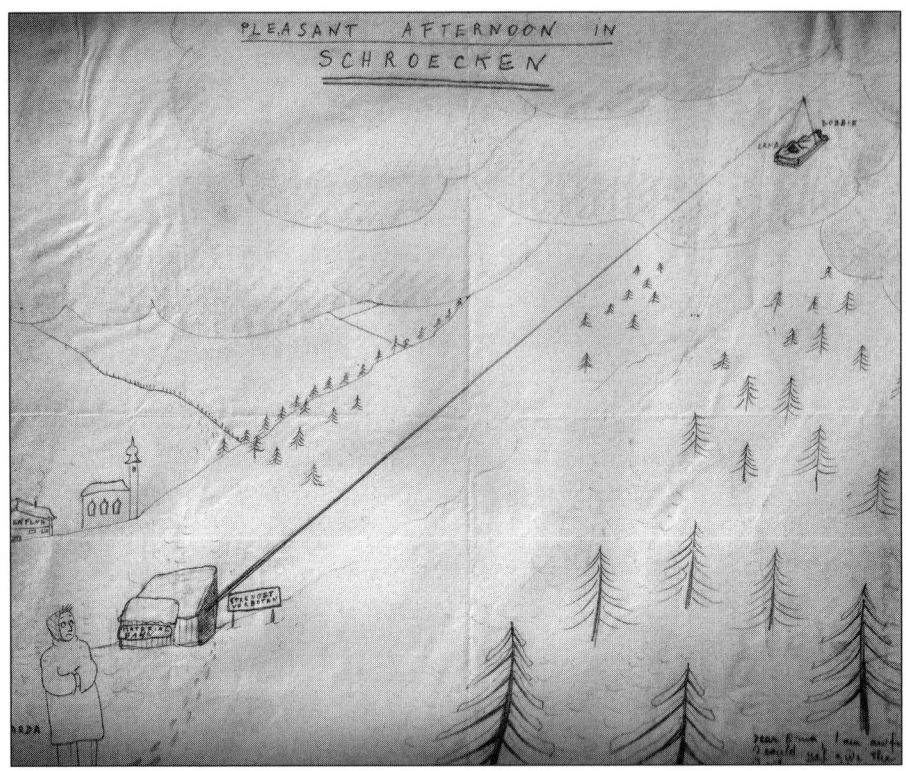

A cartoon of Erna and Bobbie's Schröcken adventure, illustration: Riccarda Ruberl

She particular targeted publications that would be read by academics such as *Isis* and the *Oxford Clarion*. Erna even established a network of academics at various colleges, such as Robin Ditchburn at St John's and Michael Arnold at Wadham, to act as agents for the company.

By 1952, all was going very well for the Erna Low Travel Service.

But Bobbie Shafto, who had been with the company since its formation, decided to leave to start a new life in Canada.

On her leaving, she wrote a poem entitled 'Low Life', explaining what life was like at the office at the time:

Our office, you know, was then in the Mews,
And as such it suffered some little abuse
For the boss, in the office, or so it was said,
Kept poodles and liquor and even a bed!

When questioned the boss would merely reply,
"Above all, my clients, I must satisfy."

***

Clients again streaming in at the door,
Appointments we made to start at four.
And so it is us that they'll have to see.
"Miss Low won't be long, won't you come in?"
And 'though I know it's a mortal sin
A lie here and there is really quite kind
If it puts to rest their troubled mind.
Especially the clutching handbag type
Asking one such a lot of tripe.
"The weather at Windsor, will it be hot?"
(Oh God, this woman, she ought to be shot).
And, "Can I have a single room?"
"Oh yes," in reply one has to boom.
(I'm sure there's a room which has only four
But goodness this woman ain't half a bore).
"And could you tell me, are there REAL men?"
My answer is, "Yes," but I'm thinking of Len.
Now what's she asking – "Will there be snow?"
"Why? Oh for skiing. Yes I hope so.
It's always a help in case you should fall."
And, "No, you shouldn't require a shawl."

***

It's hard, you will see, to hide from one's friends
The hours and hours and hours that one spends
Sorting out things in the peace of the night
Until one can finally see the light.
And then it's a job to try and pretend
One was spending a glorious naughty week-end,
An event which certainly couldn't be missed.
But, my dears, if that's life then 'il est triste.'

***

And then there are house parties – Oh such fun –
One moves all the beds around, one by one.
Driving for hours in a car packed so full
That, on hills, it simply refuses to pull.
One arrival, you find that the staff are not there
So you heave and you push; you curse and you swear.

It was to prove to be a short-lived move and Bobbie was soon back, juggling Erna and clients again with great skill and finesse.

***

In March 1952, Erna was advertising "Easter holidays with a Difference". An ad in *The Times* reads, "Enjoy a gay holiday in interesting company with a small party to Paris, Majorca, Spring Ski-ing in AUSTRIA or an Easter party in HAMPSHIRE BY THE SEA, or at Stratford." Through that summer she was offering "informal parties" to the Tyrol and Salzburg.

The company was doing so well in fact that the company needed to expand beyond the cramped conditions of 9 Reece Mews and Erna took out a lease on a building at 47 Old Brompton Road, in what is now a branch of the cupcake firm Hummingbird Bakery.

Old Brompton Road had an accounts office and post room in the basement, a "cupboard" where the telephonist sat and an office next door that would eventually become the home of Uli Lloyd Pack, one of Erna's right hand women.

Upstairs, in a converted loft, were packed far more employees than were allowed by the regulations.

Former tourist director of the Austrian resort of Lech, Hubert Schwärzler, was one of those who worked at the cramped 47 Old Brompton Road office.

"There was not enough room," he remembers. "There were three desks but there were ten or eleven people working at them. When the inspector from the authorities came to check, everybody had to go to the coffee shop next door and Erna would say 'The drinks are on me'. However, by the time we had all reached the coffee shop, the inspector would have gone and Erna would be in the shop before we had time to order."

He remembers one of these inspection visits in particular. "I thought I would get the better of Erna and ran to the coffee shop as soon as she asked us to leave and ordered drinks for everyone. Erna arrived as usual and said it was time to go back and I said, "But Erna, we have already ordered". She replied, 'You will have to pay, you know what business is like.'"

***

Although business was booming, 1952 was to prove a very difficult year for the company.

Winkfield Place, a school run by society florist Constance "Connie" Spry and cook Rosemary Hume in Cranbourne in Berkshire, was one of the locations for Erna and Bobbie's house parties that year. In the following year, Spry would be asked to do the flowers for the Princess Elizabeth's coronation while Hume's students invented a dish to be served to the foreign dignitaries that became a British staple – Coronation chicken.

Winkfield Place was "a rambling Georgian house with a large stable block midway between Windsor and Ascot, perfect for the Home Counties families who were their target market. There was a large dull looking garden dissected by a rectangular lake, the remains of an eighteenth century canal."[45]

It was intended to be a "middle-class continuation school... neither a domestic science school nor a finishing school like the 'French' schools which turned out fully polished young ladies... it would be a 'beginning' school for a new generation of wives, mothers and professional women".

"Much of the furnishing was surplus... [with] curtains made of butter muslin parachute fabric, rolls of braid stitched together and any unrationed textiles they could find... offcuts from [society couturier] Victor Stiebel's workrooms... sewn into wild and flamboyant patchwork quilts and curtains. Connie's needlework carpet... was laid on the drawing room floor."

Guests enjoyed staying at Winkfield Place and it became a regular feature of the company's house party programme for several years, with parties at New Year and an "international house party" each summer.

The house party was set for July of that year and one of the guests was a twenty-two-year-old Parisian student called Camille Maille.

Roma Black recalls: "It was a hot day and we were all in the garden and there was a swimming pool. At tea-time they called us in and said somebody was missing, a young French girl. We went all over the gardens looking for her and couldn't find her and we couldn't understand what had happened. One of the boys said perhaps she's in the pool. We couldn't believe it when he dived in and pulled her out. It was a horrible thing to happen."

Erna wrote later. "I was, of course, very upset but was greatly relieved that at the inquest it turned out that she had been told by her parents not to go swimming as she suffered from a heart disease. She had never told me. The Coroner's verdict was 'death by misadventure'. This unfortunate incident taught me a useful lesson. Thereafter I insisted on house party members informing me if they suffered from any kind of illness. I also asked them to supply me with a doctor's certificate to state 'that the bearer is healthy and can swim in local pools with or without supervision'."

Upsetting as the incident was for Erna, something much worse was just around the corner.

Guests enjoying the sun at Constance Spry's Winkfield Place, a regular venue for
Erna and Bobbie's house parties

Chapter 8

The 1952 Arlberg Disaster in which eighteen people died, including eight travelling with Erna Low Travel Service (see Prologue), could have spelled the end for a company still in its early growth years. Despite their natural causes, avalanches and other incidents like this can shatter public confidence in a travel company, sending it into insolvency through no fault of its own.

The dead who had travelled from Britain were named in the press [46] as Miss Doris Maud Cheyney of Battersea, Ann Mary Agnew of Hemel Hempstead, Charles Morris, a student at University College Oxford, Audrey Lewin of Ashford Girls' School, Kent and her sister Stephanie of Empress Avenue (tragically celebrating her 21st birthday on the trip), D A Marks an employee at the Ministry of Supply, Brenda Littlefield of Carlisle, New Zealander J W Campbell of Old Brompton Road and Miss Penrose and Miss Johnstone, both of New Zealand. The injured were B Venning of Plymouth, Louis Hyatt of London and John David Gard of Bude, Cornwall. Anthony Campion, the eleven-year-old son of party leader Lloyd Campion, also later died in hospital.

The fact that it did not have more of an effect on the company was perhaps due to the Erna Low name being kept largely out of the newspapers in connection with the incident, a situation which would be unlikely to happen in today's world of the internet and 24-hour news channels.

Despite the serious setbacks of 1952, Erna applied herself with even more zeal. Erna started advertising on a daily basis in many national newspapers, including *The Times* ("four lines for 20s"), *The (Manchester) Guardian*, *The Observer* as well as *The Irish Times*.

In 1953, the ski programme included Davos, Zermatt, Champéry, Kitzbühel, Lech, Obergurgl and a number of smaller centres with prices at "off-season rates" (perhaps to encourage bookings after the avalanche) with prices starting at 28 ½ guineas for sixteen days' for an inclusive holiday.

How the 1952 Arlberg disaster was reported,
credit: Vorarlberger Nachrichten

Erna had also massively expanded the company's summer programme. By this time, the company was organising sunshine holidays in Spain, Majorca, Yugoslavia, the Italian Adriatic, Brittany and the south of France, mountain and lake holidays in Austria and Switzerland, city breaks to Paris and Amsterdam as well as "music lover's parties".

Erna was also promoting her holidays through film shows (tickets 2s 6d) held at Chelsea Town Hall where she would hand out brochures for both skiing and summer holidays.

***

It was in the 1950s that another innovation in travel, and skiing in particular, occurred – the chalet holiday.

Dennis Fabri answers a delicate question very carefully.

He says, "It's all very well to say that Alan Turing invented the computer, but its invention was not just down to him."

"It is Colin Murison-Small who made the chalet holiday what it is today but Erna had a few chalets in mind and she always had somebody on the spot," he goes on.

The question being asked is "Who invented the chalet holiday?", a controversy that has rumbled on for a few years and may never be satisfactorily answered.

In the later years of her life, Erna told ski writer Peter Hardy that it was she who had run the first chalet party. "In the beginning we didn't even provide a chalet girl. The guests all shared the cooking and the cleaning – they were very happy to do this, and it saved me a lot of money."

What is reasonably clear is that in early 1953, Erna took the natural step of combining the two elements of her business: ski trips and house parties. The trip went out to Obergurgl, along with a group leader.

A brochure from the mid-fifties explains how it worked: "Our special parties for professional and university people, their families and friends, have made quite a name for themselves… Our parties are equally suitable for those joining alone or for small groups of friends joining together… Several of our parties are conducted throughout, others are met and looked after at the resort by resident hosts or hostesses. Our leaders or hosts are generally members of former parties."

Three years after this trip, a man named Colin Murison-Small completed his National Service and came across an ad in the personal columns of *The Times* offering villas to rent in Blanes, Gerona. He got together a group of eight friends, took the boat over to Belgium and hired a VW Minibus in Belgium to make the two day journey down, with brief stops in Paris and Avignon.

"The whole holiday cost us each about £35… having our own minibus meant we spent nothing on excursions—a lesson which stuck firmly in my mind," he writes in the autobiography he is working on.

The guest list from the first ski house party, in Obergurgl

After organising another trip to Yugoslavia, he then went to see Erna at Old Brompton Road in January 1958 to apply for a position as a ski party leader. "I implied that I spoke French and German, in fact I had A-level French (like everyone else) and a smattering of German I had picked up during National Service."

Murison-Small's first trip was taking twelve members to the Hotel Central in Verbier, "all of whom had a note saying that the party leader was a Mr Smart (office procedures were never Erna's strong point)".

The trip went without a hitch although Colin was flattered to receive some uninvited attention from two girls on the trip. "I could only conclude that the enormous authority which representing Erna Low conferred on me through my appointment as *Gruppenführer* gave me a macho image to which I could not, and never subsequently did, aspire."

He then turned his thoughts to whether he might be able to organise his own trips. "I began to wonder whether by renting a chalet, finding a girl to run it and investing in a minibus I might be able to get a free skiing holiday the following winter and perhaps even make a profit."

With a £200 personal loan in his bank account he set off for Grindelwald to check out potential chalets.

Colin Murison-Small's 1958-9 Winter Sports Holidays brochure – if you can call three typewritten and copied foolscap sheets that – describes what a Murison-Small chalet holiday offered. Rail travel from London Victoria on Friday, a ferry from Dover to Dunkirk, then a train to Grindelwald via Bern and Interlaken.

He says, "I have hired two chalets close to each other in Grindelwald. One of the chalets is over an ironmonger's shop and is owned by Herr Schlunegger, who speaks excellent English, is very helpful and happens to be a ski instructor as well as an ironmonger. Two English girls, Lovedy Moule and Rosemary Reece, who will be living in the chalets for the whole season, will feed you and do all they can to make you comfortable and keep you happy."

The chalet party classic of afternoon tea and cake, "You will be welcome to have tea with bread and butter and jam at no extra charge, although you will have to buy your own cakes: also included is tea or coffee after lunch or dinner, and wine at dinner."

"The chalets are comfortable, though not luxurious or spacious."

The chalet holiday cost 30 gns per person with no high season supplements or low season reductions although ski lifts, he admitted, were "expensive" at 63 Sw. fr (at a then exchange rate of £1=12.2 Sw. fr) for an eight-day pass on the mountain railway.

Erna certainly organised house parties in ski resorts but the question is, were they chalet parties?

Colin Murison-Small does not believe they were chalet parties as such.

"On one of these supposed chalet parties to Austria, there was a note left in the kitchen telling people what they should eat that night and where they should buy the food or the food was left on the table and they were meant to cook it themselves. You couldn't possibly run chalet parties where a whole group of people who probably didn't know each other at all got together. It would have been a total disaster."

Perhaps the answer is to redefine the question. Does a chalet holiday mean a property booked for a whole season with live-in staff (probably from Britain) or can ad-hoc weeks with staff travelling out with guests count too?

What is certain is that Erna never advertised these trips as chalet parties – the few lines in the personal columns or the travel classifieds always talked about "winter sports parties" and "inclusive holidays".

Why did chalet holidays become so successful?

Colin Murison-Small says, "Nobody had been able to go abroad at all between 1939 and 1945. You had a group of young people, say in their twenties, who were beginning to earn enough money to go abroad by the late 50s. People were so excited about going abroad at all. If you put them in a Viking going to Athens with three stops on the way and taking ten hours, they just got off at the other end and went straight into a taverna and enjoyed themselves. They didn't say, oh what a tiring journey – it was exciting."

Whoever was there at the birth – and it was probably a combined effort – chalet holidays have certainly taken off from those early days. Of the million or so people who go skiing from Britain each year, a third of them now stay in a chalet[47].

Insurance broker Michael Pettifer, who went on early Erna Low holidays and who has provided ski insurance for most of the companies in the sector, has what may be the last word on the matter. "Erna invented the chalet house party; Colin invented the chalet party."

***

One day in 1952, Erna came out of her room at 47 Old Brompton Road to see someone dressed immaculately with dark hair and a kindly face leaving the offices.

"What did she want?" Erna asked the receptionist.

"Work," she replied.

"Well, get her back," said Erna.

"From that day she never did anything else," says her son, the actor Roger Lloyd Pack. "Uli, my mother, was her right-hand woman."

Uli Lloyd Pack was born Ulrike Elizabeth Pulay in Vienna in 1921 and married the actor Charles Lloyd Pack, best known for appearing in several Hammer horror films, in late 1941. By the 1950s the couple were living in Neville Street in South Kensington, just around the corner from the offices of Erna Low Travel Service.

Roger says, "Erna was very fond of my mum and she became indispensable to Erna. My mum was very good at her job and she went on all the trips with Erna. My dad was very jealous of her because she was so demanding, so very, very demanding. If Erna wanted something, she had to have it. If she wanted mum to go round there, mum would just go – and dad used to get very angry and upset. He resented the demands that he made on mum and I have some sympathy for that because mum would attend to her every whim. "

As well as working long hours in the office, Uli also took work home with her, which upset Charles.

"Erna and my father had one colossal row and he started to call her the Mad Woman of Old Brompton Road or MWOBR."

Uli Lloyd Pack, who joined Erna Low in 1958

He adds, "I think Erna felt very proprietorial of my mum, and my dad was very jealous of her – and of us, of his sons. He was jealous anyway as a person and it was difficult for my mum. It was a demanding friendship, it was part employer-employee, part maternal and maybe there was a physical attraction too."

Despite both coming from Vienna, Erna and Uli – whom one colleague called "the perfect example of chic, especially when she had wooden framed glasses" – came from very different social circles.

Roger says, "They spoke very differently and other members of my mum's family rather looked down on Erna because she was from lower echelons and my mother was quite high up in Viennese society in the artistic circles; her dad knew Freud and Kafka. But she was very good friends of my mum and I don't know what we would have done without her – she was very generous."

Roger, born in 1944, worked for Erna a lot in the school holidays. "I worked with the Roneo printers in the printing rooms and downstairs in the office doing the post. I also did proof-reading for her. She also offered me jobs as a rep which I didn't do – I feel I missed out on that, I could have repped her holiday tours," he says.

Uli's other son Christopher, who went on to become a successful stage manager, says, "I don't remember a Christmas morning without Erna being in our house and being part of our family. I think my brother and I may have been her surrogate children."

"Before Christmas morning, it would be Christmas wrapping in her house, where some of her staff would gather and we would spend an evening wrapping presents for all her staff with the occasional naughty sherry. Those were times of joyful happiness, a reflection on her ability to have fun and laughter which she loved.

"My brother would always make her laugh – ridiculous things, silly sayings and intellectual humour as well. I don't think practical jokes were much appreciated, she liked to have a good time and she was the kindest and most generous person I have ever met. I would get basically anything I wanted from her. She was overwhelming in her generosity."

***

In the year of that chalet house party in Obergurgl, someone special came into Erna's life. Nick was black, curly haired and Erna first met him in Knightsbridge. He also had four legs and a tail. Nick, you see, was the great canine love of her life.

Nick, the poodle, came into Erna's life in 1953 and was one of
a succession of canine companions

Erna met her beloved Nick one day after her and Bobbie Shafto had waved off
a party at Victoria – perhaps even that Obergurgl trip.

Bobbie recalls, "On the way back from Victoria, I said I wanted to stop at
Harrods and so we drew up. There was a pet shop opposite and little puppies in
the window and we stopped and looked. This little bundle of fluff ran across the
floor to Erna and we both fell in love with it. We bought rugs, baskets and all that
sorts of stuff and took him home. But Erna didn't have a clue how to train the
dog – she spoilt him and ruined him in the end."

Erna said, "I saw Nick first when he was a puppy and looked quite forlorn in
the window of a dog shop. He became my faithful companion until he died aged
seventeen years."

Erna would often not have time to walk Nick and this job fell to anyone who
was in Erna's vicinity, including the young Lloyd Pack brothers who would come
into Erna's life in the 1950s.

He also travelled extensively. There are pictures throughout her scrapbooks of
this fine-looking black poodle being cuddled by dozens of people and was clearly
a regular participant in the house parties organised by Bobbie.

Bobbie says, "She was mad about the dogs. They would go everywhere with
her. If a restaurant wouldn't let them in, she would never go there."

An article in the *Kensington and West London Times* of 8 September 1961 by a
correspondent identified as C.L.P. (which is almost certainly Charles Lloyd Pack,

the actor husband of Erna's long time friend and co-worker Uli) gives a fine insight into her character.

"Early last Saturday evening, in Neville Street, the silence was broken by the high pitched moan of a black poodle, whose ear was being devoured by a largish bull-terrier. Had it not been for the prompt action of Miss Erna Low, a well-known travel agent, the fight could have been prolonged. She hit the bull-terrier with her handbag, the contents of which were scattered on the ground and finally separated the two dogs."

The report concluded with the observation "Neither dog was injured".

***

One day, at the Old Brompton Road office, a Polish-born girl who had spent much of her life in Germany turned up unexpectedly.

Erna remembered this first meeting, "Halina Hodi was a very attractive but penniless girl who came from Germany as an au pair and was given my address when she was in search of a new job. I liked her immediately and offered her a job as an extra office help. Fortunately she likes animals and became a great favourite with my various dogs."

Speaking at her South Kensington "cottage", Halina – smartly dressed with piercing eyes – remembers things differently.

She says, "When I first met Erna I thought of myself as footloose and fancy free. With ten shillings in my pocket, I was ready to conquer the world. Erna saw me differently. To her I was a penniless waif who needed rescuing. That is how I began my career as girl Friday with the Erna Low."

Halina had worked as a secretary in Germany to support her widowed mother but it didn't suit her.

"I was supposed to be a secretary but I couldn't think what you could do for eight hours in an office so I kept falling asleep. A friend of mine suggested I go to England and learn a bit more English."

With a reference from the friend, Halina went to work in a boarding school in Hindhead, Surrey, opened by three Jewish headmistresses before the beginning of the war. The school had opened before the war and took in Jewish children sent by their parents to England. After the war, the school took in boys and girls from Germany doing their year's service.

Halina quickly gained a good grasp of English and realised that she did not want to return to her former sleep-inducing role in Germany. The head of her school gave her three letters of recommendation for jobs in London. "One was Universal Aunts, one was a domestic agency and the last was an obscure thing called Erna Low," says Halina.

She initially dismissed the latter and first tried the other two but realised domestic service was not her calling.

"I called on Erna who was just in the process of leaving for something or other but as was her wont she said 'Bobbie will take care of you and find you somewhere for you to stay. Don't do anything till I come back.'"

Halina didn't do anything – apart from a brief brush with the police when she tried to register her new residence in a boarding house. "The police said I couldn't do that so I just ran away."

Erna returned a few days later and rushed in the room, turned to Halina and said, "Hey! Take the dog, go to the park and don't come back!'"

"With this I thought 'It's a sunny day, no worries' and went to the park and had a lovely time. At six o'clock I rang Erna and asked if I could come home. She said, 'Who are you?' and I thought there was no point in saying Halina but rather that I was the person with her dog. "

Halina would become Erna's "girl Friday" – making coffee, lunch for whoever was visiting that day and taking the dogs for a walk. Erna applied for a work permit for her, arguing that she needed a diet cook despite Halina "not knowing even how to boil an egg".

***

Halina shared the tiny Reece Mews house with Erna for the next year.

It was cramped but at weekends there were the house parties and Erna would send Halina off all over the country to help out.

This was typical Erna style – if she trusted you enough to take you on, you were handed responsibility immediately.

"My first overseas assignment was to take a group of English people to Yugoslavia," says Halina. "We had a fabulous time although I lost a couple in Paris."

Halina would be a regular companion on Erna's scouting missions in the car and the two would talk and talk to while away the hours as they drove across the Continent.

"We talked endlessly about everything and anything. I was not interested in talking about work – I preferred to fall asleep – although she would have liked me to take an interest."

One time they were driving through France and could not find a hotel for the night.

"It was around 2am and we were considering sleeping in the car," says Halina. "Then we came to a hotel and asked if they had a bed. They looked at us and said no. I said it doesn't matter what kind of bed. They took us to a huge room with four king size beds, a wash stand and a naked bulb. On one of the beds there was a wedding dress and we just fell upon one of the beds each laughing."

Halina also helped with the ski parties.

"We had to go by bus to Lech and I arrived at the station and there were 600 children there and an avalanche had blocked the road. Erna took charge and got hotels for all of them. Everything fell into place – she just put herself in charge and that was that."

Erna's organising nature later almost caused a family feud in the Hodi family.

When Halina's son Nick got married, Erna arrived at the hotel and immediately started to organise the guests into rooms.

"The next day, after the wedding had happened and Erna had left, Nick realised that Erna had put everyone into different rooms than he had planned. My brother was absolutely livid and both he and Nick were screaming at me. I said to myself, 'Thank you Erna' and then had to spend hours sorting it out."

Halina was also helping Erna with her German correspondence but lacked shorthand and went off to the Germany Embassy to learn it. While she was taking her courses, the Embassy asked Halina to go and work for them, which she accepted. This did not go down well with Erna, who demanded unswerving loyalty throughout her life.

"Erna was very cross with me; when you were in her 'doghouse' she was furious. But leaving the office was when our friendship began," says Halina.

The doghouse became a running joke between her and Ernst, who both found themselves in Erna's bad books from time to time.

Halina remembers, "Ernst and I were in the same league, partly because we were both German and she wasn't very fond of Germans. One of us was always in the doghouse. One day we got bored of this so in front of her we said to each other 'Oh, you are in the doghouse today, I thought it was me?' She overheard this and took more care afterwards."

Erna became something of a surrogate mother to Halina in England. "She

Erna and friends learning to ski, photo: Rob Wrate

Erna, Christmas 1918

Teenage Erna on a summer trip

Erna's mother
Emma in
Vienna

The days before she found her
Zurich suitmaker

Erna's Bloomsbury years

The Ruberl family at home in Milan.
From left, Uncle Rodolfo, Claudio,
Riccarda, Guido, Liana

Riccarda Ruberl, Erna's Italian "cousin",
regularly accompanied her on trips

Erna's brother Fritz

Ernst Litthauer, photo: Lisel Haas

Happy times for Erna and Ernst

A rare shot of Erna relaxing

Erna's clients usually became friends

This group of Erna's clients lost a bet and
had to ski "bare-chested"

A ski party in the 1930s

Erna in the days before
laminated metal skis

One of the early ski
parties in Zermatt

Erna, friends and
canine companion in
Saalbach, Austria

Erna preferred being behind the
camera to in front of it

Surprisingly fashionable on the slopes

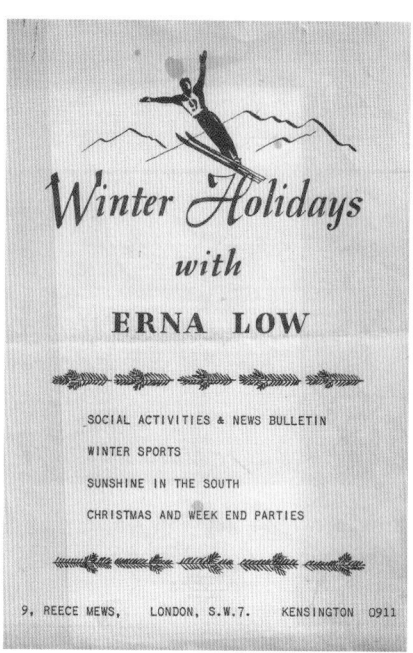

One of the earliest Erna Low brochures

The 1950/51 brochure, which advertised Festival of Britain holidays

Erna's response to Wilson's "pound in your pocket" speech

One of the early ski parties in Zermatt

Erna, friends and canine companion in Saalbach, Austria

Erna preferred being behind the camera to in front of it

Surprisingly fashionable on the slopes

House parties were large affairs. A young Roger Lloyd Pack is front left

A thank you card from a happy guest at a house party

Erna, between hotel visits, on an
early scouting trip to Majorca

An early scouting trip with Riccarda and Bobbie

Slippery Sam, Erna's Morris 8

Walks in the countryside
were regular features of
Erna's house parties

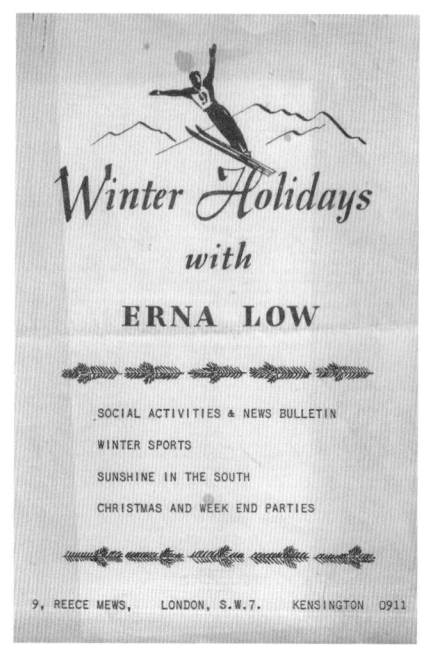

One of the earliest Erna Low brochures

The 1950/51 brochure, which advertised Festival of Britain holidays

Erna's response to Wilson's "pound in your pocket" speech

INTERESTING HOLIDAYS

Our holiday arrangements appeal to people with discriminating tastes who appreciate personal recommendations and up-to-date knowledge of good places in Britain or the Continent.

Independent arrangements, small groups, Church and School parties.

Details from

ERNA LOW, 47 Old Brompton Road, London, S.W.7

Telephones: KEN 0911 and KEN 9225/6

Holidays were always "interesting" with Erna

Erna personally visited hundreds of hotels before putting them in the brochure

An **Erna Low** Recommended Hotel

Erna Low

47, OLD BROMPTON ROAD,

LONDON, S.W.7.

Telephone KENsington 0911/8881/4

A summer brochure from the 1960s

PARTIES
FOR YOUNG
SKIERS
(8 to 18 YEARS)

SWING 'N SKI

1970-71

ERNA LOW TRAVEL SERVICE LTD
47 Old Brompton Road, London, S.W.7
Telephone : 01-589 8881/7 Telex: 24303   Cables : ERLOTRAVEL, LONDON

Swing was the thing in the Sixties

Erna's office was usually strewn with paperwork

Erna with Maxi, who loved nothing better than nipping at people's ankles

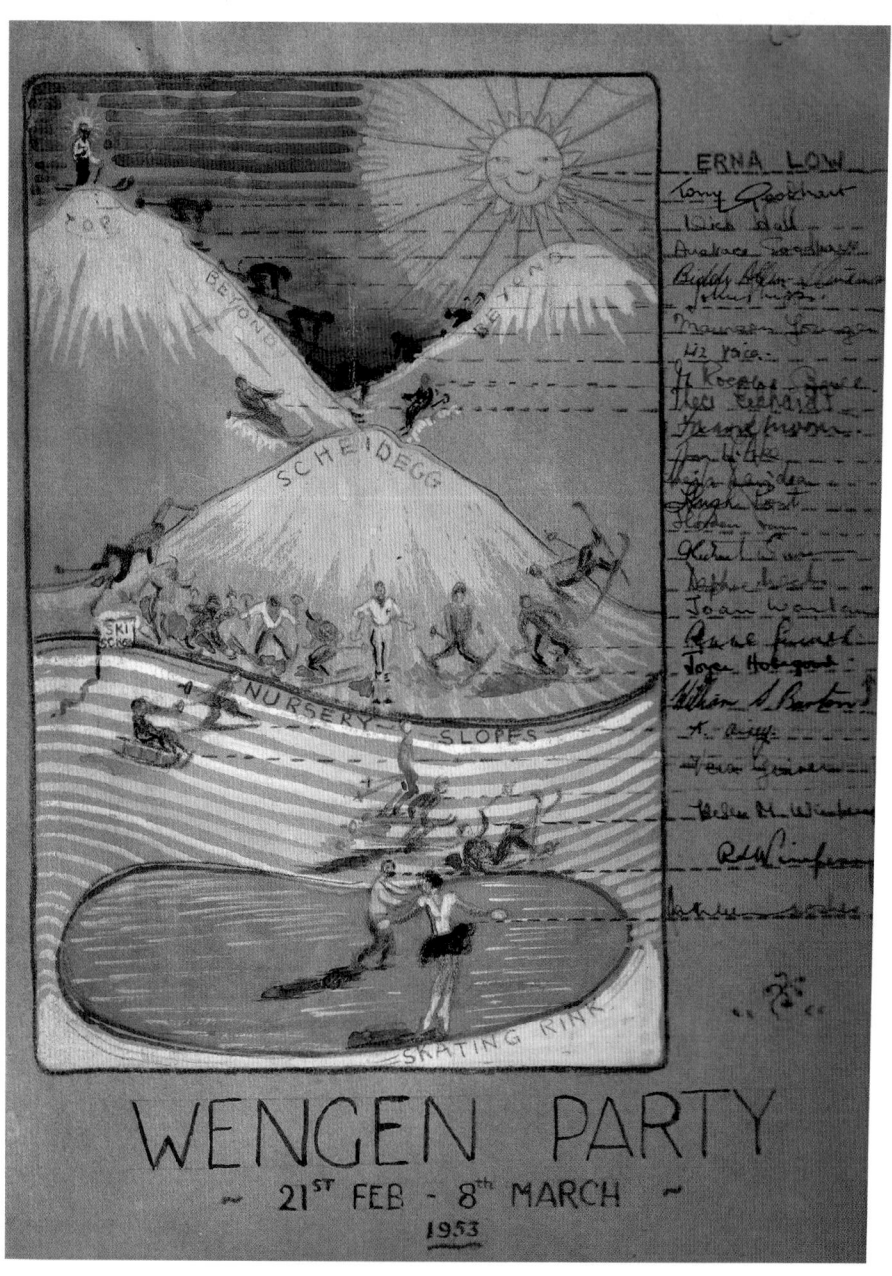

Sun and snow on a 1953 trip to Wengen

One of the mules that in earlier days might have carried skis up the mountain

Erna chartered Tube trains for her schoolgoers, photo: Times Educational Supplement

School ski trips were an Erna Low innovation

Ernst Litthauer on the day he received his OBE with sister
Hilde Himmelweit and Erna, photo: Monitor Press Features

Driving a piste-basher in later years

Erna was still
active into her 80s

guided, scolded, encouraged, scolded. Quite a lot of scolding actually," laughs Halina.

In this mother role, Erna was very protective of Halina.

"When I met a man I wanted her to meet, she was very crusty and said she didn't' want him to come to her house," says Halina with a laugh.

Speaking at Erna's funeral much later on, Halina said: "In time, Erna became the rock in the stormy seas of my life and co-mother of my son – ever critical and always supportive. Among other less flattering things she called me was her teenage mother – that was the latter part of her life. One of her favoured travelling companions who would drive her all over the world. So much I learnt from Erna. Not always did I take her advice – but always she was there to guide and console."

***

Erna's relationship with Ernst – although not her friendship – came to an end in 1956.

After breaking up, they didn't communicate for a while but Erna must eventually have written to him saying she missed him.

Ernst replied on 3 March: "I too, miss you. I missed you very much at first, then I became somewhat less aware of it, and recently I began to miss you more again. I certainly haven't forgotten you – what a word! How could I ever? But it is too early to meet again and to go again over the old ground. I will therefore not 'phone, but I will think of you as indeed I do every day. Try to think of some of the things you liked about me, rather than the things which you disliked."

The break-up happened after Ernst had consulted with the psychoanalyst Hans Erich Haas, a fellow German Jew who had been forced to leave his homeland in 1936. Hans Erich's sister, Lisel, was a successful photographer and was Ernst's landlord in Moseley in Birmingham.

Halina Hodi says, "Ernst was a very complicated person but they complemented each other very well. She was a leader and he loved to follow so that worked well. But then his psychoanalyst told him that what he needed was a gentle little woman who would sit at his feet and cook his food and that Erna was definitely not right for him."

Erna wrote to Ernst in May, keeping a copy of her desperately sad letter in her personal correspondence file.

"I hope you will soon find that peace and happiness for which you are so much

longing," she wrote. *"Haas was deliberately leading you to believe in [an] ideal which was absolutely the opposite of me, the person who you pretended o care for. Your ideal is nothing unique – in fact the average young man longs for exactly that – a little house, garden and children with the only difference that they go all out to get it when they are about twenty-four or twenty-six. You must remember that you known me now for thirteen years – eight of those intimately… when we were so much more apart than together [and] there must be masses of nice young girls in Birmingham who would have been perfectly suitable for such a domestic idyll.*

"Perhaps you do not realise it now but in the beginning of our relationship you told me again and again that I was the only person you could let yourself go, who spurred you on to things and with whom you managed to have an all-round relationship in spite of great initial difficulties. In my opinion, the reason for this lies just in the difference of our respective mental make-ups. We happen to supplement each other and therefore our attachment has lasted so long. I may have energy and drive but these are quite largely due to a deliberate attempt to overcome shyness and an inferiority complex.

"Fortunately I have good health and physical strength and have managed more or less to make a fairly good 'substitute' existence for myself. Fundamentally, I also long for a home and children – why then does my professional success mean so comparatively little to me and why I am always longing for something else and talk of adopting children. I found in you someone who cared, who helped me in lots of small and big ways, who believed in me far more than I believe in myself, who was always pleased to see me and who – in fact – gave me the moral support I needed and still need."

*" Bobbie, for instance, knows this very well and always tells me that I am a funny mixture and my mother always said that outwardly I was the go-ahead go-getter type and inwardly a little girl who wants to be reassured and loved. Strangely enough, instinctively you understood this and read me like an open book until the analysis interfered and presented me to you in the wrong light. You stood out against this for a remarkably long time until you finally capitulated. You, on the other hand, saw in me the strong, active person who had drive and energy and you admired just that – until you were told that I wanted to keep you dependent on me and hindered your development. If you really had become self-assessed under the analysis you wouldn't have minded my being more active – in fact – it wouldn't have worried you in the slightest. But as it is, I am afraid, the mischief has been done and what could have been a real great good fun time for both of us – to have found a person to understand and love who would have been willing to reciprocate these feelings – has now been destroyed. This is a lot of male **and** female in each man and in each woman – in some more of one and less of the other and vice versa. With us it seems to*

me possibly wrongly proportionate in each of us and therefore the mixture between us is all right. I am willing to accept this state of affairs and have realised this for a very long time – you are not and I believe that Haas is deliberately trying to make you into something which you are not and may never be – instead of making yourself accept yourself as you are, I might, of course, be quite wrong in this and only time will tell. As it is, I have never seen you so determined and so obsessed by anything and what Haas has deliberately wanted you to believe appears to you now completely your own ideas. As you feel like you do, there just is no alternative – you must have your complete freedom and I must not stand in your way in any way. Please remember always that there was and still is someone who loved you very much and tried her best to understand you and to help you overcome your difficulties and who now brings perhaps the greatest sacrifice to walk out of your life at your own bidding with nothing but good wishes for you in her heart.

"I, for my part, am not looking for anyone else. How could I after all these years together? – happiness and sadness, good times and miserable ones, I shall just carry on as I am and will try to make the best of it. It will be a lonely road no doubt and at present there seems little point in anything – so please don't believe or let yourself be persuaded in believing that I will have no difficulty in replacing you or that I will be just as happy without you – I only wish this were true but it isn't… Our last meeting made me realise once and for all how much you meant to me and just because of this, those lost years when I felt you being taken from me through Haas was such hell. If you were less fond of me or I less of you, the position would be far easier but our last meeting has convinced me

Erna and Ernst together in happier times

even more that a very real attachment still exists between us which could have meant so much to both of us . What more can you expect in the way of stability?

"I hope that you will find happiness in your life and in your job soon. To me, real happiness means the acceptance of oneself as one is without struggling for ideals or to achieve the impossible, to find the right balance between one's ambitions and one's capabilities. So let me wish you that above everything. Remember that there are alternatives to the analysis and remember that there are other analysts apart from Haas.

"I am afraid there is nothing else we can say to each other now. It would not be fair to you if we kept reminding ourselves of each other by letters or cards or presents. You know how I feel and my feelings are not likely to change now having lasted so long. With all my love, may your peace of mind not be long in coming, Erna."

One of the passages in the letter, where Erna talks about the balance of male and female, also raises another issue that was a stumbling block in the relationship – Ernst was bisexual. "He was queer, but not a very active one," says someone close to the pair.

Roger Lloyd Pack says the signs were always there.

"When I was in Birmingham I went to a rather dodgy sauna for treatment an injury and I thought 'This is a little bit, hmmm, well if Ernst goes here, then perhaps he is gay'. I think to me they both seemed pretty asexual. I don't think Erna had time for sex anyway, it just wouldn't have happened, every hour was accounted for."

One very odd thing about the correspondence they had at this time was that despite the hugely emotional missives that were flying backwards and forwards between South Kensington and Moseley they were interspersed with very businesslike letters. One in March of 1957 matter-of-factly talks about Ernst trying to find a Birmingham representative for Erna's company with no mention whatsoever of traumatic breakdown of the relationship.

***

What is perhaps surprising is that Roger Lloyd Pack, son of Uli, is not more of a skier, given Erna's generosity.

He says, "I went on one skiing holiday in 1957 and broke my leg on the last day – and never went again for thirty years. It was unfortunate as I could have gone on so many ski holidays."

The Lloyd Pack brothers and friend on an ill-fated ski trip

His brother Christopher remembers the trip too but for different reasons. "My first ski trip was in Serfaus, stayed in a pension run by a charming family. At the end of the two weeks on the last day of skiing, my brother was messing around at lunchtime and broke his leg. A friend came running into the restaurant shouting for help and we ran out, there was Rog lying in the snow with a fracture. I remember him being loaded into the Blutwagen and being taken down to the town and then the ski instructor turning to me and saying I should go down on the lift. I refused and skied down behind him; whatever the ski instructor did, I did. It was one of the best experiences I ever had. Rather than being at the tail end of fifteen kids in the ski class, I was with him and followed in his tracks."

***

Ski equipment changed dramatically from the late 1930s to the mid 1960s, making it much easier for recreational skiers to enjoy the mountains and – crucially – not hurt themselves as much while doing so.

Early ski racer and jumper Hjalmar Hvam was born in Kongsberg, Norway in 1902. Like many expert skiers of this time, he suffered from broken limbs because of the primitive equipment they were using – largely caused by twisting while falling. In the 1920s, Hvam emigrated to Canada before moving to Mount Hood in Oregon.

In 1937, "Hvam had a 'Eureka moment' in a hospital bed where he was being treated for a leg fracture of his own. Arriving home, he used part of a bay window stud and some steel to make a prototype that became the sport's first releasable safety binding"[48].

He went on to promote the binding – which became known as the Saf-Ski – in the Sixties using the slogan Hvoom with Hvam".

By the 1940s, skiing safety had improved to the point where "about one per cent of skiers were injured on any given day, and by the end of the season about ten per cent of all skiers were out of commission due to ski injuries", mainly lower leg fractures[49].

An engineer called Mitch Cubberley recognised that binding technology could be improved further and invented the Cubco binding. It was a step-in binding and did away with the heel cable, which released the foot unreliably if the boot was wet, replacing it with a spring-loaded latch. He also invented the first ski brake, "a single blade-like prong significantly longer than today's [that] was designed to flip the ski on its side when released. Because of its knife-like appearance the brake became known as the 'toad-stabber'". They eventually became so popular they were selling 200,000 pairs a year[50].

The move from long wooden skis to ones made from composite materials took its first step just after the Second World War. In 1947, aircraft engineer Howard Head began experimenting with making skis from a combination of aluminium, wood laminate and honeycomb plastic. While he was able to make skis lighter this way, they often broke when used for ski racing.

He solved the problem with the Head Standard ski, produced in 1950. This replaced the lightweight honeycomb with heavier plywood which gave the ski strength but without adding too much weight.

Another advance in ski equipment was taking place at around the same time across the other side of the Atlantic. In 1948, Frenchman Jean Beyl invented a metal plate which could be embedded into the ski. The revolution was that the plate twisted with the skier's foot and then returned to the centre[51]. By 1950, members of the French ski team started using Beyl's system.

Although the new plate increased safety, it also added extra thickness to the ski which the French racers deemed undesirable. Beyl then took a new tack, developing the Look Nevada toe binding "the first recognizably modern binding design, with a long spring-loaded piston to provide plenty of lateral elasticity for shock absorption".

As skiing became more popular and reached an audience wider than the early devotees, skiers started to want better and more comfortable equipment.

The time it took to lace up your boots was an inconvenience that found a solution in 1955 when the Swiss German firm Henke developed the first buckle-up ski boot, promoting it with the advertising slogan "Are you lacing when others are racing?"

It was inevitable that the post-war love for all things plastic would eventually touch on the skiing world and it did so in the late 1950s.

In 1958, Bob Lange was running a small plastics company in the city of Dubuque in Iowa making toy cars for General Motors, hula hoops and fridge interiors. A keen skier, Lange was convinced that the future for ski boots was plastic not leather and created the first all-plastic ski boot, albeit still a lace-up, top-entry boot, the following year.

The first boot "was an extremely stiff ski boot that could only have been used by a powerful ski racer. In 1959, a new blue and white lace-up version, with hinged cuff came out of production; in addition to forward flex, it offered more control, but still necessitated two persons to tighten-up the laces."[52]

A happy marriage of the two technologies finally came in 1965 – plastic ski boots with fast-close buckles. The move to the ski equipment that we would recognise today was complete.

Chapter 9

By the late 1950s the company was growing fast and taking on new employees to cope with the increasing demand.

In 1957, Erna learned of the existence of the Shell Travel Club, which offered discounts on holidays to employees of Shell International. The secretary of the club was a man named Colin Trigger and Erna offered club members a 10% discount off her prices in order to encourage bookings.

Trigger says his first impressions of Erna were "not favourable".

"Her temper was bad and with that guttural Viennese accent she actually came over worse than she actually was. Yet a heart was there, even if it was hidden," he says.

At the time, Trigger was living in Ennismore Gardens in South Kensington, a short walk from Erna's office on Old Brompton Road.

Trigger explains how he ended up working for Erna. "My knowledge of the tour industry was, at best, limited and she asked if I would like to work evenings 'to gain knowledge' (but of course no payment). The evening work often lasted until the early hours and could involve walking the dogs. In 1958, just prior to my getting married she made an offer to work full-time at an interesting and better salary, which I accepted."

Trigger worked for the company for the next five years on both summer and winter holidays but mostly as manager of the summer holidays department.

"The clients were usually well off and educated; many from the Kensington/Chelsea area. Most were a delight to deal with because they were so appreciative of her style of holidays and could certainly afford them."

He remembers that many of the clients were long-time customers and friends of Erna. "She enjoyed a large degree of repeat business, probably more than her main rival, Inghams. Of course, these people were not always the easiest to handle."

Trigger, who went on to found Scantours in 1984 and was president of the

Association of British Travel Agents for three years in the 1990s, says that his time working for Erna "taught me more or less everything I know about tour operations".

"This was because we became adept at covering up for errors and dealing with sometimes irate clients," he says. "Of course that behaviour changed later with the licensing of tour operators (and *Holiday Which?*)"

***

A letter that Erna sent to the editor of *The Times* in early 1958 showed an early unease about what was soon to happen in the world of travel – the arrival of cheap, mass tourism, a new wave that she herself had helped create.

The letter appeared in the paper on 30 May under the heading *The English Abroad: Need they behave as they do?*

As well as expressing her distaste of rude British tourists, she still managed to use the opportunity to promote her own business.

Sir – While travelling in Switzerland and Austria during the last winter sports season, I came across a great many British people on winter sports holidays. They belonged mostly to the professional classes and were sufficiently well off to embark on a holiday costing £30-£50.

However, once they set foot on foreign soil they developed a strange habit of counting the groschens or cents (sic) to such a degree that they became the laughing stock of hotelkeepers and skiers from other countries.

People [who] would never dream of brewing their own afternoon tea or after lunch coffee in an English hotel were known to ask for hot water to set up a private canteen in their bed rooms, families of four would share one bath and people would bring their own bottles of drink into a hotel bar.

The main topic of conversation was 'bargain hunting' – one frequently heard remarks such as "I only paid one franc for my tea"… The usual retorts were "How clever, how did you manage that?…In fact, the British skiers seem to enjoy the new sports – 'bargain hunting' and 'beating down the locals' as much as the winter sports themselves."

… A certain amount of tipping is expected by the hotel staff as tips constitute a substantial portion of their wages. This is not sufficiently realised by some British holiday-makers, who think nothing of leaving a hotel or restaurant without leaving a farthing for the staff.

… Needless to say, all this does not exactly further British prestige abroad and it explains the recent reluctance of hotelkeepers to make reservations for British travellers, who used to be their favourite guests.

The letter sparked a lively debate over the next week.

Count Ladislau de Hoyos, the director of the Austrian State Tourist Department in London, responded: "I have never known British visitors to be the laughing stock of any Austrian hotelier. Our sense of humour does not work that way; we would rather applaud anyone who has the skill to avail himself of a bargain when he sees one… it is definitely not the British who have introduced this sort of thing. I know of one Austrian hotelier who has had to fit very special plug points in the bedrooms of this establishment so as to prevent guests from using his electric current for cooking whole meals and ironing anything from handkerchiefs to evening dresses."

"There cannot be any doubt that the overwhelming majority of Austrian hotel-owners regard British visitors as their most welcome guests."

Gordon Cooper, "a Scot and frequent traveller", wrote to say "I always take… a small outfit for making… a *real* cup of tea. The prices charged for their so-called tea presents a good reason for a Briton to practise a sensible economy."

D L Reynolds wrote from the Reform Club to say "To economize honestly on tea and baths by brewing the former or sharing the latter is not by any means unreasonable… [when] a portion of tea may cost up to 3s a head and baths 5s a head. This is not to say that ordering hot water to be sent up to a hotel bedroom or slipping surreptitiously into a bathroom is anything but reprehensible and tactless."

R O Hobhouse argued, "Isn't it time that Alpine hoteliers gave up their archaic attitude towards baths, and realized that a hot bath after a hard day's skiing is a necessity, not an excuse for an extortionate charge?"

Charles Holt, general manager of Thomas Cook, weighed in to say "Dr Erna Low seems to have been singularly unfortunate. I and my colleagues frequently travel on the Continent and… we have not come across the intensive "bargain-hunting" and even more questionable practices to which reference is made. In any case… it is for the individual to judge what he can afford."

Taking a new tack, Frank Day waded in: "It is not unusual – especially in Austria – to come across a part of high-spirited young British folk abroad for the first time, in the charge of a so-called 'courier' as young and irresponsible as themselves. The young man or woman dignified with this title is probably an arts student taking the chance of a cheap holiday. More often than not these 'couriers' are as new to foreign parts as their troop of tourists… Moreover, they are themselves out for a good time and tend to encourage rather than to control the high spirits of their charges."

Another correspondent, Nigel Daw, wrote to explain what he thought were the root causes of 'bargain hunting': "Some travel agents try to drive a hard bargain with the hotel-keeper, since their custom depends on their ability to quote a lower price than the travel agent next door. Then, of course, the hotel-keeper has to make up his profit by charging extras for sundries. Many British tourists do not realize this, and it is quite a shock to them on their first visit, after absorbing the usual advertisement about 'inclusive price £40,' to find that they have to pay 5s extra for each bath."

Veteran of the ski industry, Arnold Lunn, joined in the discussion too. "The travelling Englishman has far less money to spend than was normal when I first began to ski, sixty years ago, and to that extent is less welcome to those hoteliers the warmth of whose welcome is nicely adjusted to the wealth of their clients, but it was only the other day that a hotelier in the Bernese Oberland remarked to me that he still preferred the British to the clients of any other nation."

***

One of the best elements of Colin Trigger's job was to take what became known as the Skimobile, a sort of ice-cream van without the ice-creams, around the country on tour.

"We bought a Bedford Dormobile, renamed it the Skimobile, and did a deal with Vauxhall so that we could position the vehicle in a town's car showrooms to which potential winter sports clients were directed thus helping the showroom (perhaps)," he says.

The Skimobile would stay on the road for up to three weeks, visiting cities such as Birmingham, Edinburgh, Exeter and Newcastle, only returning to London to stock up with brochures.

An article in the *Kentish Gazette* in 1960 said the Skimobile contained "a variety of ski equipment… and also some very eye-catching Norwegian sweaters". The van also featured "a special TV-style automatic colour transparency viewer [showing] ski-ing scenes continually".

"I am not sure if the tour secured many bookings but it certainly attracted a lot of attention in local newspapers and the loud alpine horns I had fitted and the roof rack signage certainly did," says Trigger.

Colin Trigger and colleague with the Skimobile

The Skimobile was rather unreliable, according to former employee Jane Stevens.

"We would 'peddle' around Great Britain in the van, laden to the gunnels and nearly always on the brink of breaking down. One time when Ellen [Fleming] and I were in the Lake District, en route to Glasgow we stopped for a picnic in some field miles away from anywhere. The inevitable happened and the van wouldn't start. We ended up being pushed by a milk tanker."

Stevens recalls that the budget for accommodation on these tours was "minimum minimum". "[Erna] got frightfully mad if we were extravagant and one time en route to Manchester I had to share a room with a parrot."

While the Skimobile was in town, the team took the opportunity to show a promotional film called "Ski-ing and All That".

Christopher Lloyd Pack remembers these film shows well. "The wonderful thing about the film shows was her lack of self-consciousness. She had this ability to talk without training into a microphone and tell you what the picture was about. She would just talk as if she was talking to a friend about this place or that place or how it came to be that this was here or that was there."

"They would have a panel of experts and people would ask questions to find out about the holidays. All the brochures were on display, there was a brochure about everything that you wanted to know."

The team would also show films made by the ski cinematographer Warren Miller. Jane Stevens says, "Erna herself produced films but we preferred those which had been made professionally and so did the public. A whole load of super action packed films arrived from the USA and those were really exciting, even to me who had seen them night after night."

Some places were not ready for such excitement.

"One time we tried to do a publicity show in Carlisle, of all places," remembers Jane Stevens. "It wasn't a hub of activity and there were very few in the audience, mostly OAPs in from the cold, two of whom were fast asleep and the other did her knitting. Carlisle was then crossed off the list."

On one Skimobile trip, Erna showed her hidden heart – despite her seemingly flinty exterior she would often be overwhelmingly generous when it came to the children of her staff, perhaps because she had none of her own.

Colin Trigger says, "My son Stephen was born just before we left and experienced an intestine problem while in hospital. We were at that time in Scotland so Erna asked Walter Leonard [the company air guru] to fix me flights down to London and back up to wherever the team were two days later."

In 1962, Colin's wife, a mezzo-soprano opera singer, was granted a scholarship to study in Vienna for three months and Erna agreed to his taking a short sabbatical to accompany her since it was over a winter period and would not conflict too much with his work.

Erna writes in her autobiographical notes, "After a few months, Colin returned full of ideas but he had outgrown being an assistant and I didn't persuade him to return."

Colin remembers things slightly differently. "On returning to England I found to my surprise I had been sacked in my absence and so claimed one month's salary which was eventually given if reluctantly. Typical."

***

The 1950s saw the advent of a new form of travel that would eventually totally disrupt Erna's way of doing business – charter flights.

The defining moment was the creation of what would become known as package holidays by Vladimir Raitz of Horizon Holidays. In the summer of 1950, he successfully launched holidays to the Camp Franco-Britannique in Corsica using chartered DC3 Dakotas[53]. The first group assembled at King's Cross Coach Station early in the morning, took a coach to Gatwick and then the plane for the journey to Calvi, stopping off at Lyons where they "refuelled the plane and… stomachs".

Despite the Spartan nature of the accommodation and initially slow sales, the first packages tapped into a desire for escaping from Britain to the impossibly exotic Continent.

By 1954, Horizon Holidays was taking thousands of holidaymakers to Corsica, Majorca, Sardinia and the Costa Brava. The era of mass tourism, although few suspected it, had begun.

Ski charter flights were an obvious extension and these came in the 1960-61 season when both Ingham's and Poly Travel started running services to the key gateways of Innsbruck, Geneva, Zurich and Basle[54].

Despite the change to the core business model, Erna embraced the idea of running ski holidays based on flights, getting skiers to the mountains far quicker and more cheaply than by rail. The change dramatically changed the whole winter sports industry and the following decade would see Erna Low Travel Service turned upside down.

***

In 1959, Erna expanded the company's ski programme considerably, in conjunction with the Ski Club of Great Britain. Over the next three years, the company's winter programme would be expanded to contain 150 principal ski resorts[55].

The company was doing very well indeed as the swinging Sixties began. An article in the *Financial Times* of 25 July 1960 reveals that the company's turnover had reached half a million pounds, it had a staff of thirty-three and was making travel arrangements for 10,000 people a year.

A year later, the *Sunday Times* said, "Miss Erna Low, who specializes in holidays for the intellectual" had fourty staff and 12,000 clients.

As a result of the expansion, yet more space was required and Erna took out leases on a row of connected shopfronts on Bute Street, just off Old Brompton Road.

In June 1961, the company veered in a new direction, opening a business travel centre at 7 Bute Street under the responsibility of Walter Leonard.

At 9 Bute Street, Erna opened the Ski Dive, "a spot where people can talk skiing, meet the experts, make new friends and see the latest wear on the slopes' equipment", according to trade paper *Travel Topics*. It opened to the public on 22 October 1962, just in time for the coming winter season.

The Ski Dive was open at lunchtimes and evenings on Tuesdays and Thursdays and visitors could also use the opportunity to take a lesson on a 30-foot-long plastic slope that had been set up at Philbeach Hall in nearby Earls Court by Simpsons of Piccadilly at a cost of 12s 6d a lesson. Instructors included "well-known Swiss expert Dolf Wachter and Caroline Sims, a recent member of the British Ladies Ski Team"[56].

***

The company's expansion meant finding new premises in Bute Street,
photo: Jack Wilson, Jatony

Dancing your way across the Continent is what many people remember about going on an Erna Low ski holiday in the 1960s. The disco carriage was not an Erna innovation (or perhaps Erna-vation) like some other concepts but was pioneered by Ingham's in 1950. Erna Low shared the trains – which both called the Snow Sport Special – and the company had its own branded carriages.

Ski writer Peter Hardy had his first taste of skiing on an Erna Low holiday to Lech in the 1950s, staying at the pension Sandhof and remembers well the introduction of the Dancing Car or Disco Carriage as later hipsters might have called it.

"The record player worked on gimbals and bounced around gyroscopically, although not always very successfully," says Hardy.

"One of the problems with using old train rolling stock was that you felt every corner you went around and you had to clutch onto things and people. It was extremely difficult to stand up. As a result, the floor of the dancing car was awash with drink."

In *Ski Time is Here Again!*, the introduction to one brochure in the 1960s, Erna wrote: "There is no holiday like a ski holiday. You start enjoying yourself the moment you enter the Bar/Dancing Car on one of the fast Special Trains, shaking and twisting your way across the Continent to the tunes of the latest pop music."

The 1967 brochure trumpeted: "Your holiday starts when you board the train… you will find a gay wintersports atmosphere in the Dancing Car, which is now attached to most Ski Specials."

Insurance broker Michael Pettifer, whose company arranged ski insurance policies for many tour operators, was an early guest on the ski trains. "The carriage nearly fell over on one occasion it was so full," he remembers with a laugh.

Tim Clarke of wine tour specialists Arblaster & Clarke was another who took the ski train in the late 1960s as part of a school group.

"On the way out, we were wandering around the train and I remember sitting at the back with our feet dangling out of the back of the train. It was going so slowly I think one of the kids jumped off and walked alongside it," he says.

"On one trip my sister and some of the older boys were in the disco car the next morning. Near Basle they uncoupled the carriage and they were shunted all around and taken off into a siding. Luckily, we were later reunited."

The arrival of ski charters posed another challenge – how to transport the large amount of equipment you need to go skiing. Erna, ever innovative, came up with an idea that would resurface more than half a century later when the low-cost airlines started charging for all manner of extras.

Ski insurance guru Michael Pettifer says, "When aeroplanes first started, Erna suggested that people wear boots onto the plane to save money. I can remember going on an aeroplane with lace-up boots on when I was nine or ten."

He says that as a result, when personal effects were added to travel insurance policies in the Sixties, ski equipment covered skis, bindings and sticks. "Boots were always in the baggage section because you wore them on the plane," he says.

***

By the 1960s, Erna had recognised that catering for holidaymakers with specialist interests was a lucrative business; the sheer variety of what the company was offering at the time is breathtaking.

In one leaflet entitled *Holidays With A Purpose*, Erna explains, "Every year more and more people seem to prefer a holiday which gives them a chance to acquire some specialised knowledge or to improve their already existing knowledge."

The leaflet includes painting and sketching holidays in Yugoslavia, Spanish courses in Granada, Austrian culture courses in Vienna, botanical tours in Norway and geographical visits to Perthshire.

Every new year seemed to bring a new direction for Erna's innovative take on the specialist holiday.

The Daily Sketch of 6 January 1962 reports: "It was bound to happen sooner or later – the holiday by helicopter...Erna Low have dreamt up two heli-holidays." On one you see the Lake District by air, spend the night at a lakeside hotel, two days sightseeing in a chauffeur-driven car, and then first-class restaurant car train back to London. The second trip leaves Battersea on Saturday morning and lands at Yarmouth, Isle of Wight, for Totland Bay. Again a chauffer driven car tour on Sunday and back to London. The first trip costs £85, the second £29."

Another offering at the time was luxury slimming holidays at Rodmell House in Tunbridge Wells proposing "steam baths, massage [and] slimming diets"[57], the first of Erna's health holidays, which would become an important part of the business in later years.

The Ipswich Evening Star of 24 January 1963 shows the company offering "inclusive weeks for gourmets… house parties for teenagers, language courses at home and abroad, touring in horse drawn caravans, pony trekking in Scotland and Wales and canoeing holidays on the River Wye".

Erna also had plans to launch "sightseeing" tours for another specialist group.

In late March of 1963, *The Observer* reported that "Erna Low, the South Kensington travel agent… is starting these blind tours this summer, [and] flew out to Vienna last week to arrange for parties to be allowed to run their hands over the groaning giants, pigtailed sphinxes, classical rapes and other baroque statuary of the city's parks and museums."

Another innovation was a holiday for sixty teenagers, half from England and half from France, to learn each other's language. It was priced at 9½ guineas per week.

Teenagers Rowena and Verity, from Harrow and Guildford respectively, said they "learned quite a lot of French". "We go into Wallingford and pretend we're French. They were quite taken in… "[58]. The French girls, meanwhile, were more interested in the English teenagers' make-up. "The girl in our dormitory has a drawer FULL of make-up," said Catherin and Danielle both seventeen, from the outskirts of Paris. "FOUR tins of talcs, FIVE lipsticks and a lot of eye make-up and she's younger than us."

Her skill in developing tourist trade brought her to wider attention. In December 1962, she was invited to the Jordanian Embassy to meet King Hussein "to allow His Majesty the opportunity of meeting members of the British travel trade to discuss Jordan's present and future plans to attract more tourists".

By 1964, Erna – "one of Britain's most resourceful agents" – was offering motorists ski packs[59] including hotels, insurance, ski-hire and lift passes, ski gift vouchers – and snowsports combined with language lessons in Austria or Switzerland or with operas and concerts in Austria or Italy."

Christopher Lloyd Pack says, "She wanted everyone to have an opportunity. She didn't want just rich people to do this, she wanted everyone to be able to enjoy or fulfil something in their life. If you were interested in birds, she would like you to come and develop your interest. She was selfless. She loved people to enjoy themselves and may have made a buck or two out of it. It was for them to have a good time."

Long-term friend and journalist Eithne Power says, "She was always urging people to educate themselves. I remember once rebelling on a press trip to Verona. It was really hot and one of the visits was to a Palladian villa and I said I would rather read a book. Erna was outraged and told me it was a unique opportunity to see this wonderful villa. Naturally, I went and it was absolutely beautiful. I don't ever remember her being wrong in her recommendations."

***

Anyone who met Erna would be surprised to hear her name and the word "fashion" in the same sentence. She nearly always wore the same standard outfit.

Roger Lloyd Pack says, "She always wore a suit, a skirt and a jacket. I don't think I ever saw her in anything else and she certainly never wore trousers."

The suit was made of "good tweed", recalls Jean Yellowlees, mother of Joanna who would later take over the company. "She bought one every six months or so and would always go for the classic four square cut things. She had her own style."

Bobbie Shafto encouraged her in this standard "uniform". "She was not an easy shape to dress and used to have her suits sent from Switzerland," she says. "The shops had her measurements there and she just used to order them."

In one article[60], Erna explained her distinctive style, "I like loose, comfortable clothes. The only place I seem to be able to buy readymades is in Zurich."

Despite this standard outfit, she was being solicited for fashion ideas in the Sixties.

"If you are my size and go to Switzerland, you will find a vast selection of not-at-all dowdy outsize jersey suits," she told *Housewife* magazine in 1962

In the same article, she recommended teenagers to buy slipper socks from Yugoslavia, "much thicker and sturdier than ours because they are worn by the peasants and not meant for soft living. They are in very gay, if rather loud, designs."

Norwegian sweaters, meanwhile were "irresistible, especially those for children with stylised reindeer across the chest".

Men also received a fashion tip, although quite how many were reading *Housewife* at the time is an interesting thought. "For sartorially-enterprising males, Spain has just the thing: antelope ties in olive greens, deep blues and reds… washable, brush-up-able and wonderfully cheap".

When asked about what to wear while travelling, she said, "Comfort is the backbone of a travelling wardrobe. English tourists spend far too much time abroad looking for somewhere to put their feet up. Wives can be seen leaning wearily against the Acropolis, obviously suffering from a surfeit of tight corsetry, and easing aching feet out of high heeled shoes."

Her advice was to take a handbag "big enough to hold passports, two purses (one for foreign currency and one for British)". Her advice on shoes was to take "two comfortable pairs… which do not pinch from the word go" and that "high heels are fine for dancing but not for cobbled streets".

On planes, she recommended a scarf because "many people suffer from stiff necks due to the blasts of draught from those little whistling things above each head".

"Nylon [underwear] in hot climates is quite unsuitable," she continued. "Slacks and jeans are for young girls. Middle-aged ladies in trousers look especially grotesque on the Continent."

Her most useful outfit was "a four-piece set: shirt, skirt, bathing suit and shorts, all made from the same material".

For skiing, ladies "must take a little cocktail dress for dancing and dinner. Hotels are becoming more fidgety about ladies clumping around in trousers and boots, even though their sweaters flash with fashionable après-ski glitter."

A few years later, as London became the centre of the Swinging Sixties, she made her views on a particular fashion at the time very clear in a letter to *London Life*[61].

"Last week, I was horrified to see a large display at a well-known store in the centre of Zurich called the Young London Look—girls in absurdly short mini-skirts, with Beatnik boys either lounging or lurking in the background. The remarks of Zurich spectators were anything but complimentary, and I am positive that the British image abroad suffers considerably by such displays. Isn't it time that the young British look became a little less provocative?"

Two weeks later, a Freddy Silberman replied as follows:

"I could not disagree more with Erna Low's anti-mini letter. Britain must export or die, and the way to export to Switzerland is to offer them something as far away from Calvinism as possible. Vive la mini-skirt!"

Erna's was also being asked for her views on design[62]. "I think men should do most of the designing," she told TTG. "After all, have you ever heard of a woman designing an engine?" On internal décor: "Women should certainly be consulted; after all they have the practical touch. Supposing, for example, a bar was being designed. Would a man ever stop to think about where a woman could rest her handbag? These things are important."

By the 1980s, Erna had branched out from her Swiss readymades and had a British Guyanese dressmaker come to her South Kensington home for private fittings.

"At present, my dressmaker's making me a silk jacket to match a dress," she told a magazine at the time. "It's the second jacket I've had made. I gave away the first one to the Italian Earthquake victims [the 6.9 magnitude Irpiona quake of 1980] by mistake. I was in Naples shortly afterwards and I kept a sharp eye out, but no luck. I had to scour Venice to find the shop where I'd got the original silk three years ago – they shinned up ladders and earthed it out. After a lifetime of travel, I'm only now getting the message about travelling light and planning my wardrobe accordingly."

***

Erna was constantly on the road, looking for new destinations, particularly those that were untouched by mass tourism. She was regularly accompanied by Uli Lloyd Pack, Bobbie Shafto and, indeed, anyone who happened to be hanging around the office at a loose end.

Historian Christopher Black, before he became famous, accompanied her on many a scouting trip "You might be sitting around in the car waiting for her to conduct the negotiations. You never knew when you were getting a meal," he says.

Erna's friend from the BBC, Ellen Fleming, also returned to Erna Low at this time.

"One day at the Ski Club, there was Erna," remembers Ellen. "She said 'Oh, you're unemployed, you can drive me round the ski resorts'."

Ellen agreed but insisted that there be no permanent employment contract, the memories of her earlier year in the office still fresh in her memory. Ellen drove Erna around ski resorts in Austria, France, Switzerland and Germany for the next few seasons. "She would tell you where to go even though she had no sense of direction and then would fall asleep," she recalls.

On one trip to see a hotelier, Ellen remembers having to sleep in the swimming pool complex. "There was a room for Erna but not for me," she says with a laugh.

On another trip to France, Ellen woke Erna up as they arrived in Chamonix and Erna quickly barked out directions – "'Left, right, whatever," says Ellen. "And then we were at the biggest chocolate shop ever."

Another year they were driving up to the mountains and were slowed down by heavy snow and were still driving late at night. "We couldn't get into the town because there were terrible avalanches and what we had meant to do was go up the pass and down the other side. Erna said we would have to go through the tunnel instead. We got to the tunnel and the attendant said that we had to take the chains off the car. By now, it was midnight and I was done for so I said I couldn't. Finally the attendant let us through but told us we must drive through very slowly. When we came out the other side, the snow was up to the second floor windows. Erna eventually found somewhere we could stay and she turned to me and said 'Would you like a drink?', a very unusual sentence for Erna to utter. 'Schnapps now', I replied".

She adds, "Working for her, you felt that you had been correctly evaluated and then when you did whatever it was you felt that you had achieved it. It was very satisfying. She did take advantage of you but she wanted things done the way she wanted, and might be critical if it did not happen that way. She also had a very soft heart and was very kind to many people."

***

Jane Stevens, who repped for the company in Villars, was another who accompanied Erna on these trips.

"Erna always fell asleep as soon as we started off and so was useless as a navigator," she says. "We found ourselves doing contracts at all hours, onward to the next place, a snooze in the car, and then at it again. We went to all sorts of places, Erna did the business side while I looked at the skiing side – or else had to see the bathrooms, view the bedrooms and count the hangers in the cupboards just to make sure all the claims made by the various hoteliers were correct."

Christopher Lloyd Pack remembers, "I myself went on one contract mission to Austria and went round all the people she had dealings with to fix contracts with. She tried to do it in a way that no-one knew she was coming. She liked to catch people out to see what the hotel was really like, not just a show. But once she arrived, everyone knew she was coming."

"When we went to every place, everyone was ready with schnapps on the table," says Christopher. "Because she didn't drink, I had to drink it all. I didn't understand what was going on because I didn't understand the language. Everything about [these trips] was joyful. You didn't realise it was a business meeting, there was always laughter and joy and she had this exceptional relationship with hotel and pension owners. She helped them by arranging both winter and summer holidays."

In a brochure from this era, Erna writes of the "Special Features of our

Service", which promised "personal inspection of centres by Erna Low and her senior staff (usually two carefully chosen young men)".

Erna generally received a warm welcome on these scouting trips. "When I took Carol Wright, the well-known travel writer, on one of my annual trips of inspection and exploration, she commented 'They greet you as a long lost sister'," wrote Erna later. "This is, of course, not only pleasant but also very useful as at present the negotiation of cheap rates is of prime importance and that's why I always go myself and usually succeed in bringing back a good many contracts."[63]

Colin Trigger, an employee for five years in the 1960s, says "I suspect that many hoteliers agreed to her terms just to escape or end the discussion."

Celia Fielder, former editor of the *Army Ski Association* magazine agrees with this. "I was on a golfing trip with Erna to St Cyprien in the south of France, near Perpignan, a golf trip, which I wrote up for *The Key*, a Forces publication in Germany. Nicolas Boissonnas, who owned St Cyprien and most of Flaine, was hosting the dinner. I remember him telling me the following day that he was exhausted, after a very tough evening with Erna who had argued over rates and terms until 3am. She was over eighty at the time, but had lost none of her business acumen, or tough dealing and thrashed out a hard bargain."

Erna's trips were not all about business though. Sylvia Antunovich (née Jones), who worked for Erna in the 1960s, says Erna was "a stickler for getting the tough negotiating and decisions over first" but that then they would move to "the best *Konditorei* in town also had to be checked out… I still believe that Erna enjoyed checking out the *Konditorei* more than anything else".

Always the innovator and keen to make new finds, Erna discovered many places that are now firmly established on the tourism map, such as Torremolinos.

In 1962, she told Ruth Miller of *Housewife* magazine[64] that finding the right places was "Hunch plus map reading, rather than method which leads you to this sort of discovery".

She explained how she came across one particular Portuguese gem. "I arrived later at night for a routine hotel inspection. As I loathe spending night in towns when I'm abroad, I took a little road which looked as though it didn't lead anywhere in particular and suddenly came upon Sesimbra, a tucked-away fishing village with golden sands."

She would rarely spend more than two days in any one place. "Where the roads are good we give the once-over to three small resorts in a day. In a large place, we might charge in and out of ten to fifteen hotels in twenty-four hours; we inspect things like kitchen equipment, the wattage of the bulbs in the bedside lamps, and we never forget to pull the plugs. We even test how soundproof the bedroom walls are."

Erna wrote later, "We were among the first to promote Spanish holiday centres but the Spanish Embassy could not guarantee that traveller's cheques would be cashed in Spain… Obtaining a Spanish visa was a morning's work, to obtain Insurance Cover for Spain was practically impossible."

America was another destination added to the programme at this time. Erna also decided to start trips to America and called on Ellen Fleming to be the tour leader, who had just travelled around the country with a friend and co-written a book called *Introducing America.*

The other leader on the tour was Lorna Braithwaite, the then travel editor of *Good Housekeeping* magazine. "I asked her whether she had done anything like that before and she said no. Neither of us had and we both fell about laughing. Erna would always say to people 'You would be good for that', even if you hadn't ever done it before."

"We took them all round the States and had a wonderful time. They loved it so much we took them back again the next year."

***

Despite the new directions for the company, house parties were still at its core.

However, by now the focus was firmly on families as many of the couples who had met and fallen in love at her earlier parties had now gone on to have children.

Christopher Lloyd Pack says the parties were "an opportunity for families to have a holiday together in a safe environment".

"There would be a host and hostess who would put on concerts, beetle drives and there would be fancy dress. They would also organise coaches to go to the beach "Once a week, we would go to one particular beach and have a barbecue. It was great fun. The grounds were fantastic and wonderful for children to play in. We would have tennis and table tennis tournaments. It was wall-to-wall fun."

One article states[65]: "Erna Low likes to meet parents and children beforehand to make sure they will fit into their particular party, and reserves the right—never yet used—to send the child home if he won't obey the few rules laid down, which includes set bedtimes and no drinking or smoking under the age of sixteen."

One of the popular venues for the parties was at Moulsford in Berkshire, which had tennis courts and the use of a swimming pool[66]. The 1962 Christmas party there cost ten guineas for four days. Other destinations at the time included Highclere (now famous as Downton Abbey), Barford in Warwickshire and St Peter Port, Guernsey.

In an article in the *Daily Telegraph* [67], the paper's first ever full-time travel writer Elisabeth "Minky" de Stroumillo recounts one of these family-friendly holidays at Runton Hill, "a thoroughly OK girls' boarding-school, on the Norfolk coast" where Erna had been running house parties for more than ten years.

The party consisted of seventy-five people, two thirds of them families who had paid £15 for the week. The rest were unaccompanied children between the ages of seven and fourteen, some from broken homes, others from families where the parents were working while others were children whose parents had gone on their own holidays abroad.

The holidays offered "egg and spoon races with knobbly potatoes, sprinting races, prizes of gobstoppers and candy sticks, swimming in the huge indoor pool" followed by a "high tea of fish fingers and baked beans [and] huge helpings of trifle".

Farmers' Weekly[68] was also raving about the parties: "At her house parties in Britain it is possible to meet young people from abroad and this helps to broaden a child's outlook without actually sending him or her away," wrote Barbara Wace.

Erna's focus on the family and children at this time perhaps had her own sadness at its heart.

Roma Black, who worked for Erna, says, "Her whole life was with young people. She was marvellous with young people but it would not have been a good idea for her to have children."

Bobbie Shafto says, "She loved children; she should have had children."

However, Bobbie feels that she might not have been the ideal parent. "She wouldn't have been very tolerant," she says.

***

The historian Christopher Black, who went on those house parties, says he was greatly influenced by Erna in his career path.

Now Honorary Research Professor in the Department of Modern History at the University of Glasgow and author of the *The Italian Inquisition,* Black explains that as a young pupil, he had been interested in classics but switched to history at senior school under the influence of an inspirational teacher.

"Once Erna realised this she would give me history and art books as Christmas presents. She gave me one particular book, Garrett Mattingly's *The Armada*, which I took up with me, having got into Oxford on a scholarship in December."

Black was booked in for one of Erna's house parties for Christmas and New Year.

"I arrived at this house party, she took one look at me and said 'You do not look at all well. You are going on the train in two days' time to Sölden. So she sent me off, armed with this copy of *The Armada*. It had the effect of persuading me to be interested in the early modern period. I actually left it on the train coming back and had to buy another copy."

She also suggested to Black that he improve his modern languages.

She told him to either stay with her family in Austria and learn German or go to the University for Foreign Students in Perugia and learn Italian. He chose the latter and it was there that he developed the research interests that guided much of his career.

***

In 1962, Erna was looking for some more living space as the business took over at Reece Mews, Old Brompton Road and Bute Street.

She saw an advert in *The Times* for a 'Small house in South Kensington for sale – "ninety years lease, small garden, cost £7000." The house was 17 Selwood Terrace, just a short walk from the heart of the Erna Low business empire. It was a snip and would be worth many millions when it was sold after her death.

Selwood Terrace is named after the market gardener Richard Selwood, who owned the land on which it now stands back in the 17th century. The land was acquired by the architect Samuel Ware – who designed London's Burlington Arcade – and a house built on it by 1831.

The first occupants were humble, according to house researcher Sara van Loock, and were employed as "a stay-maker, a paper-hanger and a day washerwoman" and lived there in 1846. Two wealthy widows then lived there until it was taken on by an ironmonger from Shoreditch called Thomas Watson, who took in boarders.

After many years as an apartment house, it was bought by "Bernard Metts, a prosperous general merchant with offices in Rathbone Place".

Erna recalled later, "I hardly had £7,000 at my disposal but I was determined to raise it. I made an appointment to inspect the house, fell in love with it at first sight and immediately made a bid for it. Fortunately I did not listen to my friends who thought that it was overpriced, the rooms too small, the basement damp and the little garden neglected."

"Very expensive it was, even then," says Roma Black. "Next door to her lived a retired assistant governor of northern Nigeria; it was a good address."

The actress Julie Christie also lived on the road, paying £20,000 for a three bedroom property in 1966, a year after the release of *Dr Zhivago*[69].

The house at Selwood Terrace had a very narrow hall and a big sitting room downstairs. In the basement, there was the kitchen where she had lunch.

An article from just after she moved into the property[70], revealed that it had "sparkling white paint, overall fitted green carpet and elegant comfort, certainly reflecting her down-to-earth personality: nothing superfluous, no more rooms than she needs; everything chosen for good reason."

The drawing room was furnished with 18th century French antiques; the study was painted in tallow green and white while the bedroom was painted pink and mushroom with "one wall taken up by a large wardrobe".

She covered the walls of the house with paintings and the shelves with decorative plates she had picked up on her travels. She was particularly fond of a watercolour painted by a local artist in Hydra in Greece. "[It] will always remind me of the bright light (not lights!!) of the island and, though I don't know anything about paintings, I think this particular picture might well be a 'find'".

Christopher Lloyd Pack, a regular visitor to the house, says, "The lounge was knocked through and there was a big table covered in documents and brochures from other companies. At the other end, there was a comfortable sitting room – she liked watching television although she often fell asleep while watching it. It was a comfortable room, very warm, but the emphasis was definitely on work rather than relaxation.

"Upstairs she had a bathroom on the mezzanine floor and two bedrooms on the top floor. Her own bedroom I only saw when she was ill much later."

Her Italian relatives were also regular visitors to the house.

Erna's "cousin", Francesca Ruberl, wrote in her family history *I Ruberl*, "Her home in South Kensington was very English in style. It made a base for many of us cousins and second cousins to visit London. While we were there, we would stick stamps on envelopes for the Erna Low Travel Service. During one visit to her, the present for my work was a surprise trip to see a ballet with Margot Fonteyn, accompanied by a young man from the office who made it very clear that he would have much preferred to be at a football game."

***

In the 1960s, Erna was at the peak of her business success and the Old Brompton Road office was a regular haunt of the famous and influential.

According to former employee Sylvia Antunovich, the opera diva Dame Eva Turner was "a regular client and personal friend of Erna". Antunovich also talks of one summer on Derby Day. "The staff had stopped for a brief moment to listen to the race when the front bell [at 47 Old Brompton Road] went. Richard Baker, well known presenter and music buff, had come to collect the tickets for his honeymoon."

Asked by *The Lady*[71] her secret, Erna replied: "I just did what I liked. A lot of people came to like the same things."

Halina Hodi, Erna's "girl Friday" from the 1950s and friend for life said: "There were always difficulties but she never looked back. She cut her losses and went forward and put the trouble behind her. Everything that she touched was made possible."

Halina believes that Erna's success as a businesswoman was instilled in her by her mother Emma.

"Her mother always supported her," she says. "When Erna came back with a failed school report, her mother would not scold her. She would take her in her arms and say 'Don't worry, better luck next time.' That way she learnt to be positive. She had no doubts in herself in the male-dominated business world."

Halina adds, "A business grows or stagnates. So she had to always build up, up, up – at some points there were over sixty people working for her. Yet she couldn't have anyone strong beside her, not when she was in her 'bloom' or prime."

This is something that Roger Lloyd Pack agrees with. "She was quite indomitable and not everyone got on with her. She was quite a ruthless business woman and she didn't suffer fools at all. But she was loyal, very loyal and she expected high standards. I got away with things because I made her laugh."

"Yet she could be incredibly rude to people. Was it intentional? It is hard to say," he says.

French Tourist Office marketing director Dennis Fabri says, "I was very fond of Erna but she could be abrupt. She would be on the phone to my secretary asking to speak to me and they would say not at the moment. Erna would reply brusquely 'Why not?'"

Erna also found it very difficult to delegate, something that would become a crucial factor in the decade that was to follow.

"She wouldn't trust anyone to do anything," says Roger Lloyd Pack. "It was also very hard for men to work for her. There were a few men who found it too difficult because she would humiliate them and they just left," he says.

Often these departures followed a trip to the front room at 47 Old Brompton Road. Former employee Jane Stevens later wrote to Erna to share her memories for the would-be autobiography, "Being summoned to the front room was always taken in fear… It seemed a huge room, always full of files and papers and more often than not [Erna was] not in the best of moods. Things were never done fast enough – and [Erna] always insisted on writing loads of notes by hand which were never easy to decipher."

She continued, "The post room was a refuge, as you never came down those narrow stairs. If we heard your footsteps in the corridor it was immediate silence in case one should be summoned for a task (usually at 5.25pm). One time I dived for the safety of the post room and landed on the fire extinguisher, which didn't exactly remain silent."

One anonymous former colleague wrote in 1985 that "In spite of the few divergences of opinion we sometimes had, I always admired you for your work, your courage, your willpower and your zest of life, and I must say, I am glad I have met you. The years I worked at E.L will never be forgotten."

Roger adds, "She wasn't worried about pleasing people or people liking her. She never ingratiated herself with anyone and she could spot anyone who tried to ingratiate themselves with her."

Despite the size of the company, it was not at all corporate. Ruth Miller in *Housewife* magazine said that by 1962 "with the enormous growth of winter sport's traffic, seasons now overlap alarmingly and all the bookings have to be dealt with at once. She copes magnificently but there is still something endearingly amateurish about her set-up."

Erna added: "I have no ambitions to make a lot of money I already have all I want: sympathetic friends, a comfortable home and a good car!"

So why did she work so hard? "I suppose it must be because it gives me satisfaction to think I have started a new way of holidaying, and it's a challenge to put new ideas into practice," she told Miller.

***

A typical day in the life of Erna would involve getting up between 8am and 9am and then off to the office at about 9.30am to 10am[72].

She would then work till very late, meeting journalists and tourist directors for lunch and, most of all, writing the copy for the vast number of brochures produced by the company, which she would not delegate to anyone else.

Sylvia Antunovich, who scouted out various new destinations for the company, said when you entered 47 Old Brompton Road there were "piles of paper in all directions, and a favourite poodle at her feet".

When writing, she would become totally absorbed. The historian Christopher Black remembers: "She would sometimes have me meet her in the office and I would sit in a corner and look at magazines while she proofread. Then at nine o'clock at night she would say 'Right, it's time to eat'. She had to finish her business tasks first and she just assumed that you would amuse yourself or just behave in a corner."

Her au pair, Halina Hodi, explains how Erna worked on her brochures at Selwood Terrace.

"I would usually pop in after work. She would take half an hour off and then open a box of chocolates and get back to writing a brochure until five in the morning. She did this year after year. The chocolates kept her going," she says with a giggle.

There was no time for socialising with this punishing schedule and true friends were few and far between. Those friends there were usually ended up working for her in some capacity.

Erna told *Housewife* magazine in 1962[73], "I have a few close friends who know I've always time for them if they need me. But I loathe small-talk evenings with acquaintances."

But back to the brochures. Uli Lloyd Pack would take Erna's reams of notes and then transform them into something that a printer could understand.

Uli's son Christopher says, "[Uli] worked after hours at home, typing up the brochures. They were all originally handwritten, Erna's handwriting almost illegible. Mum would sit at typewriter typing up the manuscript and [the whole family] would be involved in the proof-reading".

The brochures were in "her quirky style just as she spoke", he says. "The writing was just matter of fact and she would try and put over the energy of the particular village or resort and try and bring you with her."

"Everything that appeared in her brochure, she knew; she knew what the beds

Erna at her desk in 1965, photo: C O'Gorman, The Times

were like, she knew what the food was like. She knew everything about the resorts she advertised. She was adamant that nothing would appear that she hadn't personally experienced."

Roger Lloyd Pack remembers making suggestions for inclusion. "They were jokey things but she didn't go for them. She was always looking for slogans – To Sun and Snow with Erna Low, that sort of thing. I would suggest 'Earn A Low Cost Holiday' or some pun like that but she wouldn't go for it."

He says he became a good proof-reader as a result. "It was good training and I became one and did lots of it. I used to like the sessions and we would go through her text, usually with one other person. We would just go through all these exotic places like Saas Fee, Innsbruck and Serfaus."

The brochures were written in a first-person style, as you might expect from someone whose name is synonymous with the experience you hope to find, a sort of TripAdvisor before the age of the internet. They include countless recommendations garnered from those endless scouting trips around Europe.

An article in *Travel Agency* magazine[74], said "Her greatest feat is writing all the firm's brochures – a dozen a year, not counting many other small leaflets – in friendly terms which clearly pull in a lot of business."

"Not many managing directors do their own proof checking. Miss Low writes her brochures as well which accounts for their distinctive chatty style. They read a bit like an account of travels round Europe and this is, in fact, what they are."[75]

Writing about Obertauern in the 1967 brochure, the introduction reads "When I visited the centre last March, in spite of arriving in the middle of a snow storm, I confirmed my view that this indeed is a paradise for all standards. Many new hotels had been built since I had last been there and après-ski entertainments, which had been practically non-existent, have caught up with the ski life."

The brochures were also full of fun little titbits. The 1967 brochure included the exhortation "Make Your Camera Pay For Your Holiday" asking holidaymakers to send in their photos and 16mm films. "If we publish any of your photos you will receive a £1.1.0 reproduction fee."

She told a journalist in 1982[76], "I suppose my brochures were a bit different, very personal, very family. I wrote and did all the photography myself, but I didn't see anything unusual about them at the time."

***

In 1963 a travel trade magazine decided to do a review of one of her brochures.

In *Travel World* [77], someone hiding behind the nom de plume "Candidus" wrote: "Erna Low produces a fat little brochure. I'm sure if she sees anyone else has a good idea, she pops her own version into her book. While she lifts the better ideas – and I give her full marks for doing so – she always ends up with a jumbled brochure in which prospective bookers must get hopelessly lost and this must cost bookings. Spend time sorting it out and you could do well. Her brochure is loved by travel writers seeking something different… [It]tells you how to sunbathe and things like that."

Candidus' review apparently did not sit well with Erna. Writing again the following year, Candidus wrote:

"I did hear on my private grapevine that after my review of her brochure last year Erna Low almost committed *hari-kari*, but stopped herself in the nick of time to see whether she could make me eat my words in 1964."

Candidus added: "She consistently finds new centres. Just ponder these… Serfaus, St Johann im Pongau, Carteret, Bernkastel-Kues, Paleokastitsa, Thasos, Procida, Ponza, Camino, Djerba, Almunecar. Where else will you find them in an agent's brochure?"

Erna Low brochures from the 1960s

Chapter 10

The 1960s were swinging indeed and not just because of the emergence of the Beatles and the Stones or of the sudden availability of the oral contraceptive pill. Skiing became sexy too as skiwear became more figure-hugging and the après-ski got rowdier. As a result, the number of people going skiing grew rapidly.

In the introduction to the 1963/1964 brochure Erna wrote, "We have indeed travelled a long way since a handful of fanatics ventured forth on the snow slopes on home-made wooden planks, much ridiculed by spectators. Skiing has fired the imagination of millions and an astonishing number of cable cars and skilifts – many of them fantastic technical achievements – come into operation every season."

As Roger Bray wrote in *Flight to the Sun*, the reasons for the ski revolution were many. "As tour operators expanded their summer package programmes to the sun, so the industry looked increasingly for ways of squeezing more productive work from charter aircraft in the interim. Minimum price regulations prevented operators from organizing holidays cheap enough to attract the mass market to winter sunshine destinations but seemed not to deter skiers. Improvements in equipment and clothing helped, too."

Although around a million people go skiing each year from Britain these days, mainly to France, things were not always this way.

In the mid Sixties[78], Austria and Switzerland were by far the most popular places to go. At the time, Ingham's was sending 16,000 British skiers to Austria, where the company featured twenty-five resorts. Erna Low featured an incredible forty-seven Austrian resorts in its brochures in the early 1960s.

Yet this was the decade in which France started its long march towards dominance over Austria and Switzerland, countries which had held sway for most of the 20th century.

Roland Huntford in the ski history *Two Planks and a Passion* writes, "With state subsidies, and supervised planning, a bumper crop of shining new artificial ski resorts sprang up to develop the French Alps during the 1960s. Beautiful most of them were not; all concrete and high rise in a Le Corbusier lampoon."[79]

Bray says, "The skiing take-off was given afterburn by the development of a new generation of purpose-built resorts, high in the French mountains. They lacked the soul of those small Austrian villages but the snow was more reliable and the lifts were linked, so that guests could ski for many kilometres without walking, catching buses or covering the same piste twice."

Field magazine reported[80] that "more than ten times the number of Britons will go [skiing] this season as went before the war. The cause of this stampede to the mountains is partly, of course, that more people can now afford to go... New resorts have sprung up in previously lonely valleys. Mountainsides, once closed to all but climbers, are now covered by a network of lifts. Comfortable hotels cater for the now indispensable après-ski parties."

In one of her brochures from the time, Erna wrote, "The French resorts are... becoming more popular with the more experienced skiers. For the slopes in places like Val d'Isère and Méribel are a challenge to even the best skiers."

At the time, the breadth of resorts in Austria offered by Erna was still impressive, ranging from tiny, barely known hamlets to big-names resorts such as St Anton, where Erna was a great friend of Lilli Stein. Stein was another Viennese who ran the famous Rosannastubl, where a zither player entertained guests with the theme from *The Third Man*.

Erna Low ski trips could be booked in two different ways: as Free-Lance Ski Holidays or Ski parties.

She wrote, "Free-Lance arrangements are intended for those who want to be entirely independent when they arrive at a centre but wish to benefit from our advantageous hotel allotments at pre-arranged fixed rates".

The brochure goes on, "The secret of our success lies in the great care we take in forming our ski parties. We invite our clients to come and see us if at all possible so that we can advise them personally which party or centre to choose."

It was still early enough in the days of ski charter flights that holidaymakers needed to be reassured. "Viscount aircraft carrying sixty-five passengers will be used. This means a short and comfortable flight. All flying arrangements are in the hands of BUA (British United Airways), a reputable air company of high standing."

There were other changes happening to the typical ski holiday.

Insurance broker Michael Pettifer, a regular guest of the company, says, "The two main things that are significantly different from then to now is people's way of skiing and duration. Without question, we would go to ski school; there was no question of free skiing. It would have been anathema."

"Today's one week is like two weeks then," he says. "If you go back even further, to the 1930s, you used to go for a month because it took so long to get there."

For anyone brought up in the 1970s and 1980s, there was one feature of the school year that everyone looked forward to – the annual school ski trip. In fact, the boom in skiing that would happen in those two decades is often put down to the fact that many people had their first experiences on snow at school and were bitten by the bug, with an annual ski trip a fixture of the holiday calendar after they left school.

With her love of children, her successful family holiday and ski businesses, who better to conceive the idea than Erna Low?

In the mid 1960s, Erna received a visit at the Old Brompton Road office from Brynmor Jones, the deputy chief education officer at Glamorgan Education Authority, who wanted to see whether Erna could arrange ski training courses for groups of up to 800 teenagers, many of whom had never been abroad nor seen snow-covered mountains.

Erna had met Brynmor Jones on an earlier trip to the resort of Fierberbunn and had gotten on famously in one of the hotel bars. "I enticed him back to the table and ordered G&Ts to entertain him and asked the staff to bring some sausage to accompany it. Meanwhile, the band started playing The Last Post."

The sausage came at the same moment and Jones said solemnly, "I suppose this is the Last Supper then."

The company would go on to organise ski trips for Glamorgan schoolchildren from secondary moderns and grammar schools for the next decade to the Austrian resorts of Ischgl and Fieberbrunn.

"It proved a great experience to be in charge and to watch over groups of hundreds of boys and girls at a time. It was not easy to watch over such a large number but a pleasure to see how much they enjoyed skiing and how quickly they progressed on the slopes," said Erna.

Each child would usually bring a little pocket money – perhaps £10 to £15 – while the Glamorgan Education Authority contributed £5 per child for a year or two but eventually withdrew this contribution. Despite the ending of the subsidy, the courses continued to be popular. "The courses became so popular and the children so enthusiastic that parents were persuaded after two years to contribute as much as £45 per child to cover travel, accommodation, food, ski tuition and medical expenses if they occurred," said Erna.

The winter of 1965/66 was the first time that another innovation occurred – using coaches rather than trains and planes to ferry schoolchildren to the mountains, something that is now almost universal. The change of transport mode meant that the company could offer seven nights in the Austrian resort of St Johann for £24 3s rather than £27 3s by train.

A *Times Educational Supplement* article at the time[81] explained what the pupils would expect on such a trip. "The organization… was like a well-oiled clock. The children and their teachers (roughly one to fifteen) had been wafted from Wales in special trains and by cross-Channel ferry. Couriers and 'reps' bobbed up here, there and everywhere to smooth the way and warm the welcome."

One of these special trains was "a private Underground train which conveyed the party from Paddington to Victoria and was much enjoyed by all"[82].

Christopher Lloyd Pack was one of those who helped out on those school trips. "I was once a courier for a group of 500 schoolchildren who arrived in London and had to be ferried across. The Tube network was halted so that her train of children could pass through to get to Victoria and from there I couriered them out to Austria."

Once there, the schoolchildren took to skiing with aplomb. "The more advanced [pupils] were doing fearsome things with an élan which suggested an un-Celtic acquaintance with the art of manoeuvring safely on slippery slopes. The beginners were being taken through their preliminary paces with patience and good humour. All were having the time of their young lives," reported the *TES*.

Glamorgan education chief Barry Edwards said he was "convinced of the value to the children of the ski course" and elaborated on "the importance of acquiring a new skill, of making friends in strange places and breaking out of insular moulds". Another teacher, a Mrs Walters of Bangoed Girls' School, added that "nothing but benefit had accrued to those who had taken part".

The arrival of so many guests was also welcomed by the resorts. The Glamorgan Education Authority acquired a good reputation in Austria and continued to go to Ischgl and Fieberbrunn "although many other Alpine resorts tried to entice them away and change their centre".

Other education authorities soon became interested in the scheme.

"An Inner London Education Authority teacher from London, Mrs Olwen

Calland, became interested in organising ski training courses but insisted that they should not be completely divorced from academic work. She arranged ski training courses for several years but two hours per day had to be devoted to German language classes," said Erna.

As well as organising the ski holiday, Erna also helped with the gear. In the September 1966 edition of *School and College* magazine, Marion Harris wrote[83], "[Erna] can also offer advantageous mail order arrangements for ski clothing—a complete outfit consisting of ski trousers, anorak, mitts, goggles and two pairs of oiled socks can be obtained from around £12."

By the mid Seventies, Erna was handling courses for schools in Glamorgan, Cheshire, Surrey and London and was offering skiing in nine different centres across Austria, particularly smaller resorts such as Oberperfuss, Krimml and Grossarl. By 1974, a place for a schoolchild on one of these trips was around £50, plus a few pounds for a lift pass and an extra 50p if the teachers wanted to have a Tyrolean evening during their stay.

Some children made their own entertainment. Former employee Jane Stevens remembers one school trip in which one of the children was found to be "under the influence of hash (how tame these days)". "We had to get the parents to meet the child at the airport as he was in no condition to travel and I think the father was a gentleman of the cloth too," she says.

One of the biggest attractions for teachers, particularly those who liked skiing, was the offer of a free place for them for every fifteen children.

***

One school trip that Erna organised was for a group of about twenty girls from Benenden School to Davos in Switzerland in early 1966; one of the schoolgirls was the fifteen-year-old Princess Anne.

The cost of the trip, including couchettes, accommodation, ski school, ski and boot hire and insurance, is under £50. "But the girls are advised to take about £14 pocket money," wrote the *Daily Telegraph*[84].

John Samuel shares an incident that arose during the trip in his 1988 book *Bedside Skiing*[85].

To all good veterans of the slopes, a day comes when it is time to stop. Skiing, that is. Erna Low's own last day is firmly etched in her mind. The circumstances, mind you, were not exactly ordinary. She had been informed, in the special circumlocation of those times, that the girl with the famous mother would be in the Benenden School party.

She was in no doubt who they meant. The problem was that, as with the rest of the party, Princess Anne would have to share a room with three others. A further problem was that the allotted room had three good beds and one camp bed. Next. . . goodness! The daughter of the famous mother was going to arrive late. All three decent beds would be snaffled by the three who got there first.

By the time the advance detective arrived to scout things out, everything had been arranged. Somehow a fourth decent bed had been crammed in. The three other girls dutifully turned their faces to the wall when appropriate. Good behaviour was maintained for the duration – but they were anxious moments for those in charge.

Erna, still a touch distracted, hung herself around with her usual camera gear and set off for the slopes. She knew the press were not supposed to be around. She also knew that no pictures were allowed in the papers. But some photographic record was permissible, she felt. The equipment was heavy, and made skiing difficult. Suddenly she caught an edge and slipped into a river.

'I thought I was going to drown. "Hilfe! Hilfe!" Erna shouted. Some Germans were passing and they came over to help but as one tried to pull me out, he fell in too. It was a terrible mess, and terribly dangerous. Luckily the others managed to get both of us out. But that was it. No more skiing.'

The young Princess Anne found love on the trip, according to a German magazine report from the time. It reported: "A gold brooch in the form of an edelweiss has revealed that Princess Anne of England, sixteen, is in love. The brooch is a gift of eighteen-year old student Michael Cox from Shrewsbury. He met Anne in the last winter while skiing in Davos. Since then, they have been writing to teach other. Michael has also been invited several times to visit Anne at Windsor Castle. 'All I can say is that I love Anne very much and that the Royal Family has been very kind to me,' says Michael."

***

The story of the Sterling devaluation crisis of the 1960s, to which Erna had some innovative ideas on how to get around its consequences, began in, of all places, a ski resort.

Yet the visitors who came to Bretton Woods in New Hampshire in the US in 1944 were not there for the skiing.

That year, delegates from forty-four nations convened at the resort's Mount Washington hotel for the Bretton Woods International Conference, whose goal was to try to bring order to the flow of currency around the world because of the economic instability of the inter-war years.

At the conference, the International Bank for Reconstruction and Development (now the World Bank) and International Monetary Fund were founded, a so-called "gold standard" of $35.00 an ounce established and the United States dollar designated as the backbone of international exchange. The plan, intended to free up international trade and stabilise exchange rates, was largely drawn up by the British economist John Maynard Keynes.

On 20 July 1966, the Government was forced to introduce a range of harsh economic measures. The crisis was unleashed because of Britain's ballooning balance of payments: exports were increasingly falling behind imports because of labour shortages.

The amount tourists (although this included business travellers) were spending abroad had risen from £38 million in 1961 to an estimated £95 million in 1966[86]. As a result, the Prime Minister announced a measure to start on 1 November 1966 that would introduce a basic allowance of £50 per person for a foreign holiday. Holidaymakers were also permitted to take £15 in cash with the amount taken written into the traveller's passport.

"This allowance will have to cover all the foreign exchange requirements of the traveller, whether paid for in sterling or a foreign currency, except for fares paid for in sterling," said Wilson.

The Bank of England asked travel companies "not to put too much stress on the fact that the £15 sterling notes can also be spent abroad".

As well as introducing restrictions on what travellers could spend, the government increased the deposits that people had to pay if they wanted to buy things like domestic appliances, furniture and cars on hire purchase. Duty on cigarettes, wine, beer and spirits was hiked by 10%.

However, the Government's 1966 measures proved not to be enough. The balance of payments continued to worsen and a series of events conspired to increase the pressure on sterling to breaking point.

The Six Day War of 1967 between Israel, Egypt, Syria and Jordan led to the closure of the Suez Canal for eight years, meaning that trade routes through the

Mediterranean to Britain were disrupted. This was exacerbated by weeks of dock strikes during 1966 and 1967, which led to up to a third of exports being blocked[87].

The pressure was relieved late in the evening on Saturday 18th November when the Government did what many believed was inevitable after three years of currency crisis and devalued the pound by more than 14%, cutting its exchange rate from $2.80 to $2.40.

The next day, Wilson made one of his most famous speeches in which he said, "From now on, the pound abroad is worth 14% or so less in terms of other currencies. That doesn't mean, of course, that the pound here in Britain, in your pocket or purse or in your bank, has been devalued." Most people remember this as "the pound in your pocket" speech.

The 1967/68 Erna Low brochure included a panel showing how this affected holiday prices – there were supplements of 10% to Ski-Air and Special Flight Arrangements and 12.5 % on scheduled air and train arrangements.

The combination of the travel allowance and the devaluation of sterling was catastrophic for many companies involved in travel. Somewhat ironically, 1967 was the United Nations' International Tourist Year.

The new rules meant that many travel companies had to drastically rethink their programmes. Lunn Poly, for example, had a £635 a head round-the-world air cruise in its brochure. As a result of the restriction, the company had to throw £3,000 worth of brochures into the bin[88].

The devaluation led to the re-introduction of the so-called V Form, which Erna had used in the post-war years.

For package tours, the operator would enter the cost of the elements of the holiday paid in foreign currency for the hotel and other services abroad onto the V Form. A holiday might be advertised as costing £90 but might have a V Form amount of, say, £41 for the hotel and other services overseas. This would keep it within the £50 restriction.

Colin Trigger, former Erna Low employee and president of the Association of British Travel Agents, says, "We had to deal with the famous V Forms of course [never really taken seriously and never checked to my knowledge]; the deductions did not seem to affect the number of clients or their destinations."

Erna's 1967/68 ski brochure was called "Ski-ing within the £50 allowance" and the introduction, penned by Erna of course, promised "All out arrangements will leave you ample Spending Money, approximately £1.10.-£3 per day after deductions for hotels and local expenses… There may even be a silver lining to the clouds which temporarily darkened the winter sky, and you may meet the challenge by trying one of the new centres off the beaten track. You will be amazed to see how you can stretch your allowance if you steer clear of the fashionable resorts."

The brochure includes a table at the front showing how to work out the V Form amount. Quite how prospective holidaymakers worked out exactly what they had to pay is anyone's guess.

The currency restrictions were particularly challenging for skiers because of the higher basic cost of the holiday than a summer holiday. Ski writer Peter Hardy says, "I can still remember my mother getting out all the pfennigs, counting up how much we could afford to spend the next day."

The Hardy family was one of those that Erna disapproved of in her letter to *The Times* on bargain-hunting too.

"Most two to three star hotels had a bath at the end of the corridor and the key to the bathroom was kept at reception. A bath cost öS20. You booked a bathroom slot but then went in one after the other to reuse the bath, although there was sometimes a woman at the end of the corridor dressed in white who would try to stop you. I can remember now getting into the scabby water."

However, Erna was very innovative in the application of the limit on foreign holiday spending.

Erna's trick was to pay for as much as possible in advance in sterling, giving holidaymakers the highest amount of spending money once they were there, says Hardy.

"Erna's great success is that she understood all the red tape – we'll do everything here. It was the definition of the package holiday," he says.

One of the ski holidays she introduced that year was to Sallent in the Valle del Sol in the Spanish Pyrenees. An article in the *Nursing Mirror* at the time said: "As Spain has devalued to the same extent as Britain, your pound will be really worth a pound in a country where drinks, coffees and night life are already astoundingly cheap".

Erna was asked to write about the devaluation[89]. In her article, she writes, "There is no denying that the devaluation came as a bombshell to skiers who had booked their holidays, and to others who were on the verge of doing so… Now that one has come to terms with the situation, things do not look as bad as they seemed at first. Spain and Austria are, of course, the obvious choices this year, but other countries have shown willingness to reduce prices in order to make a skiing holiday possible for British skiers."

There were clearly many holidaymakers who were not open about how much they were spending while abroad.

John Samuel wrote in *The Guardian*[90], "Under one of Ingham's arrangements, for instance, a fortnight at the Sporthotel, Pontresina, one of the superior Swiss resorts, costs a total of £70 15s and the hotel, or V Form part, will be £39. These are low season (January) rates and about as much as the honest Briton will be able to afford. With the addition of ski lift and other essential expenses, this will leave about £1 a day spending money, and anyone who has paid 6s for a coffee or 4s for a beer in one of the smarter Swiss bars will know just how far this will go."

The same article talks about chalet parties organised by Colin Murison-Small and Erna Low and a group spending "a fortnight in Verbier at £62 a head, V-Form content rather hazy, but probably around £30". He writes, "[The group has] been smart enough to include a Republican Irishman in their party. His reserves of sterling will cover any emergencies."

There were no restrictions on travel to the so-called Sterling Area, which included Britain as well as Malta, Gibraltar, Cyprus and – somewhat bizarrely – Iceland. The first chapter in Erna's summer brochure in 1968 was devoted to holidays in this region, including an Archaeological tour of Malta, visiting Valletta St Paul's Bay and the Blue Grotto.

In November 1968, the travel cash restrictions were eased for the over seventies as well as children under eighteen travelling in school and youth organisation parties, meaning they could take an extra £25 on top of the £50 foreign travel allowance. An article from the time said, "Further allowances of different amounts will also be considered for students, teachers, cripples and businessmen in appropriate cases."[91]. The foreign currency restrictions were eased over the next few years but they remained in place until the election of a certain shopkeeper's daughter hailing from Grantham as prime minister in 1979.

As someone who gave other people so much good advice where to go on holiday, it was inevitable that people would ask her for her favourite places to go on holiday. In an article in *The Times*[92], she tried to answer – despite never really going on holiday as such.

"The answer is difficult when one has discovered so many wonderful places over the years and knows also that many of them have become completely spoilt over the past decade… I usually suggest a compromise and first mention my old favourite Corsica and then follow it up with an exciting new discovery – Porto Novo in Portugal.

"My favourite three places [on Corsica] are Porto Pollo on the Golfe de Valinco, Porto at the head of the Golfe de Porto and St Florent, a picturesque little town easily reached from Bastia... All three places have wonderful sandy beaches and some of the hotels are built directly on the beach – children love it... The hotels are small and family-run."

Summer tourism played an increasing role in the company during the Sixties and there are a succession of colourful brochures featuring destinations such as Yugoslavia, the Italian lakes, Majorca and more.

Erna was already trying to adapt to the new world of mass tourism. In 1964, she visited the Costa del Sol with her sales chief Uli "Pack Lloyd" (sic)[93] and was impressed by the then new Caribe hotel in Almuñecar. She told the paper, "My goodness how the place has changed. It's true it's quite a number of years since I was last here but even so I should scarcely have recognised it. Very nice of course, but personally I follow my company's preference for the smaller off-beat places."

She still managed to find new and unusual places. In 1968, she introduced the island of Mljet in Yugoslavia. "Here on a lake reached by lonely wooded paths is an island-within-an-island where a 12th-centruy Benedictine monastery has been turned into a hotel of simple charm," wrote Sebastian Cash in *Ideal Home* magazine[94].

***

Turkey would soon be added to the programme thanks to Sylvia Antunovich, who worked for Erna in the 1960s and eventually became a local councillor in Brighton.

In the 1990s, Sylvia offered to write a chapter for Erna's would-be autobiography and in it she describes how she met Erna on the 24-hour journey to Sölden by train from Victoria.

She spotted a "smiling jolly woman … in the corridor of often, talking to the travellers" and engaged her in conversation. It turned out to be Erna and they were soon discussing their love of travel and were sharing dinner. "By the time the train reached Austria Erna had offered me a job."

Antunovich went on to work as an Erna Low rep in Ischgl. She recalled "In those days, Ischgl was a small friendly unsophisticated resort, centred around the traditional Hotel Sonne and the Hotel Post. The ski slopes were so close that one could sit in a window seat indulging in mouth-watering Sachertorte and watch the skiers tumble and soar only metres away. Down the road was Magnus' ski shop and up a winding side path Serafin and Rosa's Konditorei the best for miles around."

Sylvia recalled that one winter a client arrived in Ischgl by car to meet up with his friends. "He was most embarrassed to discover there were two very different resorts with similar names – Ischgl and Ischl, easily confused in those less famous days – and he was in the wrong one."

"Sometimes there was a trip over the mountain border into duty-free Samnaun in Switzerland where the ski instructors would fill their rucksacks with cigarettes and brandy. On the return journey, they would hide their contraband under rocks above the Idalp to return later when the little ski lift had stopped and visiting skiers were already on their way down to the valley and the sole customs official had moved on."

These days, the trip over to Samnaun from Ischgl to return with a rucksack laden with duty-free whisky and cigarettes is positively encouraged.

In the late 1960s, Erna sent Sylvia off to Turkey to see whether it would make a good addition to the programme at a time when few tourists visited. Sylvia found a country where no-one spoke English and everything was incredibly exotic. She spent her time touring pensions and houses, taking copious notes and photographs, and ending up spending three weeks rather than one week there. Erna would have been proud of her diligence.

***

Villars in Switzerland was another resort featuring in the Erna Low ski programme at this time. A rep in the resort from the time was Jane Stevens.

"When I started as a rep I was paid the enormous salary of £5 a week. My lodging at the Pension Gentiana was free, as were the ski lifts. My car expenses were very minimal – I covered Verbier some seasons, and eventually had the whole of the Swiss Romande, from St Cergue to Saas Fee."

The rep "uniform" consisted of a red arm band with the words Erna Low Travel Service on it. "I think we even went so far as having jackets with a badge some place. Now reps are equipped from top to toe with magnificently styled garments – how times have changed."

The Villars' guests were accommodated at Aiglon College, which had an early curfew.

"I remember one New Year's Eve when the guests had to be in by 12.30 – we thought we were generous – and I spent most of the night tramping in the snow and rain to make sure the dears were all right. They were all indoors as instructed but they climbed out of the windows as soon as we had turned our backs."

Fondue and raclette nights were always a popular fixture during a week in Villars.

"One time we had a party at the restaurant at the Col du Soud," says Stevens. "They were a very sporting group and thought the Swiss white wine was very poor and low in alcohol and drank it quite freely. When it came to putting on skis to ski back to Villars with lighted torches, one guy put his skis on back to front and one of the instructors ended up walking down with him."

The Swiss resort was also the centre of an outbreak of scarlet fever one winter while the company had guests staying.

Sue Himmelweit, the niece of Erna's long-term friend Ernst Litthauer, says: "There was an epidemic during a ski trip and we all piled down to help people. Erna was very concerned that everybody was alright and we were all roped into help in some way or other. It felt a bit like she was sending friends or family away rather than paying guests and she was very concerned and rushed to get her people back. She went beyond the call of duty."

***

In the late 1960s, Reece Mews was an eclectic place. An Austro-Hungarian émigré was at number 9 selling holidays. At number 7, the artist Francis Bacon had his studio. Next door, at number 6, was the composer Lionel Bart, most famous for his musical *Oliver*. As a result, famous friends of Bart and Bacon – although the two did not see eye to eye and were always having an argument about something – were often to be seen swanning up and down the Mews.

Another neighbour was car dealer John Spero, who got called upon by his neighbours to fix cars but also anything of a practical nature.

"Those kind of people didn't know about ordinary things like changing light bulbs. Clever people like that just don't bother. Erna would say the lights have gone out and what would I do about it. She wouldn't want to get an electrician in. Another time, a box would arrive for Francis Bacon and he would ask 'How do you open it?'"

"There was always something wrong with Erna's car and I would have to try to fix it. One time, I got in the car but didn't realise the dog was on the back seat. He was a nasty dog and just started growling. 'Come and get the dog out, Erna' I yelled. She replied in her sweetest Austrian accent, "Oh but he'll never hurt you.""

He remembers Erna as a terrible driver. "She would park right in the middle of the mews so no-one could get past and you would spend half the day getting the keys off her."

Spero, who still lives in the Mews, got to know Erna well over time. "I liked Erna," he says, "but she would tell you what she thought about you."

***

By the end of the 1960s, unprecedented numbers of people were going skiing.

In 1967, the *Financial Times* reported: "At present, about 250,000 people take winter sports holidays and the number does not change much from year to year. However, efforts by the agencies to widen the appeal of skiing holidays have helped to dispel the sport's rather classy image."[95]

The democratisation of skiing was helped by the arrival of some very large tour operators into the skiing market, which offered ski holidays at historically cheap prices. However, their arrival into the market had a serious implication for Erna Low Travel Service.

Roger Bray, in *Flight to the Sun*, says: "The arrival of the mass tour operators [particularly Clarksons] forced a major upheaval in the way operators such as Erna Low did business. Previously she had never needed to make down payments to hoteliers. Now it became the only way to secure beds."

In 1969, the *Financial Times* reported, "The dreaded Clarksons… is now taking its own winter holiday business very seriously… within the next week it will produce a winter sports programme aimed at carrying 15,000 people. It is a highly profitable business. Last season, Clarksons had a 96 per cent occupancy rate with 9,000 people; the year before, 99.6 per cent with 3,246."[96]

The same article shows how skiing had grown through the Sixties. It reported that in 1963/64 Lunn Poly "carried 6,200 winter sportsters at a time when skiing was strictly for the enthusiasts. By 1968-69 this had reached 13,600; this year it was 16,000." Ingham's believed it would carry between 22,000 and 25,000 in winter 1970.

"The reasons for the upsurge in winter sports are many," said the *FT*. "More money, more time, and more inclination on behalf of the customers; more economic pressure on the operators. There has also been a noticeable swing away from the ski to the *après-ski*. Brochures tend to have a strong sexual undertone about them which is successfully attracting the free-living, free-spending young."

Former employee Colin Trigger says, "She had a niche market and this only started to suffer when air charters became more usual than the special trains at that time; however most tour operators lacked her experience, contacts and reputation for value for money holidays, summer and winter. She was, in her way, a sort of legend; feared but respected."

Erna still felt there was a market for her brand of holiday. Speaking to the *Financial Times* in 1969[97], she said, "Obviously we must keep our prices as competitive as possible. But I have found that our customers are prepared to pay a few pounds more because they know they are likely to find congenial company on our holidays, because our hotels are carefully chosen for their local flavour, or because we cater to suit all tastes."

Yet the writing was on the wall. Roger Bray says, "She covered that crossover from the age of exclusive and upper middle class to the working class tourist. Skiing went through an enormous metamorphosis. The only people who went skiing in the 1950s spoke the Queen's English. Then suddenly, you got people going to Söll from Camberwell and Sauze d'Oulx began to develop its reputation [for après-ski]. She must have felt that coming. Although she may have played an important part in the early development of ski holidays, Erna Low was tiny in comparison to these new companies. I have no doubt she would have felt overwhelmed."

Chapter 11

Erna's love affair with the French that would culminate in her promoting a number of French resorts in the 1980s probably began thanks to one man – Robert "Bob" Hollier, the UK director of the French Government Tourist Office (FGTO) in the late 1960s.

Bob was married and a father of five and held a Master of Art Degree from the Sorbonne and a doctorate of Philosophy (Linguistics) from Montreal University. He was a Free French officer with the British Eighth Army in Libya and the US Forces in Normandy in the war and gained him the rank of Officer of the Legion d'Honneur.

Bob Hollier and Erna at his farm Sahune

Erna met Bob at a FGTO workshop on the Côte d'Azur in 1967. In a travelogue she wrote entitled *Travels with Bob, How to Live Dangerously and Enjoy Yourself*, she said he was "attractive, knowledgeable and entertaining". Bob acted as chauffeur to a small group of travel's great and good, including Horizon's Vladimir Raitz, around Renoir's villa, Madame Rothschild's museum near Beaulieu and some fancy restaurants.

Former FGTO Marketing Director Dennis Fabri remembers that "Erna was very fond of Bob".

"Bob didn't see her a bothersome old biddy. He saw her as a clever woman who had made a success of her business. He too was loyal to old friends and she appreciated that. Erna saw me as a sort of son but she saw Bob Hollier in a different way. She was girlish in front of him."

Erna visited Bob many times at his French country hideout, Sahune, in the south of France and they became firm friends, meeting regularly in Paris after he left Britain for a job as executive director of the European Travel Commission.

She said Hollier and his team, which Fabri, ran an "enormously successful PR campaign for France" at the time. "They taught us all *joie de vivre* and turned us into gourmets with a great love for France and all things French."

Fabri worked for the French Tourist Office in the UK for many years, becoming its marketing director, and first met Erna on a trip to Corsica in 1969.

"We invited some of the top names to Corsica and Erna Low was among them," says Dennis. "I was with Erna Low and I said I was the chauffeur. Erna quickly realised that the chauffeur knew a lot more than he should."

The group was staying in a series of gîtes at the Hameaux de Pietragione near Porto Vecchio, with each person staying in their own. Erna went out and left the light on.

"Before dinner, I heard a scream and it was Erna," recalls Fabri. "I ran to her gîte and there she was, standing up on a chair, with loads of little frogs leaping all over the place."

Erna wrote later, "I had underestimated the animal life in Corsica – frogs, snails and grasshoppers had come out from nooks and crannies. The French Government Tourist Office – in the shape of Dennis Fabri – came to our rescue. He was the hero of the day [and] evicted invader after invader by hand."

Fabri says the excitement didn't stop there. "The next day we stopped to see the Hotel Asia. To my mind, I thought it looked more than just a hotel. There were loads of French Legionnaires, who had a garrison nearby, and loads of

Vietnamese girls with split shirts. I said, 'Erna, I don't think it's the sort of place we should stop'. She kept insisting that she wanted to stop and take a look around. It took a long time to convince her that this was really a sort of glorified brothel".

Erna never touched a drop of drink on any of these travel workshops, remembers Fabri. "In travel in those days, that was a plus. You wonder how some companies were run. There was the head of one large travel company and if you wanted to ask him anything, you had to do it before eleven o'clock."

"Erna never took risks, even if she was urged to do so. She was very much the sort of person who travelled to do the contracting herself. Her personality gave her so much leeway. She was known all over France, Austria and, to a lesser extent, in Italy. Erna opened so many doors and invariably got very good prices. The proof of the pudding is that the company still survives."

***

Erna was an early proponent of French skiing. It is hard to imagine now that France was not always the dominant destination for British skiers, a country which now accounts for around a third of all ski visits from the UK.

Back in the 1970s, Austria was by far the most popular destination and the presence of French resorts in Erna's ski brochure was seen as distinctly odd.

A *Guardian* article[98] in September 1971 said: "France is expensive and, in competition with Austria and even Switzerland, has failed to capture a sizeable share of the British market and is still largely neglected by the tour operators, with the notable exception of Erna Low, who optimistically features no fewer than eighteen French resorts in her brochure".

One of these resorts was Flaine, now a very popular ski destination for British families, but then only newly opened. Flaine is a classic example of the French purpose-built resorts of the era and has famously 'brutal' architecture that you either love or hate.

Writing about the resort in *The Lady*[99], Jean Ryder called it "one of the most exciting modern ski stations to appear recently. Created by three talented men with vision, Flaine is thoughtfully designed, allowance being made for the terrain, weather conditions, and the ever-present hazards of pollution."

Erna discovered the resort in 1969, on a private trip to the resort organised by Bob Hollier. Erna related later that the four people on the trip were not on speaking terms with each other. "[Flaine architect] François Gassan sorts out the

Flaine in 1968. Erna would introduce many British skiers to the new purpose-built French ski resorts, credit: Flaine – Centre Culturel

affair in the tradition of French diplomacy and introduces me to Flaine, thus paving the way for our French ski programme, the first to feature the new purpose-built French ski stations". In 1970, there were just two tour operators offering French resorts – this number had ballooned to twelve, four years later.

***

In September 1970, the actor Roger Lloyd Pack, to whom Erna had become something of a surrogate aunt, honoured Erna by asking her to be godmother to his daughter Emily.

Erna's scrapbooks are filled with pictures of Emily as a child but also with cuttings from magazines and newspapers that proliferated when she was chosen to play the role of the young brothel madam Cynthia Payne in the 1987 David Leland film *Wish You Were Here*.

Roger says, "Erna was very fond of Emily and she certainly financially sorted her out, as I didn't have a bean, nor did my wife Sheila. She supported her generously as she always did with children and friends."

Emily was chosen to hand Princess Diana a bouquet at the Cannes Film Festival in 1987. Erna said, "She was not at all embarrassed and invited the royal couple to come and see the film in which she featured."

In 1995, Erna wrote, "[Today] she is still as charming and uninhibited as in 1987 when she was at the centre of a great deal of publicity."

The request to become Emily's godmother came at a time when Erna was very down – her beloved black poodle Nick had died at the grand old age of seventeen.

"We all were very sad and there was only one solution and that was to buy another dog. I finally did but it took me a long time to recover from Nick's death," said Erna.

The new dog was another poodle – Charlie, Nick's grandson. Charlie was adored by Erna and her staff but Nick remained her favourite: she kept a photo of Nick in her sitting room for the rest of her life. "None of my dogs was so close to my heart as Nick had been," she said later.

Erna's god-daughter, the actress Emily Lloyd

This era also gave rise to one of the most often repeated anecdotes about Erna.

At the instigation of her friend Bob Hollier, Erna attended the 1971 Conference of the Association of British Travel Agents in Cannes.

Among the other delegates was holiday park pioneer Billy Butlin and he invited Erna to join him on his yacht for a cocktail party. One of the other guests was Harry Goodman, the founder of International Leisure Group, which went on to become Britain's second largest tour operator. The group's Intasun and Air Europe divisions became enormous in time but it all went badly wrong in 1991 when the first Gulf War led to the group's collapse.

During the yacht party, Harry approached Erna and said, "Ah Miss Low! I once applied for a job with you and you rejected me. Erna looked him up and down and said, 'I would still reject you'."

Another example of the dry humour for which she was well known by those who knew her and was unexpected for those that did not.

***

The 1970s was the boom era for package tourism and Erna did not like what she saw, whether that was in predicting the effect it would have on her own business or the end of the personalised approach that she championed.

In an article in *The Observer* on 15 August 1971, she said "The future of tourism fills [me] with horror".

The journalist writes "[Erna] had just returned from Corsica. She had been looking for unspoilt places to recommend to her clients, the former being harder to find than the latter. She said *something* must be done soon to control tourism. She would like to see an international body for it equivalent to the World Health Organisation."

The comments were made at a time when the company, founded on Erna's strength of character, her exquisite networking skills and a business model that relied on tailor making nearly every single holiday, was starting to look a little shaky.

Despite the boom in skiing and other tourism, the end of the 1960s had been a tough time for the business. Turnover had risen from £733,893 in 1967-68 to £912,467 in 1969-70 but pre-tax profits had slid from £21,485 to just £8,006 over the same period[2].

An interview with Erna in the *Sunday Telegraph* [100], said that the company was turning over £1 million a year built up "with her own money – no loans from anywhere, ever – with her own energy and, above all, her own enthusiasm". It reports that her profit margins "are a little above the 4% or so the average operator expects".

The article also helpfully added that Erna was a lapsed follower of Weight Watchers – all those chocolates and cakes at *Konditorei* in Austrian resorts over the years had clearly taken their toll.

Even for a workhorse like Erna, the workload was becoming hard to manage. "There was pressure from all sides to try and offload at least some of it," said Erna.

In 1969, Erna sought the advice about how she might exit the business from industrialist Professor Peter Jost– whom she referred to in her autobiographical notes as "a tycoon friend of mine [with a] CBE".

He wrote to her saying, "I for one would not suggest that selling at this juncture was the perfect solution to the problem".

He suggested that another course of action might be to transform the business from an owner-entrepreneurial one into an organisation.

"This means that you will have higher overheads and – unless the re-organisation is excellent – lower profits. The business will, however, carry on, and the pressure on you will ease."

"Since the impetus which is derived from your presence seems to be one of the most important factors of your business, you may build up a larger empire, which – when sold one day – will give you in this way quantitatively the financial independence that makes a sale worthwhile."

He said that the latter route "would appear the most attractive" but concluded the latter by saying, "However, I have really insufficient evidence on which to advise an exceedingly successful businesswoman. There, please regard the above as being personal thoughts only, and not an attempt to be impertinent or interfering."

***

In October of 1969, Erna received an approach from Vladimir Raitz of Horizon Holidays. He wrote with a slightly jocular turn of phrase but was in earnest. "We are now between seasons when, traditionally a middle-aged man's thoughts turn to subjects of purchasing other tour operators. So how about it?"

In a later letter, he emphasised that if he did buy the company, it would continue under the name Erna Low, that all of the existing activities, including the British division, would continue to operate and that Horizon would like to buy all of Erna's shares.

She did not follow it up and instead, another exit from the business presented itself.

Erna said later, "I had a telephone call from a certain young man whom I had briefly met at a travel function. He said that he would like to come and see me as he had a proposition to make which he thought might interest me."

Thirty-six-year-old Simon Green had a background as a management consultant, working for both Orr and Boss Partners and Arthur D Little Ltd, but he also had a sideline in skiing. In his spare time, Green and his wife Sarah developed Skicentre, "an organisation running private ski parties to the Alps".

Green's idea was to acquire the Erna Low business, keeping her on as a consultant but investing in the business.

She said, "To start with I was not at all keen on the idea but when I had repeated calls from him I gradually relented and arranged an appointment. He came together with the uncle of his future wife who was a well known gentleman."

The "well known gentleman" was Niall Macdiarmid. Macdiarmid, fifty-two at the time, had served with the Argyll and Sutherland Highlanders in the Second World War and had been chairman of Corby-based steel giant Stewarts and Lloyds, one of the companies that became part of the British Steel Corporation upon the industry's nationalisation. Macdiarmid – who opposed nationalisation – had ruffled feathers in the Labour Party at the time with a newspaper article that said he believed Stewarts and Lloyds would "rise again from the ashes", just like the phoenix of the company's logo.

As well as his steel interests, Macdiarmid had been involved with the Duke of Edinburgh's Award since its launch as well as youth charity, the Brathay Hall Trust. This is likely to have impressed Erna.

The proposed deal would be financed by the Coronado Investment Corporation and its subsidiary the Development Banking Corporation of America through a vehicle specially developed for the acquisition called Travellers Guaranty (Holdings). Robert Clark, senior vice president and director of Coronado, was a graduate of Princeton and had previously worked for management consultants Booz Allen Hamilton and investment bankers N M Rothschild and Sons.

Erna wrote later, "[The trio] proposed to take over my firm and offered me £70,000 to start with. They promised me the blue from the sky. I was by no means enthusiastic and told them that I wanted a period in which I could consider their offer and discuss it with my solicitor. They kept on bombarding me with telephone

The Travellers Guaranty trio:
(from left) Niall Macdiarmid, Simon Green and Robert Clark,
photo: Goodchild Photography

calls, increased their offer to £98,000 and offered me a position as joint managing director [shared with Simon Green]."

Erna canvassed various friends in industry and the travel business on the proposal. "They all thought that the offer was a good one and persuaded me to think carefully before refusing it. So I dithered and dithered but finally decided to refuse the offer," she recalled. "More telephone calls followed, more money was offered and finally I gave in and accepted their offer. Bobbie Shafto and Uli Lloyd Pack were not at all pleased with the idea of a takeover but kept silent as they thought that it might be in my interest."

The deal was done for £85,000, a shade under a million pounds in today's money. Erna's Enjoy Britain company, which was formed in 1970 and organised house party holidays in the UK, was not part of the deal.

The new owners had big plans for restructuring the business to take account of the changing ways that people booked holidays. According to the press[101] at the time, the company was selling 92% of its holidays direct to customers. The new owners "would be very unhappy if we sell 50% ourselves in between three and five years' time," according to Simon Green. They were also keen to implement new reservations systems and "in the development of educational and young people's travel which at present accounts for about one-quarter of Erna Low's business"[102].

In what seemed like a dig at Erna's management skills, Macdiarmid told the FT at the time[103], "The travel industry has suffered from management problems. Its difficulties are largely the result of rapid growth, with small companies outgrowing their management capacity."

Erna wanted to know who she was selling her company to and turned to graphology, the analysis of handwriting in order to gain an insight into personality, to do so.

She engaged handwriting analyst Brian Kennett, a pupil and associate of Dr Eric Singer who popularised graphology in Britain after the Second World War, to study Simon Green's handwriting.

Kennett produced a page of analysis of Green's handwriting, finding that "his mind functions at a tempo that is too fast for his physical actions to match" but with a "quick grasp of the essentials". He added "his unwillingness to compromise may cause him difficulty in negotiating with some people, especially those who are at all sensitive".

Summing up Green's character, Kennett said "If relieved of supervision and control he may well be liable to bite off more than he can chew".

Historian Christopher Black says, "She was interested in handwriting. I remember writing to her from Nigeria but my family had been complaining about my handwriting so I tried to alter it. I got a letter back from her immediately saying 'What the hell have you been doing?'"

Friends and others in the travel industry were quick to congratulate Erna on the sale and her impending retirement.

A letter from Walter [Leonard] at Travis Travel said, "You most certainly deserve a rich reward for all your many wonderful ideas and for the unbelievably hard work you have devoted to your firm… The repercussions of this will no doubt shake the travel world and the general public for many, many years – things will never be the same again in many ways. In lots of ways, they have completely changed already in the last few years, but one of the last remaining bastions of personal service and individualism will disappear when you eventually leave the travel world."

The Rev William Baddeley, rector of St James's in Piccadilly and known as the

Racing Dean from his time in Brisbane, Australia, wrote to say "I hope that this move will relieve you of the burden of responsibility and give you more leisure to enjoy things for yourself" calling the company "a remarkable concern".

Another person contacted her after the sale too. A literary agent wrote to say that "I see from *The Times* that you may be slightly less busy in the future … My purpose in writing is to enquire whether you have ever considered writing your autobiography and, if you have whether I could be of any assistance to you as a literary agent".

It was an offer, as we know, that she did not take up.

***

The company now faced another challenge on top of the devaluation a few years earlier – Value Added Tax.

Some suspected an April Fool Joke when, on 1 April 1973, Labour Chancellor Anthony Barber introduced VAT at a rate of 10% on most goods and services, including holidays. VAT replaced the previous purchase tax, introduced as a "temporary" wartime measure in 1940, which was levied at different rates according to how much of a luxury they were considered.

Erna was also concerned that the floating pound would dampen enthusiasm for winter sports holidays[104]. Speaking to the *Evening Standard*, she said that the annual 10 to 15% increase in the number of skiers could disappear. "I think [the number of skiers] will remain static. I will be surprised if there is an increase. The question is – will the new skiers come in?...Rising prices on the Continent, especially in Austria and Switzerland coupled with the downward floating of the pound, has made winter sports packages fairly expensive when you consider all the extras involved."

Despite the challenges, Erna did her best to generate interest in winter sports. Her film shows were a regular advert for skiing at the time, which included "hearty advice about preparatory exercises and insurance in case of broken limbs... colourful slides and films of snowscapes, and of bronzed beautiful people enjoying technicolour evening *après*"[105].

***

Yet all was not well with the new owners. By the end of 1972, the signs were becoming apparent that there were disagreements between Erna and Simon Green.

An Erna Low brochure from the 1970s

A press release listing "the personalities who make your Erna Low Travel Service Holiday a success" from the time has Erna's comments scribbled on it throughout. One unfortunate member of staff who supposedly "possesses that expertise in finding the right resort for you" is punctuated by six large exclamation marks, added by Erna in exasperation. The release is headed by a cutting comment from Erna: "We laughed and we laughed and we laughed."

An article from *Travel News*[106] in one of Erna's many yellowing scrapbooks traces the money used to finance the deal from Atlanta in Georgia via Bermuda and called the deal "a good example of a financial minnow swallowing a fish many times larger than itself". Erna herself has written on the clipping "What next? The mafia".

An interview with the business press with Erna[107] at the time said she was "worried about the level of service being offered and the way in which holiday deposit money was being used".

The new brooms also changed the way the company chartered aircraft. Previously, the company had been chartering small [80-seat] BAC 1-11s to Geneva and Zurich. Dennis Fabri says, "If the bookings were not good, Erna would cancel one. Green chartered a Jumbo while she was away one time and when she came back she was totally horrified. Jumbos and the Erna Low philosophy just didn't add up."

Later, Erna would say, "In retrospect I must admit that this was a great mistake – probably the greatest I had ever made. Working with Simon Green was no pleasure and I soon regretted staying on. I found it impossible to work with him as we disagreed strongly on how to run the company. He used to call at my private residence most mornings between 8 and 9am and we had several heated discussions."

The pressure eventually gave on in August 1973 when the company issued "a blunt statement" saying that Erna was to leave both the company and board on 14 November 1973.

Fortunately for Erna, her solicitor had built an escape clause into the contract which entitled her to leave the company 'under special circumstances' with three months' notice.

The *Financial Times*[108] said the issue of the statement followed "weeks of rumours about major boardroom disagreements within the company".

***

John Boyle, who worked for Erna, was chartering the company's flight seats at the time, remembers the takeover. "Simon Green took me to lunch to the Bistingo in Old Brompton Road to say he had put together some form of consortium to take over the business.

"Green was known in the City of London as a headhunter and recruiter. He was a passionate skier but what happened was that he got in to Erna Low and his own creation ate him. He brought in this guy – a sort of Gordon Gekko type character – called Tony Weston who was a complete opposite to him to run the company financially and build up the business."

Weston was originally given the job of handling the company's marketing at a time when it was seriously in trouble, largely because of overexpansion of the summer programme. He oversaw a halving of the staff from sixty to thirty.

Writing in a memo at the time, Weston said: "Erna Low has made substantial losses since the Travellers Guaranty acquisition. Traditionally the company had made money during winter and made small losses during summer. An unconsidered summer expansion in the last two years has increased these losses to such an extent that the company's assets… are virtually nil."

Weston did recognise the value of its founder's name. "The brand name Erna Low is the company's main strength" but that the company was mainly operating in "a luxury market that is price sensitive, and whose prices are increasing very quickly due to circumstances beyond the industry's control".

Boyle relates what happened next. "All of a sudden, Green was ousted and Weston took over," he says.

Boyle and the new boss did not get on.

"He would cut out an article in *FT* and put it on your desk to let you know he had already been in an hour before you got there," he says.

"It transpired he was pretty much a crook," says Boyle. "Erna was very unsophisticated in financial terms and there was a whitewash where the assets of the company were used to pay the acquirer; he plundered the company for cash to make his payments to Erna. He and I never saw eye to eye and I told him he was an absolute arsehole."

Boyle left the company but remained as an independent aviation broker, working from Fulham Road, and it was this that led to his future career as the chief executive of Falcon Leisure, the company that eventually became First Choice.

"Weston paid me £500 to put together the planes in the way I had done previously," he says. "I put together off my own back a plane to Corsica. Erna Low took fifty seats, Waymark, a naturist holiday company, had fourteen seats to Ajaccio and the plane was all set up and I was making a couple of quid per seat."

"Suddenly, Waymark went bankrupt and I was absolutely buggered," says Boyle. "I had fourteen seats to sell again because I was the contract holder. I was between a rock and a hard place."

At the time, nobody was flying to Corsica and flying to Nice was expensive because the Civil Aviation Authority protected the national airlines while flight prices were fixed.

"The whole thing changed my life," says Boyle. "You were not allowed to sell cheap charter flights on their own so I found this campsite in the middle of nowhere and booked twenty-eight berths at a franc a night. I went to CAA and told them what I was doing. The CAA was very enlightened – a forerunner of easyJet really – and they said the manner of how you do the flights is fine as long as you are bonded. I put an advert on the back page of *The Times* and my phone went red hot. I sold fourteen seats on the first day and then the same every week for twenty weeks. It was unbelievable."

***

Tony Weston's role at the company would perhaps have been forgotten but for one thing: he became embroiled in a murder case that shocked the nation ten years later.

His new wife of the time, thirty-six-year-old Janice, was a successful solicitor practising from Lincoln's Inn. On 10 September 1983 she went to her office and received a phone call from her husband who was in France on business in his post-Erna career as a property developer.

Janice left at 4.15 that afternoon to pick up her husband's car, stopping off at home for a bite to eat and a glass of wine, and then left the flat hurriedly without tidying up. She headed for the couple's Northamptonshire home, Clopton Hall and its thirty-two-acre estate, in the village of that name. She never made it.

Her badly battered body was discovered the following day by a cyclist in a layby fifteen miles away from Clopton on the A1 near Huntingdon. Witnesses say they remember seeing a man helping a woman change a tyre in the layby. Janice's head had been subject to a blunt force trauma, which might have been caused by a car jack. Her car was missing but was eventually found back in London, in Camden Square.

A friend of the couple at the time told the *Daily Mirror*, "Tony rang me to tell me about Janice. He was shattered and didn't seem to have any idea what had happened. They had a very happy marriage and I can't imagine Janice going off into the night with anyone she didn't know."

Anthony Weston was later arrested on suspicion of involvement in the murder but strenuously denied any link to his wife's death, saying he was in France at the time of the murder, visiting a chateau he was planning to restore. He was released on 17 December after being questioned for fifty-five hours, eventually proving that he had been overseas at the time.

Suspicions about his involvement centred on the fact that Janice had entered the marriage as a rich woman and had only recently changed her will to make Anthony the main beneficiary.

The murder remains unsolved and Anthony Weston has since died. Cambridgeshire Police says that after a review of the case, there is no active investigation into the murder.

***

So what was Erna to do now that she was no longer with the company that bore her name? Retirement seemed like an obvious choice – she was sixty-four by this stage. Yet that was not Erna's way. She had never had much time for relaxation and leisure and the thought of retirement was anathema to her.

"Retire? I wouldn't think of it. I get far too much fun from the job," she told *Financial Times* reporter Emma Evans[109].

One thing she did do in her "retirement" was to write a book, published in 1974, called *Erna Low's Guide to Family Skiing*.

In the introduction by Major General Ian R Graeme, head of army recruitment in the Sixties, he wrote: "I have also known Erna Low for many years and have enormous admiration for her sincerity, her enthusiasm and her determination to do all she can to enable families and young people to enjoy skiing which has absorbed so much of her life."

The book was dedicated to the "assistants who have driven me on mountain roads, helped me to collect information and typed the manuscript – Ellen Fleming, Margaret Koenig and Uli Lloyd Pack".

***

After leaving Erna Low Travel Service, she had given an undertaking to Travellers Guaranty that she would not engage in competitive activities. The decision not to include Enjoy Britain and its Bute Street office as part of the Travellers Guaranty deal suddenly seemed inspired. The devaluation of the pound a few years before had made Britain a very attractive destination for foreign holidaymakers.

"We decided on expanding abroad to acquire an entirely new clientele in order not to clash with my old firm," Erna said, launching a scheme called Meet the British, which caught the attention of Edna Healey, wife of the then Chancellor Dennis. She wrote to Erna saying how much she admired the scheme, saying it was just what the country needed to help the economy.

In the new set-up, Erna and Bobbie Shafto acted as joint managing directors of Enjoy Britain. Bobbie, as before, handled the British house parties for families and young people, there was another team handling economy and student tours while Uli Lloyd Pack handled the individual travel and personal service department.

The year also brought some happier news. The French Government Tourist Office in London informed Erna that she was to be awarded the national medal of the French Federation of Tourist Offices and Syndicats d'Initiative. She received the bronze medal, for promotional efforts on behalf of Paris and the French regions, at a champagne reception in July that year.

At around the same time, she was also honoured with a gold medal, presented to her by her long-time friend Norbert Burda of the Austrian National Tourist Office, for her services to the Austrian tourism industry.

Both awards recognised the enormous amount she had done to raise the profile of France and Austria as potential holiday destinations among British tourists.

***

The mid Seventies was a difficult time for travel companies. Court Line Group had collapsed in August 1974, causing a crisis with the bonding system that is supposed to keep holidaymakers and their deposits protected. Court Line was the owner of the second biggest tour operator at the time, Clarksons Holidays, which had done so much to disrupt the ski business a few years earlier. The collapse left 100,000 holidaymakers out of pocket and saw the bonding rules rewritten.

Meanwhile, Erna Low Travel Service Ltd, without its eponymous founder, ceased trading on 12 September 1975 and went into liquidation five weeks later – the turnaround plan that had been instigated by Anthony Weston had failed.

The 'death' of Erna Low the company was then picked up by Erna's former employee and chalet holiday rival Colin Murison-Small, who published a leaflet to announce the sad event.

Erna was not impressed.

She wrote later, "I recently came across a leaflet from a friendly competitor – Colin Murison-Small – which started in a peculiar way, with an 'Obituary of the Erna Low Travel Service Ltd'. First I was very annoyed but then I thought what a good idea to show that 'Erna Low', the person and her Travel Service, are still very much alive and ready to 'kick' if necessary."

And kick she did.

"At the creditor meeting, I made my position quite clear," she said. "I told those present that I had never intended to leave the travel business when I sold out in 1972. I was determined to retrieve my name to prevent it from falling into other hands."

She bought back her company name from the receivers for £5,100[110] and acquired the shop premises in 3 and 5 Bute Street with the agreement of both the liquidators Cork Gulley and of the Association of British Travel Agents.

Erna reorganised the businesses: Enjoy Britain would henceforth concentrate on incoming tourists from abroad while the newly named Erna Low Holidays Ltd would focus on British holidaymakers going overseas, working from premises at 21 Old Brompton Road, where she had acquired a short shop lease.

All was back to business as usual by December 1975 – at least for another few years.

A short notice appearing in the *Evening Standard* in December 1975 ran as follows: "Miss Erna Low, *grande dame* of the ski slopes, is back in business, running a travel company bearing her name, having had nothing to do with the collapse of another such. She is opening premises at 21 Old Brompton Road and is offering various ski holidays this year – 1975 – and will get back in her stride in 1976".

Despite the failure of Erna Low Travel Service to thrive on the growing trend for winter sports holidays, Erna felt there was still a business to be made and decided to restart selling ski holidays.

Christopher Lloyd Pack says of her decision, "She had helped create mass tourism. She had helped create the package holiday and now it was taking off. Her own brand of holiday – made to measure – was falling by the wayside so she had double the work to do to get back."

Chapter 12

The British appetite for overseas holidays continued to grow in the 1970s.

The number of visits abroad by UK residents grew from 11.7 million in 1973 to 17.5 million in 1980 (and would rise again by another 4.3 million by 1985[111]). In 1973, Spain was the most popular destination, attracting 2.8 million tourists but by 1979, France was the most popular destination, attracting 3.2 million UK visitors pushing Spain into second place.

Austria and Switzerland had been popular in the early 1970s but had declined throughout the decade. In 1973, 454,000 went to Austria and 372,000 to Switzerland. By 1979, these figures had fallen to 199,000 and 268,000 respectively.[112]

This helped Erna re-establish what was now known as Erna Low Ltd within the travel industry after a rough few years. The recovery is shown in the company's accounts for the period. In 1974, the company had a turnover of £102,377 and made an operating loss of £16,452; by 1979 turnover had risen to £1,168,890 and it made operating profits of £12,998.

Yet not everyone was happy with the profitability of the business.

In 1975, Erna sought the advice of Leigh Knights, a travel industry consultant and "a friend of many years" about the state of the business.

In a letter to her, he said "Quite honestly, Erna, I don't think you need much help in making our major decisions."

He was clearly aware of the dangers of working with someone strong-willed and drew up a contract for working together, saying "I want to ensure that whatever may happen as a result of working together that friendship and respect for each other will not be impaired."

He was appointed as a director of the company in January 1976 but a heart problem put him into hospital before he was able to do much. However, he wrote a letter from his hospital bed sharing his thoughts on the business.

"I am mainly concerned with the costs and therefore profit margins of your 'made-to-measure' holidays. The mark up on such holidays has to be very high indeed to justify the time spent in research."

He pointed out the difficulty in seeking and confirming agreeable accommodation for those wanting tailor-made holidays and suggested that the mark-up should be 30 to 35% and that holidaymakers should be charged a non-returnable deposit of £10 just for the research.

Erna was not impressed with his advice, which went against her decades of personalised service to family and friends. In a note attached to his letter, she wrote: "I'm getting sick of all those bodies knocking us and me in particular and suggest they come and spend a few days in this place to see what we all do. For years, you've lost no opportunity of telling me the work I do is unprofitable and useless but so long as we advertise made-to-measure holidays and personal service so long they will ask for them."

***

Claudio Ambroso, one of Erna's Italian "nephews", was a regular visitor to Erna in London in the 1970s and 1980s.

Claudio, born in 1964, worked as a health economist from the late 1980s to 2000 before moving to Costa Rica and setting up Arte Viva, a non-profit association for education in arts and a reggae band.

He says, "There have always been four aunts (*zie* in Italian) in the family: my mother's sister and my uncle's wife – the two "true" aunts – as well as aunt Ila (Helene Herdely, another distant cousin) and aunt Erna who were just as important as the others. When Zia Erna died, I cried."

"Although formally a very distant cousin, Erna has always been considered a very close member of the family," says Claudio. "She paid frequent visits to Italy, often looking for new destinations in the Lake District in Northern Italy. She was considered in the family as an example of skills, perseverance, determination and success, a self-made woman, as well as a very balanced, objective and calm person," he says.

"In my family, anxiety abounds; Erna was always trying to cool things off. She would always defend me and my brother Guido in our quarrels with our parents. She would always tell my brother and me how surprised she was that we were apparently both normal and good boys with so much craziness and tension going around in the family."

Claudio also believes that Erna helped save his brother's life. "Guido was really sick when he was two years old and the doctors in Italy could not save him. Erna suggested he should come to London. Whether it was the change of air or God knows what but it saved my brother's life."

In the 1970s, Claudio learned English at her house parties.

"I remember going to Runton Hill in Norfolk when I was, maybe, nine. It was the first time I had ever played tennis."

At the house parties, Claudio gained something of a reputation with Erna as a "*tombeur de femmes* (ladykiller)".

"Erna would always have an au pair girl staying with her and I would almost invariably end up dating her," he says with a laugh.

***

By the end of the decade – and with her reaching the age of seventy – Erna's thoughts turned again to selling the again profitable company. Two bidders emerged in the race to snap it up. The first was Conference Services, a Mayfair-based company organising international conferences. This was founded by Fay Pannell in 1962 and taken over by Mullan Cunningham, former hotel director of Cunard Line and managing director of Mandarin International Hotels, in 1978. The second was Ross Jones of the Bradford-based travel agency Redfern Travel, whom Erna had taken to her beloved Corsica at the company's expense in order to hear what he had to offer.

Mullan Cunningham wrote to Erna on 1 June 1979 offering to buy the company for £85,000.

A week later in June, Ross Jones offered to buy the company for £100,000 and agreed to take her on as a consultant for three years at a salary of £7,000. On the 11th, the offer was increased to £110,000.

Erna replied to Mullan Cunningham on the 13th to turn his offer down. "After careful consideration... I have reluctantly decided to accept the other offer for a purchase of the total share capital", arguing that it would make more sense to merge with an existing travel business "which already holds all the appointments and licences and can take a more active part in running the business".

However, Erna was clearly playing the two bidders against each other, ending the letter with "I may well revert to your offer at a later date".

This brought a counter-offer from Mullan Cunningham and she went for it. The sale was set at a price of £100,000 with an agreement to employ Erna for

In 1979, Erna sold the business for a second time, this time around to Mullan Cunningham of Conference Services, here with the firm's founder Fay Pannell, photo Jalmar

three years after completion of the deal at a salary of £8,500 with a restriction of sixty months after termination of employment. She also would receive the use of a motor car and a commission of 10% of the company's net profits in excess of £10,000 in any one financial year.

Redfern's Jones thought Erna was making a "big mistake" and told her so in a telegram to Selwood Terrace. "Incentive conference not you. Suggest view Bradford before decision. Regards."

He followed up with a letter "I personally think you are making a mistake for there is so very much we could do together. I would have been extremely interested in amalgamating our tour operating with yours." Enclosed with the letter were the photographs from his Corsica trip – a clear attempt to sway her at the last minute.

Erna was not to change her mind. The deal with Conference Services was eventually signed and announced to the world in August 1979: "I will continue as managing director of Erna Low Ltd and in addition to expanding the company's ski and summer programmes, we propose to engender additional business in the conference and incentive travel fields."

Despite this, in June 1980, she left the boards of both Erna Low and Enjoy Britain to "act as consultant to both firms", her role being taken by Michael Edwards, head of Austrian Airlines' conference department. However, the consultant's role was merely a sop, the *Financial Times* saying that "in practice it is a badly kept trade secret that she disagreed strongly with their approach to the ski business and to their choice of resorts" [113].

Erna made use of a handy clause in her contract which said, "The Executive will have the right to terminate her employment hereunder in the event of her having a serious disagreement with the Company upon giving three months written notice of such disagreement with the Company."

Whether this was prescience on the part of the lawyer or happy circumstance is unknown but Erna certainly made use of it.

An advert in *The Sunday Times* of 1 February 1981 caused a disagreement between the two parties. It read "Spas in Italy – Abano-Montegrotto for health and holidays… The attractively situated Veneto Spas are renowned for their mud pack and thermal treatment for rheumatism and arthritis… contact the Spa representative Miss Erna Low, 9 Reece Mews. Booking through ABTA Agents."

Mullan Cunningham argued that this was Erna effectively setting herself up in competition and instructed his solicitor.

"We understand that your client is actively advertising in various newspapers and periodicals… You have tried to persuade us that your client is acting in a representative capacity only. [The advertisement] speaks for itself. There is no doubt that your client is in breach of the sale agreement… [and unless she] is prepared to give an undertaking not to insert any similar advertisements… we shall… be seeking an Injunction against your client."

However by June, Cunningham's solicitors had agreed to allow her to call herself a "Spa Consultant".

***

Whether she was prescient or not, Erna's departure was well timed. In April 1982, Erna Low Ltd went into voluntary liquidation following the withdrawal of its air tour operator's licence, the bond which covers holidaymakers in the event of a collapse of a travel company. The collapse left 300 holidaymakers stranded abroad and ruined the holidays of 800 others [114]. *The Financial Times* [115] said the collapse had left "British skiers dotted around the Alps like chamois in an avalanche".

The debts of the company amounted to a whopping £602,000 against assets of just £197,368, *Travel News* reported[116].

At the creditors' meeting, Mullan Cunningham said the firm has "effectively lost £155,000 because of the Civil Aviation Authority's decision not to renew its air travel organiser's licence in the middle of the wintersports season. If the company had not been forced to cease trading, its liabilities would have been offset by the revenue which the bookings would have produced".

Cunningham said that the CAA had originally asked for an additional bond of £100,000 but this had increased to £250,000 and the company had been unable to meet the requirement. It is believed that the increase in bond had been occasioned by the £270 million collapse of Sir Freddie Laker's travel empire at the beginning of February 1982.

A saviour for the company came in the form of Travelpoint Ltd (the company behind French Leave and Spa Holidays programmes) which acquired the trading names, the tour operating businesses and Bute Street staff. The company said it would still help people who had booked holidays to get away and continued to accept bookings for the season.

Redfern's Ross Jones was quick to write to Erna to say "[I] can only surmise that friend Cunningham did not turn out to be the man to turn his hand to what was for him a new experience." He added "Life in the travel industry at present is extremely difficult and I think it is a matter of survival at the present time and it would appear that the day of the large multiples is here whether to stay or not will be interesting to see."

Erna wrote back to say, "I have often regretted not to have sold to you" and said Cunningham "promised all sorts of things such as joining the firm with Conference Services. Of course, he never did."

She admitted that "life in the travel industry is no picnic at present and I doubt whether it ever will be again. I hope it all goes well with you in spite of the recession."

Things have gone well with Redfern. The company still thrives in its Bradford home and recently won a contract to supply business travel services to the British Government, a deal worth up to £1.4bn over four years.

For his part, Mullan Cunningham had a sad end. He committed suicide in January 1983 at the age of forty-six by gassing himself in a car in the grounds of a hotel he was managing, Abingworth Hall Hotel in Sussex. His wife told the inquest that her husband "had been depressed for some time over an incident connected with his business".

Both Jean Shafto and Uli Lloyd Pack handed in their resignations at the time of the sale to Mullan Cunningham. "When Erna sold the business for the second time, that is when my mum parted from her," remembers Uli's son Christopher.

***

The sale of the business was the basis for another much-repeated anecdote about Erna.

Ever since the 1930s there had been a healthy rivalry between Erna Low and Inghams, the company founded by fellow Viennese export Walter Ingham and which had helped establish the British ski market. The two companies would often vie with each other to get the best hotels in a particular resort, often at the expense of the other.

This friendly rivalry was highlighted in an incident in which Erna took a group of journalists to the French ski resort of La Plagne, which she had started to represent. According to ski writer Arnie Wilson, the group went for lunch at a restaurant called Le Kitchen, run by Maureen Bell who had previously worked as the public relations manager for Inghams.

Erna grumbled to Maureen, "I remember when Inghams forced me out of a resort once".

"Well," replied Maureen, "I am no longer Inghams."

"Indeed," replied Erna sadly, "and I am no longer Erna Low", a reference to the fact that she was no longer able to use her company name.

Ski writer Roger Bray remembers these press trips from the 1980s. "She would get upset because two of us journalists on the press trip would be at each other all the time. She couldn't understand that [*Observer* travel writer] Nigel Lloyd and I would send each other up on these trips. We used to take the piss out of each other but it was just an act. I don't think she quite understood; she just thought we would take chunks out of each other."

On another of these trips to La Plagne, Roger caused Erna a headache because in his rush to leave his home, he had picked up his wife's passport by mistake.

"Nobody took a blind bit of notice at Gatwick," remembers Roger. "I knew they never ever checked your passport at French border but the Swiss did at Geneva. They locked me up in a room for hours, keeping Erna fretting."

***

An Erna Low press trip to La Plagne in 1982

While the sale and subsequent collapse of Erna Low Ltd was playing out, Erna received a surprising letter from her solicitors, asking her to provide a reference for Jean-Thomas Ollandini, who worked for one of the overseas companies with which the company worked after he had been arrested "in connection with possessing a large quantity of cannabis".

Ollandini was a member of a high-profile Corsican family that had provided transport services on the French island since 1933 and had been a family concern there since 1890. The family and its eponymous company had its fingers in many pies and several of the family had ended up as influential politicians on the island.

Initially, Erna planned to write back saying she found Jean "at all times helpful, courteous, hardworking and efficient" but eventually sent back a very bland letter just saying how long she had known him. However, when she was asked to act as surety for him, she wrote back, berating the solicitor for spelling her surname as "Lou" and saying she would not.

However, Uli Lloyd Pack – who also knew him – agreed to provide surety of £8,000.

A year later Ollandini failed to surrender to his bail and Uli was ordered to forfeit her surety. She thought about appealing the decision but decided not to pursue it.

Erna clearly felt responsible and ended up paying the money on Uli's behalf, for which she was eventually reimbursed by Mullan Cunningham.

***

The death of her dog Charlie in 1978 saw the arrival in Erna's life of a new poodle, one who would test the patience of both her and her employees and friends.

In a 1982 *Sunday Times* article[117] on her life, she described the new poodle – apricot rather than the black of his predecessors – as being "a little difficult".

Speaking to journalist Eithne Power, who went on to become a great friend of Erna's, she said: "First thing after waking up I leap out of bed and let Timmy, my temperamental five-year-old poodle, into the garden. He's no ordinary dog. He eats smoke and has been to a dog psychologist. He'd like me to take up smoking but, much as I love him, there are limits."

Another of Erna's journalist friends, the radio broadcaster Wilfrid Thomas, even introduced Timmy to his listeners in a report on a weekend trip he had made with Erna to the spa town of Baden bei Wien, where Erna had a summer house as a child and which she was at this stage representing as a consultant.

His broadcasts begins, "The only dog I know who smokes belongs to my good friend Miss Erna Low. Timmy is a small poodle with an amiable smile, charming but temperamental. If anyone is puffing a cigar or a cigarette, Timmy gets on his hind legs and snaps at the smoke as it floats in the air. A dog psychologist has been consulted to no avail. Timmy is frustrated because most of Erna's friends have given up smoking."

The psychologist in question was Dr Roger Mugford, a consultant in animal behaviour who had become famous for helping the Queen with some troublesome corgis. He put Timmy's problems down to "despotic domination" and recommended a course of action that included stopping stroking him if he was the one to demand affection, stopping bribing him with food and never playing tug of war.

Dr Mugford had some sage advice, although Erna does not appear to have followed it too closely: "Never share human food with him: that is an indulgence which probably confers human status upon him. Remember Timmy is a dog!"

He also noted a worrying tendency by Timmy to wee indoors but added

"Timmy is really a great dog… a wonderful companion and amusement, but I feel that the negatives on occasion outweigh the positive."

A Christmas note that year from Robert Hollier of the French Tourist Office reads, "Our wishes for a very happy 1982 – that is all of you and friends except for that four-legged monster [which] you should keep gagged and muzzled at all times."

***

The early 1980s were a challenging time for Britain. Unemployment had reached 2.5 million and more than 6,000 were joining the dole queue every day.

The economic tension was also coupled with social tension and the two things came to a head with the riots in Brixton and Toxteth that year.

The rioting saw Erna reach for her pen to write to the editor of *The Times* under the heading *A Glimmer of Hope?*

She wrote, "Having been unfortunate enough to observe the rise of National Socialism in Germany from close quarters, I and many like me have watched the rise of unemployment, especially among the young, with considerable concern long before the riots started. [The riots] are symptoms of lack of outlets for the exuberance and surplus energy of the young, of despair and frustration.

"At this stage, it is more important to think of remedies rather than to adjudicate (sic) blame…There are hopeful signs that enlightened and enthusiastic educationists can do a great deal to work towards integration of coloured children and their parents in the local community."

She talked of the Avondale Park Infants School in north Kensington, where she was a governor, as a model for how racial integration could be made to work. She also called for funds to made available for more playing fields, skating rinks, tennis courts and swimming pools. She also complained of the introduction of VAT on school trips. "The introduction of such taxes… is the most retrogressive and deplorable attitude and quite inappropriate for the present time."

***

Deciding against retirement again, Erna decided to share her encyclopaedic knowledge of the travel industry with others, setting herself up as a "consultant to the travel industry". Long-time right hand woman Bobbie continued to help out on a part-time basis until she eventually retired.

Erna's first au pair, Halina Hodi, with the smoke-eating Timmy

Her first two clients in the new role were the ski resort of La Plagne in the French Alps and the spa of Abano-Montegrotto in Italy.

La Plagne is typical of many Alpine villages in that it was sparsely populated for centuries, unless you count the cows. Indeed, as recently as 1940, the cattle outnumbered the farmers. It was also a mining centre – for coal at Bonnegarde and lead and silver at the St Victor mine in Peisey-Nancroix, the remains of which are still visible today.

Yet both agriculture and mining were in steep decline by the 1960s.

Erna's job for La Plagne was to act as a representative of the resort in the British market. She said at the time "My main activity has been contacting new ski operators and summer tour operators, as well as journalists, to interest them in La Plagne winter and summer ski activities and in the La Plagne summer centres."

She would send out news bulletins, La Plagne marketing brochures and details of tour operators who offered holidays there (listed democratically in alphabetical order), including the company bearing her name that she was no longer involved with.

Her marketing material at the time says La Plagne "was the first of the modern purpose built ski resorts and ranks amongst France's top ski stations".

She succeeded in gaining press coverage, perhaps helped by the Christmas party she held in Reece Mews on the resort's behalf, in Ski Survey, the Ski Club of Great Britain's magazine, and in Ski Magazine.

Others were also introduced to La Plagne's charms, including journalist Eithne Power and her son Fred, Victor Gough of the Royal Naval Ski Club and Colonel Peter Kemmis-Betty of the Army Ski Association, who had also been one of Erna's first ever clients back in the 1930s.

This early trip was due to go out on a Sunday but Fred Power was in no shape to go abroad, having a temperature of more than 100. Eithne rang Erna to share the news. "Erna grunted and was clearly annoyed," says Eithne. "The next day he was fine and I rang Erna to say we would make our own way there the following day."

"After a few problems en route, we finally made it to La Plagne," says Eithne. "I walked up to her in the resort wearing a bright orange coat. She turned to me and said, witheringly, 'Have you come from Soho?'"

Eithne laughs as she remembers this first meeting. "She wanted to have a grouse at me but once that was over she conceded that I had done my best to get there. We spent that whole week together at La Plagne."

On another trip to the resort, Eithne started to suffer from altitude sickness in a cable car. "I managed to stagger back to the hotel. Erna came up to my room and she hurled a huge packet of pills at me, just like she was throwing the javelin. I was groaning, lying prone and I could hear her muttering 'Stupid girl' under her breath. She came back that night to see if I was dead and shouted form the door 'I'm not coming in there to catch what you have'."

"We eventually became friends and it was a friendship that was to last until Erna died," she says.

Eithne remembers another trip, to the Hotel Les Vagues in Arcachon, which cemented her view of Erna.

"When we arrived at the hotel," says Eithne, "I asked the hotel owner 'Do you know Madame Low? He turned to me and replied, 'Madame Low, c'est une légende'."

***

In 1982, *The Sunday Times* ran one of its popular A Life in the Day Of columns[118] about Erna. By now her consultancy had expanded to include Hyères in the south of France and several Austrian ski resorts.

She told journalist Eithne Power: "When I'm at home – about two thirds of the year – I usually wake up to the French programme on the World Service, which I'll have forgotten to switch off before falling asleep."

She would start the day with a copy of *The Times*, a grapefruit, a boiled egg and a piece of toast. She would also have a cup of lemon tea, but never coffee, a drink that she had been turned off during childhood.

In 1984, Erna said, "Both my mother and my grandmother insisted on my drinking a large cup of coffee before going to school and ran after me with it right to the front door of the apartment house. I never did drink that coffee and right up to now I have never drank coffee for breakfast and never will."

Erna was always very interested in politics, happy to share her sometimes outspoken views with anyone.

She would discuss Northern Ireland's problems with her Irish housekeeper Mrs McKenna. "Every day we come up with a new solution," she said at the time.

One of her Italian nephews, Guido Ambroso, says "Erna was politically and socially progressive. She used to vote Labour, but later in life she switched to the Liberal Democrats, but never Tory."

In fact, she was much affected by the unexpected death of Labour leader John Smith – she had met his wife a few years earlier. In her notes she says Smith "could have become the greatest Labour Prime Minister this century". Later in life she would make a donation to the campaign coffers of an up and coming politician by the name of Tony Blair.

But back to the 1980s when New Labour was just a distant twinkle in Michael Foot's eye.

The work day proper would begin with Erna walking from Selwood Terrace to the Reece Mews office by about 10.30. Work would involve organising film previews and parties for journalists.

Erna would regularly be out for lunch, entertaining a client or a journalist. "I prefer something simple, good English food rather than anything exotic. I have no need of alcohol, maybe because I'm an extrovert."

"Life these days is much, much easier," she told Power. "I don't have the money worries I had when I was Erna Low Travel. I don't have to worry about floods, fire, hurricanes, strikes, terrorism, recession, typhoid, avalanches and whether the buses are running."

***

Erna started to represent the Italian spa centres of Abano and Montegrotto in December 1980. She said at the time, "I met with a certain amount of resistance from the medical professions and the public. I have, however, managed to overcome some of the resistance and have persuaded rheumatologists, physiotherapists and sufferers from rheumatism, arthritis and allied diseases to try out the spa treatment."

She shared her fascination with spas with someone who was very much in the news at the time, Raine Spencer, the mother of Lady Diana, with whom she shared correspondence. A postcard from Raine to Erna at the time, "You're so wonderful and full of ideas."

Erna continued to add a number of other spas to her list, such as Salsmaggiore, Ischia, Montecatini and Sirmione, French *thalasso* (sea water) therapy centres in Brittany, St Jean de Luz, Vichy, Baden, Leuk, Leukerbad, Bad Ragaz and St Moritz in Switzerland, and Austrian spas such as Baden bei Wien, Bad Hofgastein and spas further afield in Yugoslavia, Israel and in the USA.

She visited Baden with a group including journalist Eithne Power and the broadcaster Wilfrid Thomas. Thomas described Baden as a "town which nestles among vineyards on the slopes of the Vienna Woods. Since Roman times people have visited Baden's fifteen thermal springs for treatment for stress, rheumatic, respiratory and other ailments. There are gymnastic devices of alarming design and purpose, ray therapy, mud baths, pine needle baths, massages of various kinds, inhalations and sixty doctors to supervise."

On one night of the trip, the party did not get back to their hotel until 3am and found the doors locked. Thomas related in his broadcast, "It was not Erna, nor was it me, it was the sophisticated long-legged lovely twenty-three year old Serena who climbed up the drainpipe to a window, opened the latch, got inside and came downstairs and opened the door. I couldn't have done it. It reminded me that I am not as young as… I wish I were. I must certainly go back to Baden to the Spa for their course in rejuvenation."

***

In 1981, the BBC aired a new sitcom written by John Sullivan, the man behind the successful *Citizen Smith* (which starred Robert Lindsay in the title role of "Wolfie" Smith, leader of the Tooting Popular Front).

The airing of the first episode was fairly low-key, achieving viewing figures of 9.2 million, huge by today's standards but less so in an era of just three channels.

But *Only Fools and Horses*, featuring the exploits of Del Boy and Rodney

Trotter and their friends, eventually went on to become the most popular sitcom of all time.

One of the actors in the series was Roger Lloyd Pack in his first big television role as road sweeper Trigger, who became popular for his daft utterances and for his unswerving conviction that his mate Rodney was actually called Dave. He had been cast by executive producer Ray Butt after seeing him on stage.

Roger's acting success came fairly late on. Speaking from the north London home he shares with second wife Jehane Markham, he says, "I didn't really get going till my forties. I was married and living in Islington in the late 60s, leading a hippy life and was often unemployed. I was a bit distant from Erna at that point. I split from [first wife] Sheila two years after Emily was born and I didn't see Erna so much after I moved away."

Erna loved the theatre and cinema, particularly if it was something containing Roger, but nearly always fell asleep. Halina Hodi remembers going to see one film in which Roger was acting. "Erna said, 'Tell me when Roger appears' and then fell asleep. She woke up and said, 'Oh yes, that's Roger' and then fell asleep again."

A young Roger Lloyd Pack

Roger says, "Erna was rather disparaging about my acting, believing it not to be a 'proper' thing to do. She was very disparaging about my dad too. But when I did *Only Fools and Horses*, she liked that, she liked watching comedies. She came round to respect my acting after that."

After *Only Fools and Horses*, Lloyd Pack became known to a new, younger audience, as Bartemius Crouch Sr in the Harry Potter movies.

***

Erna's contribution to outbound tourism to a number of countries was recognised yet again in the early 1980s.

In 1982, Erna received a letter from the Italian State Tourist Board stating "I have the honour and the pleasure to inform you that the decoration of the Order of Merit of the Republic of Italy has been conferred upon you".

With a growing number of clients for her consultancy business, Erna decided she needed a bit more help with the business and placed an advert in the *Evening Standard* for "a young person – keen skier with knowledge of French and German".

Two hundred people responded to the ad but application number seven stood out, saying there was an "immediate rapport" with the young Joanna Yellowlees, who at that stage did not realise the important role she would play in the history of Erna Low.

Speaking at Joanna's wedding a few years later, Erna related the story of the first interview.

"Joanna's application immediately interested me," she said in her still guttural Austrian accent. "She mentioned that she had an Oxford degree in English, a good knowledge of French and German, was a skier and also keen on somewhat crazy activities such as underwater exploration, working in a lunatic asylum and in a Berlin Kindergarten – she sounded just the sort of girl I had been hoping for!"

Joanna Yellowlees was born in 1960 in a house in Tabley Road, Knutsford where her parents still live. She lived there until the age of nine when her family moved to Brussels with her father's job as a nuclear scientist. After six years in the Belgian capital, the family returned to Tabley Road where Joanna went to the local grammar school.

From school she went to study English at St Anne's College, Oxford. Each summer, she would go diving on shipwrecks with a young Falkland Islander by the name of Mensun Bound, whom she would later marry.

"I met my husband when were in our first year on a diving course. He was an archaeologist, doing excavations of his own, while I was just learning to dive."

This travel bug translated into what Joanna wanted for her career. "I knew that any job related to English I didn't want to do. I knew it wasn't me. I always wanted to travel and do something language related."

"I had heard of the name Erna Low but I didn't know there was a Miss Erna Low behind it," Joanna admits.

"The interview was in the bottom room at Reece Mews and Miss Low was sitting in the middle of the room behind a huge round table. It was much more like a sitting room rather than an office and was very dark. Initially we didn't get on very well at all. She had this horrible little poodle called Tim who attacked me, backing me up against the wall. It was not what I expected at all."

Despite this confrontation with one of her beloved dogs, Erna's mind was soon made up to hire Joanna and decided to put her on the spot immediately, just as she had done with so many of her previous long-standing employees.

Erna said later, "I interviewed no further, asked her whether she could start at once and go to La Plagne, the French ski resort I represent in Britain, with a dashing squadron leader; she immediately accepted. Was it her strange name 'Yellowlees' which she shared with an eminent doctor, a civil servant whom I had been in touch with when promoting Italian spas, or was it that she like myself had studied English literature (she at Oxford and I in Vienna) or was it that her family lived at Knutsford where I had stayed on my first visit to Britain to collect material for my PhD thesis?"

Speaking to the *Financial Times*[119], Erna said, "Finding Joanna was pure luck: one of life's little miracles. I'd been approached by La Plagne and urgently needed someone to check out the resort. Something just clicked when I interviewed her and she was on the plane to France the following day."

Joanna's mother Jean Yellowlees puts Joanna's success down to her interpersonal skills. "She has always got on awfully well with old ladies," she says. "Unlike today, young graduates then could more or less have their pick of the job market and the travel industry had a glamour attached to it."

Despite agreeing to go away, Joanna did not have a passport but she thought nothing of that obstacle. "This was the sort of person Erna could relate to – someone who was positive," says Halina Hodi.

Jean Yellowlees says, "Joanna phoned me and I had to race to Crewe station to put it on the luggage van so she could pick it up at Euston."

"Off she went on a rather delicate mission taking a squadron leader and his lady friend," recalled Erna. "She managed to convince him that La Plagne was indeed the ideal resort for his winter sports scheme for 500 people and in fact they went there three years running. When the squadron leader returned from his inspection tour, he rang me up and said 'You have a winner there – Joanna is a fantastic girl'. Never has a truer word been spoken."

"We've worked together ever since, without a single quarrel or disagreement."

She added: "I cannot work with negative people. I like people to fall in with my way of thinking. Joanna has always been easy to work with. She's independent yet she doesn't take the law into her own hands."

***

Patrick Goyet, who was director of the French National Tourist Office in the 1980s, says in his book *Vagabondage*:

"When I knew Erna Low as representative of Flaine and La Plagne, she was already seventy-five but she was still very dynamic at the head of a company which handles 20,000 customers a year."

In that time, he spent five Christmas Eves at Erna's house in Selwood Terrace.

He says in the book, "Erna received many people at the house and especially at Christmas," he writes. "The menus of those Christmas Eve dinners was always the

The young Joanna Yellowlees with Erna in 1982

same: cauliflower soup followed by a turkey roasted for too many hours in the oven, accompanied by mint sauce and an awful bread sauce… Laurent, who took part in two of these Anglo-Austrian Christmases, forced himself politely to eat everything but once back home he vowed how much it had cost him to swallow such victuals. For dessert… Christmas pudding from Fortnum and Masons.

He goes on: "The meals prepared by one of the au pairs and about whom Erna complained ceaselessly, were invariably failures but no matter: we went to Erna's not for gastronomy but to meet interesting people: the actress Emily Lloyd, the Italian theologian Guido [Ambroso], a mathematician who was doing research on AIDS in Sweden, Ernst, a member of the OBE for good and loyal service and who was nostalgic for his industrial past in Manchester. One day, returning after a long voyage in Asia, Ernst made us look at a watch he had bought in Singapore at a good price. It was very beautiful but it could not be set to the English time. Laurent offered to help him but noticed with a laugh that the winder was welded to the dial… Erna had the habit of saying 'people are my hobby'."

Goyet also recalls going into the office in Reece Mews, hoping to catch sight of another resident, the artist Francis Bacon who lived at number 7 directly opposite.

"Erna would tease us and say, 'Will he be there today with his brushes and palette in hand?'

We would occasionally catch a glimpse, a bit of clutter out of the window of the tiny shop and a fleeting shadow of the old artist with grey tousled hair.

Mensun Bound, Joanna's marine archaeologist husband, remembers Erna and Bacon shouting at each other across the Mews – Erna would yell "Dirty poof!" and Francis would respond with "Barren old bitch!" Despite the insults, relations would soon return to normal and Erna and the artist were soon back on polite speaking terms.

Erna wrote later, "I saw [Francis] almost daily. He was a loner but we had an easy relationship and greeted each other warmly whenever we met."

Bacon died in Madrid in 1993. "He was a colourful character and he is much missed in Reece Mews," wrote Erna.

***

Erna's Italian relative Guido Ambroso, grandson of her favourite "uncle" Rodolfo Ruberl, was a regular visitor to London and Erna in the 1980s. Guido came to the capital to study in Social Anthropology and Human Geography at University College London, just over the road from Erna's wartime flat at 116 Gower Street.

He remembers an amusing incident from when Erna invited him to a reception at the Houses of Parliament.

"When I was at high school in Milan, I always wanted to have long hair, but my father did not let me. When I arrived in the UK to start university, I could grow long hair and a long beard, although this was no longer in fashion in London (the hip style was punk and new wave) and Erna did not mind at all about my hippy style."

"But when she invited me to the reception, she asked me to trim my hair and beard for the occasion. I would not comply and when the day came I presented myself without having cut my hair and beard. Erna looked at me and smiled and said 'It does not matter, you can still come, at least you have a suit' (even if there was one hole in it)".

Erna intervened with Guido's father the following year. "In my second year at UCL I got an offer to move in to a student flat with two girls," he recalls. "My father, very conservative from a social point of view, although not a practising Catholic, was opposed. Erna had to phone him and intervened saying that in the UK this was absolutely normal and so my father dropped the objection."

Guido went on to work all over the world for the United Nations High Commissioner for Refugees, including the organisation's headquarters in Geneva where he lives with his family today.

***

The last of Erna's dogs, Maxi the dachshund, was another terror like his predecessor – nipping at the heels of any visitors to Selwood Terrace. He did not, however, share Timmy's predilection for second-hand smoke.

Erna bought Maxi from the Harrods pet shop one Saturday afternoon in 1986.

"It was a Saturday afternoon in 1986 and we went to the Battersea Dogs Home but could not see a dog we wanted. We decided to go to Harrods and look in their pet department. There were only two dogs left, both dachshunds."

Erna's distant cousin Francesca Ruberl, writing in the family history *I Ruberl*, says, "The only problem was that Erna had neurotic relationships with these neurotic lapdogs. They were not considered as pets but more like children and were spoiled in an incredible fashion. The animal responded to the love that she bestowed, but guests could not react even if Maxi was biting them hard on the ankles."

She again sought the guidance of animal behaviour consultant Dr Roger Mugford over Maxi's behaviour.

He met Maxi in July 1988 and wrote back saying "Maxi's problems are only problems of confrontation, where he does not wish to do something which you wish him to. This is quite a normal trait of a dominant dog. This, I can absolutely reassure you there is nothing 'wrong' with Maxi. Only that he is dominant and the more dominant in your compliant and gentle hands."

He went on to suggest that Maxi should not be allowed to sit on Erna's lap or sleep under her bed, and that there were "convincing grounds for hormonal therapy... [through the] administration of an anti-androgen injection".

Erna dismissed this drastic course of action and Maxi continued to nip away without fear of retribution from his owner.

***

Chapter 13

The 1980s were a good time for Erna. She was enjoying being a consultant to French ski resorts, the German-speaking South Tyrol region of Italy and a range of spas across the Continent which were trying to gain a bigger foothold in the British market.

Not content with working hard on her consultancy business, Erna also acted as vice-president of both the Kensington and Chelsea Chamber of Trade and Commerce – the first time a woman had held the role – and the Women of the Year Association. She had been a regular guest at the lunches of for two decades and by this time was acting as the association's vice president.

The organisation has its roots in the Woman of the Year lunch which was launched by mother of six Antonella "Tony" Lothian in 1955, which brought together 500 women who had done good work throughout the year.

Lord and Lady Lothian were long time friends of Erna and she often organised holidays for them. (Lord Lothian wrote to Erna in 1993 to say, "I came to you for advice thirty years ago and we have followed your advice ever since. We go to Cyprus every year. We owe that to you.")

The association was formed later to give those who had enjoyed the lunches the chance to meet on a more regular basis at London's New Cavendish Club, although when Erna was active the meetings were regularly held at the Parrot Club at the Basil Street Hotel in Knightsbridge.

The lunch always attracts famous speakers. In 1984, the podium was given to Valentina Tereshkova, the Russian who was the first woman in space. She used the occasion to "beg the women of Britain to join Russia's women to end the Cold War".

Erna met Tereshkova again, along with her daughter, in 1990 at a function at the House of Lords organised by Lady Lothian when the University of Edinburgh conferred an honorary doctorate on the Russian cosmonaut.

A few years later, Tereshkova would invite Erna, along with journalists Norma

Rowlerson and Eithne Power – to visit Moscow and St Petersburg as her guest. The three were lavishly entertained and they spent a weekend at a dacha in the Russian countryside. Erna came back from the trip enthused about the idea of the company offering family stays in Russia.

Other famous speakers of that era included Martin Luther King's widow Coretta King, Lady Archer, Shirley Williams and Baroness Phillips.

Erna herself was nominated to receive a Woman of the Year award on two occasions. On the second, she was up for the Woman of Europe award but lost out to Sally Greengrass, director of Age Concern and secretary general of Eurolink. "We all agreed that she deserved it," said Erna later.

***

Over the next few years, Erna Low, the consultancy company, would continue to act as representatives for the French resorts of La Plagne and Flaine in Britain. It sold apartment accommodation directly to British skiers, and was largely responsible for the growth in popularity of those two resorts to the point where they are now firm favourites here.

Joanna Yellowlees-Bound, who had joined Erna in 1982 as an assistant and now runs the company, says the focus on French apartments was very timely.

"It was an interesting time, just before the internet boom. There was a huge awareness from these resorts of what had to be done to market them on the UK market. That was why they wanted to employ us as their representatives and our strong UK brand added to their credibility."

Joanna is unequivocal in her belief that the company's representation of them in the 1980s and 1990s helped make the names of those resorts among the British skiing public.

"Erna had set up the company to handle UK reservations for La Plagne and Flaine. When I took over the company, I managed to secure a contract with Les Arcs, pretty much following her model."

***

In the early 1990s, Erna was elated when the company published its first ever dedicated spa brochure. "I have produced Health Holiday leaflets since 1968 but our first spa brochure was published in 1991 … and our most recent brochure

Erna promoting La Plagne, photo: Tess Musgrave

features spas in France, Italy, Spain, Hungary, Switzerland, Malta, Madeira, Menorca, Cyprus, Israel and South Africa."

"We strongly recommend our clients to go to certain spas if they suffer from arthritis, rheumatism or muscle pains."

Writing in her autobiographical notes, she says that many people asked her what was the secret of the eternal youth that kept her active and interested in new activities and places all this time.

"I have finally come to the conclusion that it may be my interest in people and the enjoyment in my work in travel and in seeing new places. The fact is that I do enjoy my work and that I am always interested in new ideas, new people and new places. Travel is one answer and staying in touch with one's friends is another."

***

Erna's driving, never great, continued to draw attention.

In November 1991, she was summoned to appear before Horseferry Road magistrates for "driving a Honda Accord… on a road without due care and attention… 30 yards north of junction with Old Brompton Road".

"After the crash, I came to the conclusion that my driving days had come to an end but unexpectedly a little blue Renault 5 came my way. It was sold to me very cheaply by a journalist friend who had come to lunch and had to listen to the description of my latest car disasters."

John Samuel, the journalist friend in question and who wrote the book *Bedside Skiing*, says he was an occasional visitor to Reece Mews at the time.

"She and the French Tourist Office director [Patrick Goyet] were good friends and we would often go to the Mews together. She was very positive. She knew the means of publicity to an astonishing degree and recognised that you were nothing without publicity. She would tell a tale and worked at you.

"On time, she had taken on the publicity for a golf resort and was telling them 'You have got to do this, you have got to do that'. Not to me but whoever was needing to get in the papers."

By the mid 1990s, it was time for Erna Low to get back into the business of selling holidays directly to customers again. This was partly prompted by the arrival of low-cost airlines on the scene but also of the emergence of the internet, allowing ski resorts to start marketing themselves directly to skiers, making the representation services offered by Erna Low redundant.

Joanna, very much in charge of day-to-day operations by this time, made the decision to seek a licence to start operating as a tour operator once again, taking the company back to its roots.

"The reason we did it was because we found that people who went to La Plagne one year wanted to go somewhere else the next so we built up our name as a French specialist. It was a natural extension of what we were doing," says Joanna.

The new Erna Low was based on selling accommodation only holidays with the company acting as agents for European apartment suppliers and people driving themselves to the Alps by car or organising their own travel.

"It was very successful; there was definitely a demand for it. We fitted into a niche that wasn't being properly exploited."

Erna's generosity was still very much in evidence in the Eighties and Nineties. Her attitude to money was at the root of this.

She told *The Sunday Times* in 1982: "Money, as such, has never been important to me. It's more comfortable to have it than not, that's all. The one thing I hate spending money on is holidays – I've had so many free trips over all those years."[120]

Halina Hodi says her generosity was sometimes overwhelming.

"One day she gave me a list of places where I could park a car. I thought that was strange as I didn't have one. Shortly afterwards, she came to me in the office and said 'Here you are, these are your keys. Your car is outside.' And there was a little Volkswagen – with the steering on the wrong side – but my car! She had seen it in a street and it was not very expensive. That was Erna, she was very generous."

"The person she saved money on the most was herself," says Halina. "She would never go and buy herself a decent piece of meat but when she had guests, she would. She was very simple in her needs but could be very generous to others."

Journalist Eithne Power agrees. "You could not find a more generous person. If she thought you were in trouble, she was the first one in there and she was very astute. She could always judge when somebody was going down the wrong path or being stupid and was always trying to haul you back and rescue you from whatever stupid thing you were going to do next."

This is a view echoed by Christopher Black, son of Erna's assistant Roma.

"We adopted children in the 1970s, having had a period of not much contact with her. As soon as she heard that we had adopted children, she started sending presents up and packages would arrive the whole time. There was that kind of generosity and concern and you know, maybe she enjoyed other peoples' children in short bursts, but she would never have had the time for children of her own."

There are also countless postcards and letters in her scrapbooks from people thanking her for unexpected presents – picnic tables and even cheques to cover mortgage payments when someone found themselves unexpectedly out of work.

A letter from Christl Beran, daughter of one of her long-time friends, relates: "When… did anyone, familiar or un, come to you for money and leave empty handed?"

One person to benefit from Erna's largesse at this time was a local taxi driver who had started work in the South Kensington area and who would regularly take Erna to her house.

Jean Yellowlees recalls, "She started asking for him to pick her up and she would give him money because he told her he was having money problems. Her friends were slightly bothered because they thought she was being taken advantage of. I think it was just kindness. It didn't matter to Erna what level of society people were from. I remember going to the theatre with her and she was giving money to people asking for a cup of tea. I don't think Erna ever turned them away. She fished a note out every time."

***

Yet another rebirth for Erna Low – she was a master of reinvention – came in 1995/96 when the first Erna Low holiday brochure, rather than promotional ones for La Plagne, Flaine and Les Arcs that had appeared in the Eighties, appeared. It was the first true Erna Low brochure for sixteen years.

"She absolutely loved the new brochures," says Joanna. "It was exactly what she wanted to see."

Although the company was again issuing brochures, some things had changed.

"I was conscious of the internet boom and that we had an old brand," says Joanna. "I wanted to make sure we kept that brand integral to the company while being up to date with the online side. Websites were popping up everywhere in 1996 and I was conscious that we had to have that balance."

Joanna has since made the brochures highly recognisable, using images from the original Erna Low era of stylish skiers with their long wooden skis and poles to make them stand out on the travel agent's shelves. It is a clever way of getting across to new customers that Erna Low is a company with a very long heritage in the ski business.

***

One day in 1996, Erna was showing Beverly Byrne of *The Lady*[121] magazine her collection of scrapbooks full of "moody shots of handsome ski instructors etched against sparkling slopes". When Byrne asked Low why she never married one of these hunks, Byrne wrote of her response, "Her eyes sparkle and she drawls Dietrich style: 'I do not like my men hunky'."

Roma Black said she had men in her life but she never really talked about them. "Life was different in those days," she says. "Nowadays, young people have boyfriends and the first thing they do is to jump into bed together. In her day, you could have a lot of boyfriends which never came to anything and you could mix your boyfriends."

Erna's right hand woman, Bobbie Shafto, says you could always tell when she liked someone. "You had to make sure the office was tidy and all in order and then you would know someone would be coming."

In Erna's collection of autobiographical notes, there is a list entitled "Das

Mädchen hat kein Glück mit seinem Bräutigame" (the girl has no luck with her fiancés).

Under this heading she writes: "Friedl Apotheker, Gustav Schindler, Tom Powys Cobb, Wolfi Speiser, Reinhard Grohs, Philip Mair, William Griffith, Gustav J, Laurie Laing, Bryan Donkin, Ernst".

Friedl, Wolfi and Reinhard were all friends from Erna's youth, the other people she had met during the 1940s and 1950s.

Cupid, it seemed, was destined not to be kind to Erna. In her notes, Erna calls the archaeologist Thomas Powys Cobb an "elegant young man, well educated, well travelled, taught him German and fell in love with him but he married a young instructress of health and beauty [Jean St Lo]".

"Another friend was William Griffith – I met him in a youth hostel in Surrey. He came from a fairly wealthy family in Dublin. I visited them on one occasion but that was not a great success. His mother riled their family and was not keen on having a foreigner in their midst. William was very much under the thumb especially when his father died and he had to return to Dublin to look after his mother."

"The third young man was a keen mountaineer and my ideal of a young man – attractive to look at, intelligent, a sportsman, keen on sailing and skiing – to my mind an ideal chap. Alas the large photograph he sent me said it all – a young man looked over his shoulder and homosexuality was his problem although he tried to fight against it and always hoped someone would save him. I persuaded him to go and see a specialist whom I trusted a great deal but the result was a quick end to this episode. It was a sad end of the story – our friendship came to a sudden end and we only met once again in the Underground. Bryan shared a house with a young couple – not quite his type but the wife missed no opportunity to tell me what a lucky escape I had had."

Erna's long and troubled relationship with Ernst Litthauer we have learned about elsewhere in this biography.

Yet there remains one last story about Erna's relationships which needs to be told.

Erna was a lifelong fan of the use of graphology, or handwriting analysis, to understand people's characters; she did not hesitate to use it on potential partners.

Manfred Lowengard was a German graphologist who came undone when, in 1933, he was asked to analyse some handwriting by a high-ranking official of the SS. He characterised the writer as "unstable, neurotic, and with dangerous psychopathic tendencies". Unfortunately for him, the writer was the country's new Chancellor

Adolf Hitler and he was thrown into prison before being transferred to a concentration camp.[122] A ransom deal saw him released and escape to London in 1938.

Ten years later, he was working as consulting graphologist at the Institute of Handwriting Analysis in London and had become known as the Sage of Hampstead[123] for his shrewd insights on people's handwriting. Erna sought his opinion on the handwriting of someone who is unnamed in the correspondence.

Lowengard responded, "As to your friend I feel he has a kind of Oedipus complex – this the unfulfilled attachment as naturally the love was not fulfilled completely, whilst he on the other hand always feels he betrays his "real love" when he enters an affair with someone else. The woman to make him happy should be a shrewd psychologist herself, similar in her psychological make-up as the mother was, but patient and firm enough to lead him towards fulfilment of his sexual desires. I almost feel you could do the difficult job quite amicably. He would be more loyal and steadfast in the long run than the other friend of yours who is more of a bon-vivant as he is more vain."

There is also a cryptic comment in Erna's handwriting made to her by a man unknown: "I did not think it would be so boring to spend a night with you," it reads.

Who the man was we are unlikely to ever know. It may well be the same one who, in August 1946, sent her a telegram with a single line of text. "ACCEPT YOUR OFFER = HUSBAND," it read.

It had been sent to Erna at 116 Gower Street from Fraddon in Cornwall, just a short drive from where one of the company's house parties was being held at Boskenwyn that summer. Ernst Litthauer was one of those on the guest list but it is mere speculation that he sent it.

One thing we do know is that whoever HUSBAND was, Erna never married.

***

One day in late June 1996, at which point approaching her eighty-seventh birthday, she took a look around the Reece Mews office and turned to Joanna and said, "I am just off to watch Wimbledon."

Erna left the office for her house at 17 Selwood Terrace to turn on the television, witnessing Sir Cliff Richard's impromptu concert on 3 July and seeing Richard Krajicek's only Grand Slam success and Steffi Graf's seventh and final victory at the All England Club. The handover was complete and Erna would never return to the office for a day's work again.

Epilogue

By the time she left to watch Wimbledon, Erna had not enjoyed the best of health for a number of years. There was a triple heart bypass in the late 1980s and a number of mini-strokes throughout the 1990s, including one which happened at the London Ski Show.

Despite her failing health, Erna still wanted to keep abreast of what was going on in the business.

Joanna says "From that day she went to watch Wimbledon, I would go round and see her most days to see how she was and let her know what was happening. She would give her opinion if she didn't agree. I had also been working for her for so long that I felt I needed her approval and her opinions."

Another regular visitor at the time was Joanna's young son Cody. He says, "I remember going to visit her upstairs in her bedroom – I would only have been eight years old and I was in awe of her – she lay in bed in state like the Queen. I was always puzzled that she would praise her dog, Maxi, for snapping at me when I came in the door. I used to try and hide behind Mum but Maxi always found me. "

"Erna made it very clear very early on, within two or three years of my starting work for her, that she wanted to find someone who would carry on the Erna Low legacy after she left."

"The name Erna Low was very important to her. She nurtured me to take on the company. She made it clear that while she was alive she wanted to have total control but wanted to have it all ready for handover when she died."

How did such a strong-willed person eventually hand over the reins of the company she had built up over the decades?

"It was very delicately done," says Erna's au pair Halina Hodi.

"In the 1980s, there was both Erna and Joanna and people would come to see them both. But after a while, they just came to see Joanna and people quietly deferred to her. But it was done beautifully by the two of them."

Joanna's mother Jean Yellowlees says: "When Joanna first started going on trips with Erna to see places, Joanna would be there as her assistant. On one occasion they went to Vichy and one of the people they were meeting started speaking to Joanna as though she was the one in charge. She was effectively in charge by that time but Erna hadn't realised it. That must have been quite difficult."

She adds: "I don't think Erna entirely saw her as a natural successor. Joanna is very feminine and maternal. I don't think Erna would have seen herself as that. I remember when Erna had essentially made the business over and Erna said to me 'This is a great opportunity for Joanna'. I think Erna was awfully pleased that Erna Low would carry on in somebody else's hands."

Two qualities that Joanna believes come directly from Erna are a commitment to working hard and a passion for what the company is selling.

"She had a passionate need to share and was a very determined person. I have never met anyone who worked harder," says Joanna. "She was a leader all her life and always wanted to share what she had discovered – not just about holidays – straight away. She was always 100% passionate about what she was doing and why she was doing it."

Joanna also learned some of Erna's legendary ability at negotiating a good deal. "She was a much tougher negotiator than I am. Erna would always want the very best deal without always thinking about the other side and people would sometimes close down on her."

By the end, as well as the strokes, Erna was also in the advanced stages of dementia which had an unusual side-effect – she would repeatedly copy out her address book and her notes from the autobiography that she would never write. It was as if she had found an anchor of stability in the writing that had so consumed her working life.

Her contribution to the development of the travel industry was recognised in 2000 with her induction into travel's Hall of Fame, which exists "to honour excellence and outstanding achievement, particularly in those who have played a significant part in creating and developing the travel and tourism industry." She was honoured that year alongside Sir Richard Branson and joined the likes of Billy Butlin and Vladimir Raitz.

Erna died at home at 17 Selwood Terrace on 12 February 2002, at the age of ninety-two, two years after her long-term friendly competitor and fellow Viennese Walter Ingham. The names of both live on in the ski companies they founded.

Erna was cremated and her ashes scattered by Joanna, her long-time employee Ellen Fleming and her first au pair Halina Hodi on the cliffs of Bosigran in Cornwall, the location of her first ever house party and a favourite place to which she returned again and again in later years.

Halina Hodi says, "We wanted to take the ashes to Austria to scatter them but you are not allowed to do that. So Joanna and I took the car to Cornwall where we met Ellen Fleming and we scattered the ashes at Bosigran – right on the cliffs. Whenever we go to Cornwall now, we go and visit Erna."

In her will, Erna bequeathed the company which she had built up over the period of eighty years, notwithstanding the two changes of ownership in the 1970s, to Joanna, the woman she had identified as her natural successor.

The decision came as a surprise to some. Roger Lloyd Pack says, "Joanna was a protégée whom Erna latched onto and whom she brought up like a substitute daughter. Erna had a relationship with Joanna rather like she had with my mum [Uli]. I think Erna was pleased to find someone who could take over and hand it onto. Joanna has a very strong personality and is very dedicated and I think Erna recognized someone like herself in Joanna."

Joanna's mother Jean says, "Joanna was in her early thirties at the time and could have simply sold the company. But Joanna cared about the actual heritage and didn't do that."

So would Erna be proud of where Joanna has taken the company that bears her name?

"I think she would," says Joanna. "We have carried on the same ethos – it is very much that the client comes first and is about having excellent accommodation in best locations, which has been well researched. We have very much carried on what she developed in the first place."

Repeat business form loyal customers had always been a priority for Erna, the consummate networker, and Joanna believes that this focus on loyalty continues in the company today. "We have more than 70% of our clients returning, which is very high for a travel company. I think that is still important."

Erna had always been an innovator and after Erna left to watch Wimbledon, Joanna came up with a new direction for the company – selling property in the mountains.

Joanna says, "I think Erna would have initially been surprised by the property part of the business. She was not interested in property purchase herself."

This new departure for Erna Low the company came as a result of the growing number of people who were coming back from their ski holidays with the company and asking whether they could buy the place they had stayed in.

"The property side of the business is very much destination-led," says Joanna. "It is not just about being an estate agent but selling the property on the basis of excellent resorts – I think she would have loved that."

The company now employs more than twenty people in the winter and takes 13,000 people on holiday every year, not so different from when Erna was at the controls in the early 1960s. And, as in the days when Erna ran the company, Joanna is proud that her core management team has been there for many years. "Sharon Parish has been with the company for more than twenty years, Jane Bolton for fifteen years and John Ward for ten years," says Joanna.

One difference is that most Erna Low customers now go to apartments rather than chalets or hotels.

"Over the years we have built up the most comprehensive and best selection of apartments and self-catered chalets in the Alps," says Joanna with conviction.

And the future?

"I think the ski market has gone through a very difficult few years and the number of people skiing has definitely shrunk. I think it is a temporary blip but recovery will be slow."

The brochure, so much a part of the history of Erna Low the company, may not have long left, however.

"I believe the life of the brochure is under review," says Joanna. "Within the next few years, it will probably disappear. I think people's whole reaction to reading brochures has changed so much."

And does she believe the Erna Low name will still be around eighty years from now?

Joanna does not hesitate before replying. "Yes I do, although in what form I do not know."

***

Over the course of Erna's career, there had been enormous changes in the world. When Erna had first come to Britain, the telephone was still something of a novelty. Just as she retired, offices were just installing Bill Gates' new Windows 95 operating system on their personal computers and people were marvelling at the relatively new World Wide Web, downloading basic Web pages at a blistering

28.8k over, in some places, those same copper telephone lines that had been laid six decades earlier.

Travel had changed enormously too. When Erna started taking her fellow students out to Austria, they were among the tiny number of people of that era with the time and money to do so. By the year of Erna's retirement, the number of Britons going abroad had reached 42 million a year. Taking a holiday – or more likely, several holidays – by the Nineties was almost seen as a human right rather than as a luxury. This was also the year in which an upstart start-up headed by Stelios Haji-Ioannou – the low-cost carrier easyJet – launched its first international services.

The speed of travel had changed immensely too and not just because of the replacement of the train with the plane as the foremost mode of transport. In Erna's early years, those who travelled were often the independently wealthy for whom taking off a month or even longer to go on holiday was entirely practical. By the time she retired from the business, people were regularly flying to cities around Europe with unpronounceable names for the weekend just for the hell of it.

Skiing had changed almost beyond recognition over those eighty years too. In the early days you had to love the sport to be able to put up with walking up hills under your own steam or on the back of a mule. Now a speedy cable car can whisk you from the valley floor to the highest peaks in minutes. Many of today's skiers are more interested in the recreational side of the sport and taking instruction is now seen as an option rather than a must-have. The equipment is almost unrecognisably different too. In Erna's early days, skis were little more than curved sticks that you crudely attached to your feet with simple clips and cables. Now, barely a season goes by without some ski manufacturer coming up with a new innovation – be it snowboards, carving skis, self-moulding boots or whatever we will see next year.

One thing does remain the same: a passion among a sizeable proportion of people to go on holiday and experience something with a truly local flavour. Erna was visibly horrified by the advent of mass tourism and she would have been horrified at the Anglicisation of many of the resorts to which she took some of the first intrepid skiers. Yet there are still people who love discovering something new and different and that remains at the heart of Erna Low the company as much as it ever did. It is safe to bet that there will still be people with that passion in eighty years' time and, in that case, Erna Low's legacy will still be very much alive.

BIBLIOGRAPHY

[1] *We thought we might go to Mount Everest this year*, The Times, John Carter, 24 March 1973

[2] *23 Killed By Avalanche*, The Times, 23 December 1952

[3] Statistics from 17 nations reporting to the Canadian Avalanche Centre

[4] *Lawinenkatastrophe beim Arlberg:23 tote*, Arbeitere Zeitung, 23 December 1952

[5] *Vienna and the Jews 1867-1938: A Cultural History*, Steven Beller, Cambridge University Press

[6] Vienna city government history, http://www.wien.gv.at/english/history/overview/capital.html

[7] *Jewish Politics in Vienna 1918-1938*, Harriet Pass Freidenreich, Indiana University Press, 1991

[8] *Mein Kampf*, Adolf Hitler (James Murphy translation), Hutchison & Co, 1939

[9] *Vienna and the Jews 1867-1938: A Cultural History*, Steven Beller, Cambridge University Press

[10] *When we wore old clothes, and didn't have a ski-lift*, Stephen Wood, The Independent, 28 September 1996

[11] *A Life in the Day of Erna Low*, Eithne Power, Sunday Times, 1982

[12] *Vienna and the Jews 1867-1938: A Cultural History*, Steven Beller, Cambridge University Press

[13] *History of Hill House*, Charles Langland, St Osyth Parish News

[14] *The Legend of the Snowqueen*, Eithne Power, The Guardian

[15] *The Alps: A Cultural History*, Andrew Beattie, Signal Books, 2006

[16] *Two Planks and a Passion: The Dramatic History of Skiing*, Roland Huntford, Hambledon Continuum, 2008

[17] *Two Planks and a Passion: The Dramatic History of Skiing*, Roland Huntford, Hambledon Continuum, 2008

[18] Morning Post, 17 November 1932

[19] *Travel Profile: Erna Low*, Harold Rose, Travel Agency, January 1967

[20] *Legend of the Snow Queen*, Eithne Power

[21] *When we wore old clothes, and didn't have a ski-lift*, Stephen Wood, The Independent, 28 September 1996

[22] *The Legend of the Snow Queen*, Eithne Power, The Guardian

[23] *Obituary: Walter Ingham*, Roger Bray, The Independent, July 2000

[24] *Erna Low obituary*, The Times, 18 February 2002

[25] *Dance Host "Push the Car " Ruse Before Robbery*, unknown newspaper and date

[26] *Jewish Politics in Vienna 1918-1938*, Harriet Pass Fredienreich, Indiana University Press, 1991

[27] *When we wore old clothes, and didn't have a ski-lift*, Stephen Wood, The Independent, 28 September 1996

[28] National Archives

[29] *Assigned to Listen, The Evesham Experience 1939-1943*, Oliver Renier and Vladimir Rubinstein, BBC External Services, 1986

[30] *Britannia's Third Ear*, Ivor Brown, The Listener, 27 February 1941

[31] *The Etymologicon*, Mark Forsyth (The Inky Fool), Icon Books, 2011

[32] *Travel Profile: Erna Low*, Harold Rose, Travel Agency, 1967

[33] http://www.historicracing.com/search.cfm?driverID=8043

[34] *The Jewel in the Crown*, Ian Wall, John Atherton and others, http://www.climbers-club.co.uk/downloads/histories/CountHouse.pdf

[35] *Eye on the viewers* (obituary of Hilde Himmelweit), The Guardian, March 1992

[36] *Supplement to the London Gazette*, 1 January 1967

[37] *The Slippery Slopes to Success*, Beverly Byrne, The Lady, 12 to 18 November 1996

[38] *At home with Erna Low*, Ruth Miller, Housewife, February 1962

[39] *When we wore old clothes, and didn't have a ski-lift*, Stephen Wood, The Independent, 28 September 1996

[40] *Rigorous Limits on Travel Abroad*, The Times, 28 August 1947

[41] The Marshall Foundation website

[42] *Conquering the Foreigner: The Marshall Plan and the Revival of Postwar Austrian Tourism*, The Marshall Plan in Austria, Transaction, 2000

[43] *Two Planks and a Passion: The Dramatic History of Skiing*, Roland Huntford, Hambledon Continuum, 2008

[44] *Flight to the Sun: The Story of the Holiday Revolution*, Vladimir Raitz and Roger Bray, Continuum, 2001

[45] *The Surprising Life of Constance Spry*, Sue Shephard, Macmillan, 2010

[46] *British Victims of Avalanche*, The Times, 24 December 1952

[47] *2011 Snowsports Analysis*, Ski Club of Great Britain

[48] *Ski athlete and innovator, Hvam did it all*, The Oregonian, 19 December 2009

[49] *Gear that made a difference*, Ski Canada, 30 August 2011

[50] http://retro-skiing.com/2011/02/mitch-cubberley-and-his-cubco/

[51] http://www.skiinghistory.org/index.php/2011/08/release/

[52] http://lange-ski-boots.blogspot.co.uk/1970/01/early-days-1957-to-1963.html

[53] *Flight to the Sun: The Story of the Holiday Revolution*, Vladimir Raitz and Roger Bray, Continuum, 2001

[54] *Flight to the Sun: The Story of the Holiday Revolution*, Vladimir Raitz and Roger Bray, Continuum, 2001

[55] *Low plans biggest ever winter sports series*, Travel Trade Gazette, 21 September 1962

[56] *Ski-dive for snow sports fans*, Kensington Post, 19 October 1962

[57] The Lady, 1 February 1962

[58] *Anglo-French alliance takes a holiday*, Violet Johnstone, Daily Telegraph, 31 August 1963

[59] *Winter sports*, The Guardian, 14 October 1964

[60] *A Life in the Day of Erna Low*, Eithne Power, Sunday Times, 1982,

[61] *Anti-mini*, London Life, 15 October 1966

[62] *When women get to the top – by design*, Travel Trade Gazette, 19 March 1965

[63] *Travel Profile: Erna Low*, Harold Rose, Travel Agency, 1967

[64] *At home with Erna Low*, Ruth Miller, Housewife, February 1962

[65] *Personality of the Month*, Modern Woman, July 1964

[66] *Church and School Equipment News*, January 1963

[67] *No time for homesickness at this houseparty*, E de Stroumillo, Daily Telegraph, 7 August 1971

[68] *Getting away from it all*, Barbara Wace, Farmers' Weekly 23 April 1971

[69] *Julie Christie buys new home*, William Roland, newspaper unknown, December 1966

[70] *At home with Erna Low*, Ruth Miller, Housewife, February 1962

[71] The Slippery Slopes to Success, Beverly Byrne, The Lady, 12 to 18 November 1996

[72] An article entitled The Day in the Life of Maxi Low that Erna tried to get published in the Sunday Times without success

[73] *At home with Erna Low*, Ruth Miller, Housewife, February 1962

[74] *Travel Profile: Erna Low*, Harold Rose, Travel Agency, 1967

[75] *Other people's holidays can be fun*, Emma Evans, Sunday Telegraph, 1972

[76] *A Life in the Day of Erna Low*, Eithne Power, Sunday Times, 1982

[77] *Close of Play*, Candidus, Travel World, 6 April 1963

[78] *Austria Comes First for Winter Sports*, Financial Times, 31 December 1965

[79] *Two Planks and a Passion*, Roland Huntford, Hambledon Continuum, 2008

[80] *Some ins and outs of modern sk-ing*, Field, 10 December 1964

[81] *Young Welsh Skiers Make a Hit in Austria*, John F Grace, The Times Educational Supplement, 6 February 1970

[82] *County sends 680 to ski slopes*, The Times Educational Supplement, 20 January 1967

[83] *Putting Zing into the Dullest Term*, Marion Harris, School + College, September 1966

[84] *School ski holiday for Princess Anne Likely*, Daily Telegraph, 1965

[85] *Bedside Skiing*, John Samuel, Hutchinson, 1987

[86] Hansard, *HC Deb 20 July 1966 vol 732 cc627-55*

[87] *Dock strikes stop one third of exports*, The Times, 13 October 1967, p. 17

[88] *Beating the £50 allowance*, The Sunday Times, 3 August 1968

[89] *Devalued skiing*, Erna Low speech

[90] *To the snow without the freeze*, John Samuel, The Guardian, 17 September 1966

[91] *Travel cash eased*, unknown publication, 1967

[92] *Personal choice: where recollection leads*, The Times, Tuesday 28 December 1971

[93] The Visitors Tribune, Costa del Sol

[94] *Packages for the Particular*, Sebastian Cash, Ideal Home, February 1968

[95] *A winter rush to the sun and the slopes*, Jack Amos, Financial Times, 15 November 1967

[96] *Why the big holiday operators are going out in the cold*, Arthur Sandles, Financial Times, 28 April 1970

[97] *Filling the gaps left by the holiday giants*, Nicholas Ashford, Financial Times, 9 September 1969

[98] Travel Guardian, 11 September 1971, Travel Guardian

[99] Article by Jean Ryder of The Lady, 16 September 1971

[100] *Other people's holidays can be fun*, Emma Evans, Sunday Telegraph, 30 January 1972

[101] *Erna Low Sells Out for £100,000*, 5 May 1972, Travel Trade Gazette

[102] *£100,000 deal seals the Erna Low courtship*, Gordon Wharton, Travel News, 4 May 1972

[103] *Erna Low sells to Travellers Guaranty*, Arther Sandles, Financial Times, 5 May 1972

[104] *Rising costs 'could hit skiing holidays'*, Roger Bray, Evening Standard, 27 June 1973

[105] *Winter sports without skis*, Patsy Kumm, 1973

[106] *Erna Low-down: its [sic] that old boy network in action,* Travel News

[107] *Nice Little Erna,* Leon Hopkins, Business World

[108] *Erna Low leaves Board,* Financial Times, 25 August 1973

[109] *Other people's holidays can be fun,* Emma Evans, Sunday Telegraph, 30 January 1972

[110] *Low profile,* Financial Times, 4 February 1982

[111] *The UK Travel and Tourism industry 1986,* Euromonitor

[112] *UK Holidays and tourism report 1980,* Euromonitor

[113] *Low profile,* Financial Times, 24 February 1982

[114] *Ski Tour Operator Folds,* Daily Telegraph, 1975

[115] *Low profile,* Financial Times, 24 February 1982

[116] *Call for probe as Low debts top £602,000,* Philip Ray, Travel News, 1 April 1982

[117] *A Life in the Day of Erna Low,* Eithne Power, Sunday Times, 1982

[118] *A Life in the Day of Erna Low,* Eithne Power, Sunday Times, 1982

[119] *Partners: Erna Low Consultants,* Fiona Lafferty, Financial Times, 30 September 1996

[120] *A Life in the Day of Erna Low,* Eithne Power, Sunday Times, 1982

[121] The Slippery Slopes to Success, Beverly Byrne, *The Lady,* 12 to 18 November 1996

[122] *Parade,* 4 September 1973

[123] *I Couldn't Paint Golden Angels,* Albert Meltzer, AK Press, 2001